SQL DEMYSTIFIED

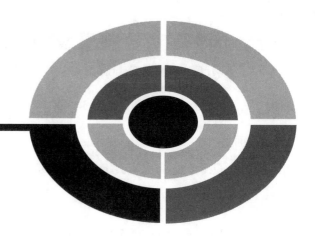

SQL DEMYSTIFIED

ANDY OPPEL

McGraw-Hill/Osborne

New York   Chicago   San Francisco   Lisbon   London
Madrid   Mexico City   Milan   New Delhi   San Juan
Seoul   Singapore   Sydney   Toronto

The **McGraw·Hill** Companies

McGraw-Hill/Osborne
2100 Powell Street, 10th Floor
Emeryville, California 94608
U.S.A.

To arrange bulk purchase discounts for sales promotions, premiums, or fund-raisers, please contact **McGraw-Hill**/Osborne at the above address.

SQL Demystified

1234567890 FGR FGR 0198765

ISBN 0-07-226224-9

Acquisitions Editor
Wendy Rinaldi

Project Manager
Patty Mon

Project Editor
Claire Splan

Acquisitions Coordinator
Alex McDonald

Technical Editor
Todd Meister

Copy Editor
Sally Engelfried

Proofreader
Paul Tyler

Indexer
Claire Splan

Composition and Illustration
International Typesetting
and Composition

Cover Series Design
Margaret Webster-Shapiro
Handel Low

Cover Illustration
Lance Lekander

This book was composed with Adobe® InDesign® CS Mac.

To the memory of my uncle, Robert E. Lee Smith, who taught me so many things about life, including never taking things too seriously. Nothing describes Robert's sense of humor better than the nickname he gave me—Darwin Data.

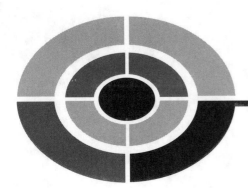

ABOUT THE AUTHOR

Andrew J. (Andy) Oppel is a proud graduate of The Boys' Latin School of Maryland and of Transylvania University (Lexington, KY) where he earned a BA in computer science in 1974. Since then he has been continuously employed in a wide variety of information technology positions, including programmer, programmer/analyst, systems architect, project manager, senior database administrator, database group manager, consultant, database designer, and data architect. In addition, he has been a part-time instructor with the University of California (Berkeley) Extension for over 20 years, and received the Honored Instructor Award for the year 2000. His teaching work included developing two courses for UC Extension, "Concepts of Database Management Systems" and "Introduction to Relational Database Management Systems." He also earned his Oracle 9*i* Database Associate certification in 2003. He is currently employed as the principal data architect for Ceridian, a leading provider of human resource solutions. Aside from computer systems, Andy enjoys music (guitar and vocals), amateur radio (Pacific Division Vice Director, American Radio Relay League) and soccer (Referee Instructor, U.S. Soccer).

Andy has designed and implemented hundreds of databases for a wide range of applications, including medical research, banking, insurance, apparel manufacturing, telecommunications, wireless communications, and human resources. He is the author of *Databases Demystified* (McGraw-Hill/Osborne, 2004). His database product experience includes IMS, DB2, Sybase, Microsoft SQL Server, Microsoft Access, MySQL, and Oracle (versions 7, 8, 8*i* and 9*i*).

CONTENTS AT A GLANCE

CONTENTS

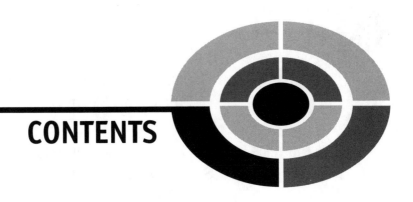

ACKNOWLEDGMENTS

I owe much to my parents for providing me with an excellent education and a love of both learning and teaching. I credit The Boys' Latin School of Maryland and the late Jack H. Williams, headmaster, with teaching me to write effectively. And I credit Transylvania University and Dr. James E. Miller for introducing me to the fascinating world of information systems and providing me the tools for continuous learning. I'd like to thank the wonderful people at McGraw-Hill/Osborne for the opportunity to write my first book and for their excellent support during the writing process. Finally, my thanks to my wife Laurie and our sons Keith and Luke for their support, patience, and understanding during the long hours it took to produce this book.

INTRODUCTION

It is often said that mathematics is the language of science. In just the same way, SQL is the language of databases. My first book, *Databases Demystified*, introduces SQL, but focuses on database design. A number of readers asked for more detail about SQL because they found writing and running database queries to be so enjoyable. So, here is *SQL Demystified*, devoted entirely to the SQL language.

I've drawn on my extensive experience as a database designer, administrator, and instructor to provide you with this self-help guide to the language that unlocks the fascinating world of database technology. This book covers standard SQL as well as the differences you will encounter when you use database management systems such as Microsoft SQL Server, Oracle, DB2, and MySQL. There are loads of examples and they all use one consistent, easy to understand database that I specifically designed for this book. And the database design and sample data that I used are included so you can try all the examples for yourself. You can test your leaning with the review quiz that is provided at the end of each chapter and the comprehensive exam at the end of the book. I hope you have a lot of fun learning SQL.

If you have any comments, I'd like to hear from you.

andy@andyoppel.com
Honored instructor, University of California Berkeley Extension
Principal data architect, Ceridian
Certified Oracle 9*i* Database Associate

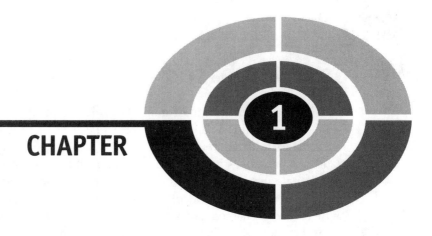

1

Relational Database Concepts

SQL is the fundamental language used to communicate with relational databases. Therefore, it is essential to understand the basic concepts of relational databases before you embark on learning the SQL language. This chapter presents an overview of relational database concepts. If you find this material interesting, I recommend you take a look at my other book, *Databases Demystified* (McGraw-Hill/Osborne, 2004), which focuses entirely on the design, use, and management of relational databases.

What Is a Database?

A *database* is a collection of interrelated data items that are managed as a single unit. This definition is deliberately broad because there is so much variety across the various software vendors that provide database systems. For example, Oracle Corporation defines its database as a collection of physical files that are managed by a single instance (copy) of the database software, while Microsoft defines an SQL Server database as a collection of tables with data and other objects. A database *object* is a named data structure that is stored in the database, such as a table, view, or index. You will find more information about database objects in the "Relational Database Components" section later in this chapter.

There is a great deal of variation in implementation across database vendors. In most database systems, the data is stored in multiple physical files, but in Microsoft Access, all of the database objects and data belonging to a single database are stored in one physical file. (A *file* is a collection of related records that are stored as a single unit by a computer's operating system.) Some other relational databases, particularly older implementations, store each database object in a separate file. However, one of the best benefits of relational databases is that the physical implementation details are separated from the logical definitions of the database objects in such a way that most database users need not know where (or how) the database objects are actually stored in the computer's file system. In fact, as you learn SQL, you'll see that the only time a physical file is named in an SQL statement is in defining or modifying the database objects themselves—you *never* need to specify a physical file when adding, changing, deleting, or retrieving the data that is stored within the database objects.

What Is a Database Management System (DBMS)?

A *database management system (DBMS)* is software provided by the database vendor. Software products such as Microsoft Access, Microsoft SQL Server, Oracle Database, Sybase, DB2, INGRES, MySQL, and PostgreSQL are all DBMSs or, more correctly, *relational DBMSs* (*RDBMSs*). Relational databases are defined and discussed in the next section of this chapter.

The DBMS provides all the basic services required to organize and maintain the database, including the following:

- Moving data to and from the physical data files as needed.

- Managing concurrent data access by multiple users, including provisions to prevent simultaneous updates from conflicting with one another.

- Managing transactions so that each transaction's database changes are an all-or-nothing unit of work. In other words, if the transaction succeeds, all database changes made by it are recorded in the database; if the transaction fails, none of the changes it made are recorded in the database. Note that some relational DBMSs lack support for transactions.

- Support for a *query language*, which is the system of commands that a database user employs to retrieve data from the database. SQL is the primary query language used with relational DBMSs and the primary topic of this book.

- Provisions for backing up the database and recovering the database from failures.

- Security mechanisms to prevent unauthorized data access and modification.

What Is a Relational Database?

A *relational database* is a database based on the relational model, which was developed by Dr. E. F. Codd. The relational model presents data in familiar two-dimensional tables, much like a spreadsheet does. Unlike a spreadsheet, the data is not necessarily stored in tabular form, and the model also permits combining (*joining*, in relational terminology) tables to form views, which are also presented as two-dimensional tables. It is the ability to use tables independently or in combination with others without any predefined hierarchy or sequence in which the data must be accessed that makes relational databases highly flexible.

Relational Database Components

Let's have a look at the basic components of relational databases. It is these components that you use to construct the database objects in our databases. The SQL statements used to create these components in the database are presented in Chapter 3.

Tables

The primary unit of data storage in a relational database is the *table*, which is a two-dimensional structure composed of rows and columns. Each table represents an *entity*, which is a person, place, thing, or event that is to be represented in the database, such as a customer, a bank account, or a banking transaction. Each row represents one occurrence of the entity. Figure 1-1 shows the listing of part of a table named MOVIE.

The MOVIE table is part of a video store sample database that is used throughout this book. The remainder of the sample database is presented in the "Overview of the Video Store Sample Database" section near the end of this chapter. The MOVIE table contains data that describes the movies available in the video store. Each row in the table represents one movie, and each column represents a unit fact that describes the movie, such as the movie title or MPAA rating code.

MOVIE_ID	MOVIE_ GENRE_ CODE	MPAA_ RATING_ CODE	MOVIE_TITLE	RETAIL_PRICE _VHS	RETAIL_PRICE_DVD	YEAR_ PRODUCED
1	Drama	R	Mystic River	58.97	19.96	2003
2	ActAd	R	The Last Samurai	15.95	19.96	2003
3	Comdy	PG-13	Something's Gotta Give	14.95	29.99	2003
4	ActAd	PG-13	The Italian Job	11.95	19.99	2003
5	ActAd	R	Kill Bill: Vol. 1	24.99	29.99	2003
6	ActAd	PG-13	Pirates of the Caribbean: The Curse of the Black Pearl	24.99	29.99	2003
7	Drama	PG-13	Big Fish	14.95	19.94	2003
8	ActAd	R	Man on Fire	50.99	29.98	2004
9	ActAd	PG-13	Master and Commander: The Far Side of the World	12.98	39.99	2003
10	Drama	R	Lost in Translation	49.99	14.98	2003
11	Rmce	PG-13	Two Weeks Notice	6.93	14.97	2002
12	Comdy	PG-13	50 First Dates	9.95	19.94	2004
13	Comdy	PG-13	Matchstick Men	6.93	19.97	2003
14	Drama	R	Cold Mountain	24.99	29.99	2003
15	Drama	R	Road to Perdition	9.99	14.99	2002
16	Comdy	PG-13	The School of Rock	11.69	29.99	2003
17	Rmce	PG-13	13 Going on 30	14.94	28.95	2004
18	Drama	R	Monster	24.99	29.99	2003
19	ActAd	PG-13	The Day After Tomorrow	12.98	29.98	2004
20	Forgn	R	Das Boot	17.99	19.94	1981

Figure 1-1 MOVIE table listing

You have likely noticed the striking similarity between relational database tables and spreadsheets. However, as you will see in the remainder of this chapter, relational databases offer many more features and much greater flexibility in organizing and displaying information.

Relationships

Relationships are the associations among relational database tables. While each relational table can stand alone, databases are all about storing related data. For example, you can store information about categories used by the video store to organize the inventory of movies in addition to the movies themselves. At the same time, you can store information about the copies of each video you have in the video store, including the date the copy was acquired and the format of the copy (DVD or VHS). By using relationships, you can tie the related tables together in a formal way that is easy to use when you want to combine data from multiple tables in the same database query but with the flexibility to include only the information of interest. This ability to pick and choose the information you want from the database allows you to tailor the information in the database to the specific needs of each individual or application that accesses the database.

Figure 1-2 shows four tables from the video store database and the relationships among them in a format known as an Entity Relationship Diagram (ERD). ERDs provide an easy medium for showing the overall design of a relational database and are easily understood by both technical and nontechnical database users. Each rectangle in the diagram represents a relational table, with the name of the table

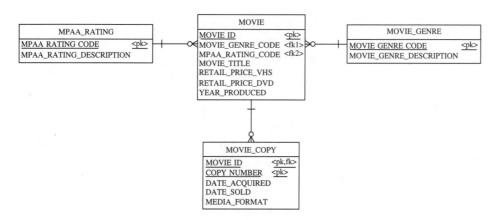

Figure 1-2   Video store database ERD, partial view

appearing above the horizontal line and the columns in the table listed vertically in the main part of the rectangle. You may wish to compare the MOVIE table as shown in Figure 1-2 with the listing of the same table shown in Figure 1-1 to help you visualize the contents of the table.

Each relationship is shown on the ERD as a line connecting two tables. Each end of a relationship line shows *maximum cardinality* of the relationship, which is the maximum number of rows in one table that can be associated with a given row in the table at the opposite end of the relationship line. The maximum cardinality may be *one* (where the line has no special symbol on its end) or *many* (where the line has a symbol called a *crow's foot* on the end, which looks like the line end splitting into three lines). Just short of the end of the line is another symbol that shows the *minimum cardinality*, which is the minimum number of rows of one table that can be associated with the table on the opposite side of the line. The minimum cardinality may be *zero*, denoted with a circle drawn on the line, or *one*, denoted with a short vertical line or tick mark drawn across the relationship line. For example, the relationship between the MPAA_RATING and MOVIE tables in Figure 1-2 is a *one-to-many* relationship, which means that each row in the MPAA_RATING table (the table on the "one" side, which is also called the *parent* table) can be associated with many rows in the MOVIE table (the table on the "many" side, which is also called the *child* table), but each row in the MOVIE table can be associated with only one row in the MPAA_RATING table. This should make sense because each movie released in the U.S. has only one rating, and each rating can be assigned to many different movies. I recognize that sometimes movies are "recut" to achieve a different rating, but this is easily handled by treating different versions as different movies, much as we do when a movie is remade using a different cast and crew. It is essential to consider such things because relational databases only support one-to-many relationships.

The minimum cardinality indicates whether participation in a relationship is mandatory or optional. All of the relationships in Figure 1-2 are mandatory on the "one" side and optional on the "many" side, which is the most common form of relationship. Looking back at the relationship between the MPAA_RATING and MOVIE tables, this means that each row in the MOVIE table *must* have a matching row in the MPAA_RATING table at all times, but that a given row in the MPAA_RATING table does not necessarily have to have a matching row in the MOVIE table at all times. If you wanted to allow movies to be in the video store inventory that did not have an MPAA rating assigned, the tick mark near the MPAA_RATING table end of the relationship line would show as a circle. While optional relationships on the "one" side of a relationship are relatively common, it is most unusual to have a mandatory relationship on the many side, which essentially means that the parent table must have at least one child in the database at all times. Consider the

consequences of making the MOVIE table a mandatory child of the MPAA_RATING table. If the Motion Picture Association of America (MPAA) created a new rating code, you would not be able to add it to the MPAA_RATING table until you had a movie to add to the MOVIE table. Likewise, you would not be able to delete the last row in the MOVIE table that matched any particular rating code without deleting the corresponding MPAA_RATING table row. These awkward restrictions are likely the reason that relational databases do not provide direct support for mandatory children in one-to-many relationships.

Relationships are implemented using matching columns in the two participating tables. On the ERD, the underlined column(s) in each table with the notation "<pk>" to their right form the *primary key*, which is a column or a set of columns that uniquely identifies each row in a table. Each table may have only one primary key. However, a primary key may be composed of multiple columns if that is what it takes to form a unique key. Primary keys are very important because they are the foundation for relationships. Whenever a primary key is used in another table to establish a relationship, it is called a *foreign key*. In Figure 1-2, note the foreign key columns in the MOVIE table that establish relationships with the MOVIE_GENRE and MPAA_RATING tables, which are noted with "<fk1>" and "<fk2>" to the right of the foreign key column names. The LANGUAGE_CODE column is also noted as a foreign key ("<fk3>") but the LANGUAGE table and its relationship with the MOVIE table have been omitted from Figure 1-2. Also notice that the primary key of the MOVIE table appears in the child table MOVIE_COPY as a foreign key to establish the relationship between those two tables.

Primary keys and foreign keys are the fundamental building blocks of the relational model because they establish relationships and provide the ability to link data from multiple tables when required. You must understand this concept in order to understand how relational databases work.

Constraints

A *constraint* is a rule placed on a database object (typically a table or column) that restricts the allowable data values for that database object in some way. Once in place, constraints are automatically enforced by the DBMS and cannot be circumvented unless an authorized person disables or deletes (drops) the constraint. Each constraint is assigned a unique name to permit it to be referenced in error messages and subsequent database commands. It is a good habit for database designers to supply the constraint names because names generated automatically by the database are not very descriptive. However, I did not supply constraint names in the sample database included in this book because, unfortunately, not all RDBMS products available today support named constraints.

There are several types of database constraints:

- *NOT NULL constraint*   May be placed on a database column to prevent
  the use of null values. A *null value* is a special way in which the RDBMS
  handles a column value to indicate that the value for that column in that
  row is unknown. A null is not the same as a blank, an empty string, or
  a zero—it is indeed a special value that is not equal to anything else. Null
  values are discussed in more detail in Chapter 3.

- *Primary key constraint*   Defined on the primary key column(s) of a table
  to guarantee that the primary key values are always unique within the table.
  When defined on multiple columns of a table, it is the *combination* of all
  column values that must be unique within the table—a column that is
  only *part* of a primary key *may* have duplicate values in the table. Primary
  key constraints are nearly always implemented by the RDBMS using an
  index, which is a special type of database object that permits fast searches
  of column values. As new rows are inserted into the table, the RDBMS
  automatically searches the index to make sure the value for the primary key
  of the new row is not already in use in the table, rejecting the insert request
  if it is. Indexes can be searched much faster than tables; therefore, the index
  on the primary key is essential in tables of any size so that the search for
  duplicate keys on every insert doesn't create a performance bottleneck. An
  additional characteristic of primary key constraints is that they can only be
  defined on columns that also have a NOT NULL constraint defined.

- *Unique constraint*   Defined on a column or set of columns in a table that
  must contain unique values within the table. As with a primary key constraint,
  the RDBMS almost always uses an index as a vehicle to efficiently enforce
  the constraint. However, unlike primary key constraints, a table may have
  multiple unique constraints defined on it, and columns that participate in
  a unique constraint may (in most RDBMSs) contain null values.

- *Referential constraint* (**sometimes called a *referential integrity***
  constraint)   A constraint that enforces a relationship between two tables in
  a relational database. By "enforces" I mean that the RDBMS automatically
  checks to ensure that each foreign key value always has a corresponding
  primary key value in the parent table. In the MOVIE table (see Figure 1-1),
  the RDBMS would prevent me from inserting a movie with an MPAA_
  RATING_CODE of "M" because "M" is no longer a valid MPAA_RATING_
  CODE and therefore does not appear as a primary key value in the MPAA_
  RATING table. Conversely, the RDBMS would prevent me from deleting
  the row in the MPAA_RATING table with the primary key value of "PG-13"
  because that primary key value is in use as a foreign key value in at least one

row in the MOVIE table. In short, the referential constraint guarantees that the relationship between the two tables and its corresponding primary key and foreign key values make logical sense at all times.

- **CHECK constraint**   Uses a simple logic statement (written in SQL) to validate a column value. The outcome of the statement must be a logical true or false, with an outcome of "true" allowing the column value to be placed in the table, and an outcome of "false" causing the column value to be rejected with an appropriate error message.

Views

A *view* is a stored database query that provides a database user with a customized subset of the data from one or more tables in the database. Said another way, a view is a *virtual table* because it looks like a table and for the most part behaves like a table, yet it stores no data (only the defining query, written in SQL, is stored).

Views serve a number of useful functions:

- Hiding columns that the user does not need to see (or should not be allowed to see)

- Hiding rows from tables that a user does not need to see (or should not be allowed to see)

- Hiding complex database operations such as table joins (that is, combining columns from multiple tables in a single database query)

- Improving query performance (in some RDBMSs, such as Microsoft SQL Server)

How Relational Databases Are Designed

This section presents a very brief overview of the database design process. When you first looked at Figure 1-2 earlier in this chapter, you may have wondered why the columns were placed in multiple tables or why a particular column was placed in one table versus another. This section is intended to help answer those questions and to get you started should you decide to design your own database tables as you practice the SQL you will be learning. However, there is a lot more to database design, literally enough to fill an entire book. If you find the topic interesting and want to learn more, you'll find many web pages on the Internet as well as other books devoted to the topic, including my first book, *Databases Demystified*.

In 1972, Dr. E. F. Codd, the father of the relational database, realized that relational tables that meet certain criteria present fewer problems when data is inserted, updated, or deleted. He developed a set of rules to be followed (organized into three "normal forms") and a process called *normalization*, which is a technique for producing a set of *relations* (Dr. Codd's term for tables) that possess the desired set of properties.

The Need for Normalization

Figure 1-3 shows the MOVIE table in unnormalized form, much the way it would look if everything known about a movie were collected and put into a single table. This example will be used to demonstrate the normalization process. Incidentally, column names in relational tables generally use underscores to separate words. I have removed them in the figures throughout the discussion of normalization in order to make them more readable.

There are three problems that occur in unnormalized tables in relational databases, and all three of them exist in the table shown in Figure 1-3. The purpose of normalization is to remove these problems (anomalies) from the database design.

MOVIE ID	GENRE CODE	GENRE DESC.	LANG. CODE	MPAA RATING CODE	MPAA RATING DESC.	MOVIE TITLE	YEAR PRODUCED	DATE ACQUIRED	DATE SOLD	MEDIA FORMAT	RETAIL PRICE
1	Drama	Drama	en, fr	R	Under 17 requires accompanying parent or adult guardian	Mystic River	2003	1/1/2005		DVD	19.96
2	ActAd	Action and Adventure	en, fr, es	R	Under 17 requires accompanying parent or adult guardian	The Last Samurai	2003	1/10/2005		DVD	19.96
2	ActAd	Action and Adventure	en, fr, es	R	Under 17 requires accompanying parent or adult guardian	The Last Samurai	2003	1/10/2005		VHS	15.95
3	Comdy	Comedy	en	PG-13	Parents strongly cautioned	Something's Gotta Give	2003	1/10/2005	1/30/2005	DVD	29.99
3	Comdy	Comedy	en	PG-13	Parents strongly cautioned	Something's Gotta Give	2003	2/15/2005		DVD	29.99
4	ActAd	Action and Adventure	en, fr	PG-13	Parents strongly cautioned	The Italian Job	2003	2/15/2005		DVD	19.99

Figure 1-3   MOVIE table in unnormalized form

Insert Anomaly

The *insert anomaly* refers to a situation wherein you cannot insert data into the database because of an artificial dependency among columns in a table. Suppose the video store wants to add a new movie genre (GENRE_CODE and GENRE_ DESCRIPTION columns) to be used to categorize their movies. The design shown in Figure 1-3 will not permit that *unless* you have a movie to be placed in that category, which you would have to add to the MOVIE table at the same time. The MPAA_RATING_CODE and DESCRIPTION columns suffer from the same restriction. It would be much better if new genres and ratings could be created before movies arrived in the store.

Delete Anomaly

The *delete anomaly* is just the opposite of the insert anomaly. It refers to a situation wherein the deletion of data causes unintended loss of other data. For example, if the first movie in Figure 1-3 (*Mystic River*) is the only row in the MOVIE table that has a GENRE_CODE of "Drama" and it is deleted, the very fact that you ever had a genre called "Drama" is lost. The same is true if you delete the last movie in the MOVIE table that contains a particular MPAA_RATING_CODE.

Update Anomaly

An *update anomaly* refers to a situation wherein an update of a single data value requires multiple rows to be updated. In the MOVIE table design shown in Figure 1-3, if the description for the MPAA_RATING_CODE of "R" is to be changed, you must change it for every movie in the table that has that rating code. Similar problems exist for the GENRE_DESCRIPTION. Even the RETAIL_PRICE has this problem because all copies of the same movie (same MOVIE_ID) and media format (DVD or VHS) should have the same price. An additional hazard related to this anomaly is that storing redundant data makes it possible to update one copy of the data item, but not all of them, which then leads to inconsistent data in the database.

Applying the Normalization Process

Usually, normalization starts with any rendering of data that is (or will be) presented to a user, such as web pages, application screens, reports, and so forth. Collectively, these are called *user views*. It may seem odd at first, but it is common practice in the design of computer systems to start with the output that the user will see and work backward from there to figure how to produce the desired output.

During database design, the normalization process is applied to each user view, with the outcome being a set of normalized relations that can be directly implemented as relational database tables. The process itself is relatively straightforward, and the rules are not very difficult. However, normalization takes time and repetition to master, particularly because it challenges the designers into thinking conceptually about the data and relationships they intend to use. As you normalize, consider each user view as a relation. In other words, conceptualize each view as if it is already implemented as a two-dimensional table, and it takes practice to do so.

It also takes time to become comfortable with the terminology used in the normalization process. During normalization, most designers avoid the use of physical terms such as table, column, and primary key. While the relation being normalized is a proposed table, it does not yet physically exist as a table, so the physical terms are not quite accurate. We use the term *relation* instead of *table, attribute* instead of *column*, and *unique identifier* instead of *primary key*. For newcomers to normalization, it's only natural to use the more familiar physical terms, but do be aware of the preferred terminology if you seek out additional information or examples from other sources. While object names in most DBMSs are not case sensitive, I have shown all table and column names in uppercase for consistency. However, I have shown relation and attribute names in mixed case because that is the custom in the industry.

The normalization process is applied systematically to each user view. At least in the beginning, it is easiest to represent each user view as a two-dimensional table with representative data, as I have done in Figure 1-3. As you work through the normalization process, you will be rewriting existing relations and creating new ones. Rewriting user views into relations (tables) with representative data is a tedious and time-consuming process. Care must be taken that any sample data used to make decisions during normalization is truly representative of the kinds of data values that will appear in real data. As you might expect, poorly constructed sample data often yields a poorly designed database. The good news is that, with practice, you will be able to visualize the sample data and avoid the tedium of recording all of it.

Keep in mind that normalization is intended to remove insert, update, and delete anomalies. The process causes more relations to be created than you would have in an unnormalized design. The additional relations are necessary to remove the anomalies, but spreading the data out into more relations naturally makes retrieval of the stored data a bit more difficult. In effect, you are sacrificing some retrieval performance and ease-of-use in order to make inserts, updates, and deletes go more smoothly.

Choosing a Unique Identifier

The first step in normalization is to choose a *unique identifier*, which is an attribute (column) or set of attributes that uniquely identifies each row of data in the relation.

The unique identifier will eventually become the primary key of the table created from the normalized relation. Normalization absolutely *requires* that a unique identifier be found for each relation. In many cases, a single attribute can be found that uniquely identifies the data in each row of the relation to be normalized. When no single attribute can be found to use for a unique identifier, you may be able to find several attributes that can be concatenated (put together) in order to form the unique identifier. When unique identifiers are formed from multiple attributes, each attribute still remains in its own column—you simply define the unique identifier as consisting of more than one column. In a few cases, there is no reasonable set of attributes in a relation that can be used as a unique identifier. When this occurs, you must invent a unique identifier, often with data values assigned sequentially or randomly as rows of data are added to the database table. This technique is the source of such unique identifiers as social security numbers, employee IDs, and vehicle identification numbers.

The Movie relation in Figure 1-3 presents us with a bit of a poser in finding a unique identifier. At first, it would seem that Movie ID would work just fine. However, notice that Movie ID values "2" and "3" appear twice each, so clearly it's not unique. The problem is that the Movie ID uniquely identifies each movie title, but the video store is keeping track of each *copy* of the movie they have in stock. This is because they rent movies and they want to be sure the renter returns the exact copy that they borrowed. After inspection of the sample data and some discussion with the store's manager, you conclude that there is no combination of attributes in the Movie relation that will uniquely identify each movie copy, so you invent an attribute called Copy Number that you can add to the relation. Whenever a unique identifier (or part of one) is invented, it is very important that everyone understands the values the unique identifier will assume. In this case, the store manager decided she wanted the Copy Number to start over for each Movie ID, which means the Copy Number is only unique when concatenated with Movie ID. The resulting relation is shown in Figure 1-4.

First Normal Form: Eliminating Repeating Data

A relation is in *first normal form* when it contains no *multivalued attributes*, which are attributes that have multiple values in the same row of data. Every intersection of a row and a column in a relation must contain *at most* one data value in order for the relation to be in first normal form. In Figure 1-4, the language (Lang. Code) attribute contains multiple values for at least some movies, so you must consider it a multivalued attribute. Attributes in this form are more difficult to maintain because the list of values must be picked apart so that individual values within the list may be changed while leaving other values in the list intact.

Movie:

MOVIE ID	COPY NUMBER	GENRE CODE	GENRE DESC.	LANG. CODE	MPAA RATING CODE	MPAA RATING DESC.	MOVIE TITLE	YEAR PRODUCED	DATE ACQUIRED	DATE SOLD	MEDIA FORMAT	RETAIL PRICE
1	1	Drama	Drama	en, fr	R	Under 17 requires accompanying parent or adult guardian	Mystic River	2003	1/1/2005		DVD	19.96
2	1	ActAd	Action and Adventure	en, fr, es	R	Under 17 requires accompanying parent or adult guardian	The Last Samurai	2003	1/10/2005		DVD	19.96
2	2	ActAd	Action and Adventure	en, fr, es	R	Under 17 requires accompanying parent or adult guardian	The Last Samurai	2003	1/10/2005		VHS	15.95
3	1	Comdy	Comedy	en	PG-13	Parents strongly cautioned	Something's Gotta Give	2003	1/10/2005	1/30/2005	DVD	29.99
3	2	Comdy	Comedy	en	PG-13	Parents strongly cautioned	Something's Gotta Give	2003	2/15/2005		DVD	29.99
4	1	ActAd	Action and Adventure	en, fr	PG-13	Parents strongly cautioned	The Italian Job	2003	2/15/2005		DVD	19.99

Figure 1-4   Movie relation with Copy Number added

Sometimes a multivalued attribute is disguised as multiple attributes. For example, Figure 1-4 could be changed to have separate attributes (columns) for up to three languages per movie, called Language 1, Language 2, and Language 3. However, they would still be considered multivalued attributes but in a special form called a *repeating group*, which is also forbidden in first normal form. A repeating group is logically no different than one multivalued attribute. In fact, repeating groups often present more maintenance problems than multivalued attributes because a column must be added whenever you want to add more values than the original designer anticipated (such as a fourth language for a movie). Relational databases expect all rows in a table to have the same number of columns, but you can have as many rows as you wish in a table. Therefore, the trick is to take repeating columns and repeating values within columns and turn them into repeating *rows* in another table, and this is exactly what the first normal form process instructs you to do.

To transform unnormalized relations into first normal form, you must move multivalued attributes and repeating groups to new relations. Because a repeating group is a set of attributes that repeat *together*, all attributes in a repeating group should be moved to the same new relation. However, a multivalued attribute (individual attributes that have multiple values) should be moved into its own new relation rather than combined with other multivalued attributes in the new relation.

The procedure for moving a multivalued attribute or repeating group to a new relation is as follows:

1. Create a new relation with a meaningful name. Often it makes sense to include all or part of the original relation's name in the new relation's name.

2. Copy the unique identifier from the original relation to the new one. The data depended on this identifier in the original relation, so it must depend on the same key in the new relation. This copied identifier will become a foreign key in the new relation.

3. Move the repeating group or multivalued attribute to the new relation. (The word *move* is used because these attributes are *removed* from the original relation.)

4. Form a unique identifier in the new relation by adding attributes to the unique identifier that was copied from the original relation. As always, be certain that the newly formed unique identifier has only the minimum attributes needed to make it unique. If you move a multivalued attribute, which is basically a repeating group of only one attribute, it is that attribute that is added in forming the unique identifier. This will seem odd at first, but the unique identifier copied from the original relation is not only a foreign key to the original relation, but also usually part of the unique identifier (primary key) in the new relation. This is quite normal. Also, it is perfectly acceptable to have a relation where all the attributes are part of the unique identifier (that is, there are no "non-key" attributes).

5. Optionally, you may choose to replace the primary key with a single surrogate key attribute. If you do so, you must keep the attributes that make up the natural primary key formed in steps 2 and 4.

Figure 1-5 shows the result of converting the relation shown in Figure 1-4 to first normal form. Note the following:

- I took a bit of shortcut with the unique identifier in the new Movie Language relation. The languages in which a movie is available apply to the movie in general, not to individual copies. Notice that the list of languages does not vary in the duplicate rows for the same movie in Figure 1-4. Therefore, the Copy Number part of the unique identifier in the Movie relation was *not* copied to the new Movie Language relation. Had I done so, it would end up presenting a second normal form problem in the new relation that I would only have to fix in the next normalization step. You'll find that experienced database designers often synthesize the three normal forms simultaneously and simply rewrite original relations in third normal form. With practice, you'll be able to do the same.

Movie:

MOVIE ID	COPY NUMBER	GENRE CODE	GENRE DESC.	MPAA RATING CODE	MPAA RATING DESC.	MOVIE TITLE	YEAR PRODUCED	DATE ACQUIRED	DATE SOLD	MEDIA FORMAT	RETAIL PRICE
1	1	Drama	Drama	R	Under 17 requires accompanying parent or adult guardian	Mystic River	2003	1/1/2005		DVD	19.96
2	1	ActAd	Action and Adventure	R	Under 17 requires accompanying parent or adult guardian	The Last Samurai	2003	1/10/2005		DVD	19.96
2	2	ActAd	Action and Adventure	R	Under 17 requires accompanying parent or adult guardian	The Last Samurai	2003	1/10/2005		VHS	15.95
3	1	Comdy	Comedy	PG-13	Parents strongly cautioned	Something's Gotta Give	2003	1/10/2005	1/30/2005	DVD	29.99
3	2	Comdy	Comedy	PG-13	Parents strongly cautioned	Something's Gotta Give	2003	2/15/2005		DVD	29.99
4	1	ActAd	Action and Adventure	PG-13	Parents strongly cautioned	The Italian Job	2003	2/15/2005		DVD	19.99

Movie Language:

MOVIE ID	LANGUAGE CODE
1	en
1	fr
2	en
2	fr
2	es
3	en
4	en
4	fr

Figure 1-5 First normal form solution

- The Movie ID was copied from Movie (the original relation) to Movie Language (the new relation).

- The Lang. Code multivalued attribute was moved from the Movie relation to the Movie Language relation as the Language Code attribute. (The abbreviated attribute names in Figure 1-4 were for the purposes of illustration—it is always best to abbreviate only when absolutely necessary.)

- The unique identifier of the Movie Language relation is the combination of Movie ID and Language Code, which amounts to all of the attributes in the relation.

- Neither Movie nor Movie Language in Figure 1-5 has repeating groups or multivalued attributes, so both relations are in first normal form.

Second Normal Form: Eliminating Partial Dependencies

Before you explore second normal form, you must understand the concept of *functional dependence*. For this definition, I'll use two arbitrary attributes, cleverly named "A" and "B." Attribute B is *functionally dependent* on attribute A if at any moment in time there is no more than one value of attribute B associated with a given value of attribute A. Lest you wonder what planet the author lived on before this one, let's try to make the definition more understandable. First, saying that attribute B is functionally dependent on attribute A also means that attribute A *determines* attribute B, or that A is a *determinant* (unique identifier) of attribute B. Second, let's have another look at relations in Figure 1-5.

In the Movie relation, you can easily see that Movie Title is functionally dependent on Movie ID because at any point in time, there can be only one value of Movie Title for a given value of Movie ID. The very fact that the Movie ID uniquely defines the Movie Title in the relation means that, in return, the Movie Title is *functionally dependent* on the Movie ID.

A relation is said to be in *second normal form* if it meets the following criteria:

- The relation is in first normal form.

- All non-key attributes are functionally dependent on the *entire* unique identifier (primary key).

In applying the criteria to the Movie relation as shown in Figure 1-5, it should be clear that there are some problems. The entire unique identifier is the combination of Movie ID and Copy Number. However, only the Date Acquired, Date Sold, Media Format, and Retail Price attributes depend on the entire identifier. This does make logical sense. It doesn't matter how many copies of a particular movie you have—they *all* have the same genre, MPAA rating, title, and production year. How did this happen? It should be clear that some of the attributes describe the movie itself, while others describe copies of the movie that the video store has (or used to have) available. Essentially, I've mixed attributes that describe two different (although related) real-world things (entities) in the same relation. No wonder it is such a mess. Second normal form will help us straighten it out.

It should be clear by now that second normal form only applies to relations that have concatenated unique identifiers (that is, those made up of multiple attributes). In a relation with a single attribute as the unique identifier, it's impossible for anything to depend on part of the unique identifier because the unique identifier, being made of only one attribute, simply has no parts. It follows, then, that any first normal form relation that has only a single attribute for its primary key is *automatically* in second normal form.

Once you find a second normal form violation, the solution is to move the attribute(s) that is (are) partially dependent to a new relation where it depends on the *entire* primary key. Figure 1-6 shows the solution. All the attributes that depend only on Movie ID are now in a relation (named Movie) with Movie ID as the unique identifier. Those that depend on the combination of Movie ID and Copy Number are in a relation (named Movie Copy) with Movie ID and Copy Number as the unique identifiers. The Movie Language relation was already in second normal form because it has no non-key attributes and thus remains unchanged.

Third Normal Form: Eliminating Transitive Dependencies

To understand third normal form, you must first understand transitive dependency. An attribute that depends on an attribute that is not the unique identifier (primary key) of the relation is said to be *transitively dependent*. Looking at the Movie relation in Figure 1-6, notice that Genre Description depends on Genre Code, and MPAA Rating Description depends on MPAA Rating Code. The danger of leaving these descriptions in the Movie relation is that you end up making Genre and MPAA rating artificially dependent on Movie, which leads to all three of the data anomalies introduced earlier in this chapter.

A relation is said to be in *third normal form* if it meets both the following criteria:

- The relation is in second normal form.
- There is no transitive dependence (that is, all the non-key attributes depend *only* on the unique identifier).

To transform a second normal form relation into third normal form, simply move any transitively dependent attributes to relations where they depend only on the primary key. Be careful to leave the attribute on which they depend in the original relation as the foreign key. You will need it to reconstruct the original user view via a join. Incidentally, any attributes that are easily calculated are removed as third normal form violations. For example, if on a sales transaction, Quantity Purchased times Price Each yields Total Paid, it's easy to see that Total Paid is dependent on Quantity Purchased and Price Each. Assuming all three of those would be dependent on the unique identifier of the relation that contains them, it's easy to see that Total Paid (the calculated result) is, in fact, *transitively dependent* on the other two attributes.

Figure 1-7 contains the solution in third normal form. Note that you have created new relations for MPAA Rating and Movie Genre, moved the descriptions to the new relations, and left the code attributes (MPAA Rating Code and Movie Genre Code) in the Movie relation as foreign keys. Many database designers call relations like MPAA Rating and Movie Genre "lookup tables" or "code tables" because their main usage is to look up descriptions for the codes that are stored in the primary key

Movie:

MOVIE ID	GENRE CODE	GENRE DESCRIPTION	MPAA RATING CODE	MPAA RATING DESCRIPTION	MOVIE TITLE	YEAR PRODUCED
1	Drama	Drama	R	Under 17 requires accompanying parent or adult guardian	Mystic River	2003
2	ActAd	Action and Adventure	R	Under 17 requires accompanying parent or adult guardian	The Last Samurai	2003
3	Comdy	Comedy	PG-13	Parents strongly cautioned	Something's Gotta Give	2003
4	ActAd	Action and Adventure	PG-13	Parents strongly cautioned	The Italian Job	2003

Movie Language:

MOVIE ID	LANGUAGE CODE
1	en
1	fr
2	en
2	fr
2	es
3	en
4	en
4	fr

Movie Copy:

MOVIE ID	COPY NUMBER	DATE ACQUIRED	DATE SOLD	MEDIA FORMAT	RETAIL PRICE
1	1	1/1/2005		DVD	19.96
2	1	1/10/2005		DVD	19.96
2	2	1/10/2005		VHS	15.95
3	1	1/10/2005	1/30/2005	DVD	29.99
3	2	2/15/2005		DVD	29.99
4	1	2/15/2005		DVD	19.99

Figure 1-6   Second normal form solution

Movie:

MOVIE ID	MOVIE GENRE CODE	MPAA RATING CODE	MOVIE TITLE	RETAIL PRICE VHS	RETAIL PRICE DVD	YEAR PRODUCED
1	Drama	R	Mystic River	58.97	19.96	2003
2	ActAd	R	The Last Samurai	15.95	19.96	2003
3	Comdy	PG-13	Something's Gotta Give	14.95	29.99	2003
4	ActAd	PG-13	The Italian Job	11.95	19.99	2003

Movie Copy:

MOVIE ID	COPY NUMBER	DATE ACQUIRED	DATE SOLD	MEDIA FORMAT
1	1	1/1/2005		DVD
2	1	1/10/2005		DVD
2	2	1/10/2005		VHS
3	1	1/10/2005	1/30/2005	DVD
3	2	2/15/2005		DVD
4	1	2/15/2005		DVD

MPAA Rating:

MPAA RATING CODE	MPAA RATING DESCRIPTION
PG-13	Parents strongly cautioned
R	Under 17 requires accompanying parent or adult guardian

Movie Genre:

MOVIE GENRE CODE	MOVIE GENRE DESCRIPTION
ActAd	Action and Adventure
Comdy	Comedy
Drama	Drama

Figure 1-7   Third normal form relation

column of the relation. However, they serve other important purposes, such as controlling the values of the codes themselves and providing a convenient source for a list of valid code values that might be used in a pull-down list on a web page form.

One other design change made to achieve third normal form had to do with the Retail Price in the Movie Copy relation as shown in Figure 1-6. After discussion with the store manager, it was determined that the price depends on the combination of Movie ID and Media Format, with all copies having the same Movie ID and Media Format getting the same price. This is clearly a transitive dependency and therefore a violation of third normal form. The normal solution for such a problem would be to create a relation named Movie Price with a unique identifier of Movie ID and Media Format, and then to move the Retail Price from Movie Copy to the new relation. However, during the discussion with the store manager, she indicated that they were in the process of discontinuing VHS format movies because very few customers wanted them, and that within a few months, the store would handle only DVDs. With that news in mind, I decided to move the price to two columns in the Movie table, one for the DVD price, and the other for the VHS price. While it could be argued that this is a first normal form violation (and technically speaking, it is), it seemed the best compromise. Database design isn't always an exact science, so there is often a bit of room for adjustments provided the designer always considers the potential consequences (measured in terms of data anomalies) of each compromise.

Beyond Third Normal Form

Dr. E. F. Codd participated in the definition of a stronger version of third normal form called Boyce-Codd normal form. Various other authors and researchers have offered their extensions under the names fourth normal form, fifth normal form, and domain-key normal form, among others. In my experience, it takes a bit of practice with normalization before these extensions make a whole lot of sense. Moreover, third normal form covers just about every anomaly you will find in everyday database design work.

Overview of the Video Store Sample Database

All of the examples used in this book are based on a database for a fictitious video store. The SQL statements required to create the database objects and populate them with data can be downloaded as described later in this chapter. Figure 1-8

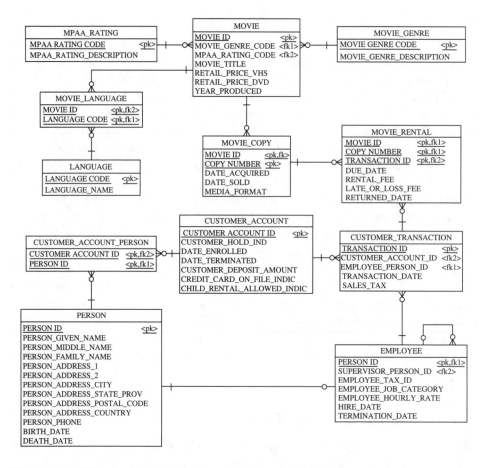

Figure 1-8   Video store Entity Relationship Diagram (ERD)

presents the entity relationship diagram (ERD) for the entire video store database. A brief description of each table appears here so you may familiarize yourself with the database design, which will help you understand the examples as you start learning SQL in the next chapter.

The video store for which the sample database was designed is a small family-owned and operated store that rents and sells videos in both VHS and DVD formats. However, the VHS format is being discontinued. The store manager expects to expand into other product lines, such as snack foods, but the plans to do so were not firm enough to be included in the current database design.

Table 1-1 gives some information about each table included in the design.

Table 1-2 gives some information about the columns in the database tables.

Table Name	Description	Primary Key	Parent Table(s)
CUSTOMER_ ACCOUNT	Contains one row for each customer account opened with the video store.	CUSTOMER_ ACCOUNT_ID	None
CUSTOMER_ ACCOUNT_ PERSON	Intersection table that shows which people are associated with each customer account.	CUSTOMER_ ACCOUNT_ID, PERSON_ID	CUSTOMER_ ACCOUNT, PERSON
CUSTOMER_ TRANSACTION	Contains one row for each transaction initiated by a customer. Each transaction may contain one or more movie rentals.	TRANSACTION_ID	CUSTOMER_ ACCOUNT, EMPLOYEE
EMPLOYEE	Contains one row for each employee of the video store. This table is a subclass of Person (each Employee will have a matching row with the same primary key value in the PERSON table).	PERSON_ID	PERSON
LANGUAGE	Lookup table of language codes and names (used to show language options for movies).	LANGUAGE_ CODE	None
MOVIE	Contains one row for each movie title. Child table MOVIE_COPY shows copies of the movie owned by the store.	MOVIE_ID	MPAA_RATING, MOVIE_GENRE
MOVIE_COPY	Contains one row for each movie copy available for sale or rent.	MOVIE_ID, COPY_NUMBER	MOVIE
MOVIE_GENRE	Lookup table of genre codes and descriptions (used to categorize movies).	MOVIE_GENRE_ CODE	None
MOVIE_ LANGUAGE	Intersection table that shows languages available for each movie.	MOVIE_ID, LANGUAGE_ CODE	MOVIE, LANGUAGE

Table 1-1   Video Store Database Tables

Table Name	Description	Primary Key	Parent Table(s)
MOVIE_ RENTAL	Contains one row for each time the movie was rented.	MOVIE_ID, COPY_NUMBER, TRANSACTION_ID	MOVIE_COPY, CUSTOMER_ TRANSACTION
MPAA_RATING	Lookup table of MPAA rating codes and descriptions.	MPAA_RATING_ CODE	None
PERSON	Contains one row for each individual associated with the video store. Each person may be a customer (associated with a Customer Account) or employee or both.	PERSON_ID	None

Table 1-1   Video Store Database Tables *(Continued)*

Table Name	Column Name	Description
CUSTOMER_ACCOUNT	CHILD_RENTAL_ ALLOWED_INDIC	Yes/No indicator as to whether or not persons under 18 are permitted to check out movies using this account
CUSTOMER_ACCOUNT	CREDIT_CARD_ON_FILE_ INDIC	Yes/No indicator as to whether customer left a credit card imprint on file to guarantee payment of their account
CUSTOMER_ACCOUNT	CUSTOMER_ACCOUNT_ID	Primary key— sequential number assigned to each customer account
CUSTOMER_ACCOUNT	CUSTOMER_DEPOSIT_ AMOUNT	For customers who did not provide a credit card, the amount of cash deposit they provided to the store

Table 1-2   Video Store Database Table Columns

Table Name	Column Name	Description
CUSTOMER_ACCOUNT	CUSTOMER_HOLD_IND	Yes/No indicator as to whether or not customer account is on hold; rentals are not permitted against accounts on hold
CUSTOMER_ACCOUNT	DATE_ENROLLED	The date the account with the store was opened
CUSTOMER_ACCOUNT	DATE_TERMINATED	If account was closed, the date of closure (null for active accounts)
CUSTOMER_ACCOUNT_PERSON	CUSTOMER_ACCOUNT_ID	Part of primary key—foreign key to CUSTOMER_ACCOUNT table
CUSTOMER_TRANSACTION	CUSTOMER_ACCOUNT_ID	Foreign key to CUSTOMER_ACCOUNT table
CUSTOMER_TRANSACTION	EMPLOYEE_PERSON_ID	Foreign key (PERSON_ID) to EMPLOYEE table
CUSTOMER_TRANSACTION	SALES_TAX	Sales tax charged for the transaction
CUSTOMER_TRANSACTION	TRANSACTION_DATE	Date of the transaction
CUSTOMER_TRANSACTION	TRANSACTION_ID	Primary key—sequential number assigned to each new transaction
EMPLOYEE	EMPLOYEE_HOURLY_RATE	Pay rate per hour for the employee
EMPLOYEE	EMPLOYEE_JOB_CATEGORY	Job category for the employee (manager or clerk)
EMPLOYEE	EMPLOYEE_TAX_ID	ID used for reporting payroll taxes for the employee (usually a Social Security Number)

Table 1-2   Video Store Database Table Columns (Continued)

Table Name	Column Name	Description
EMPLOYEE	HIRE_DATE	Date the employee was hired by the store
EMPLOYEE	PERSON_ID	Primary key—foreign key to the PERSON table
EMPLOYEE	SUPERVISOR_PERSON_ID	Primary key—foreign key to the EMPLOYEE table (to show the person to whom they report)
EMPLOYEE	TERMINATION_DATE	For former employees, the date their employment was terminated
LANGUAGE	LANGUAGE_CODE	Primary key—ISO (International Organization for Standardization) standard two-character code for a language
LANGUAGE	LANGUAGE_NAME	Name (in English) for the language
MOVIE	MOVIE_GENRE_CODE	Foreign key to MOVIE_GENRE table
MOVIE	MOVIE_ID	Primary key—values are assigned sequentially as new movies become available
MOVIE	MOVIE_TITLE	Official title of the movie (movie titles are not necessarily unique)
MOVIE	MPAA_RATING_CODE	Foreign key to MPAA_RATING table
MOVIE	RETAIL_PRICE_DVD	Retail list price for DVD copies of the movie
MOVIE	RETAIL_PRICE_VHS	Retail list price for VHS copies of the movie

Table 1-2   Video Store Database Table Columns *(Continued)*

Table Name	Column Name	Description
MOVIE	YEAR_PRODUCED	The year the movie completed production; year released by studio
MOVIE_COPY	COPY_NUMBER	Part of primary key—sequential number assigned to each copy of a movie (number unique only within a given movie)
MOVIE_COPY	DATE_ACQUIRED	Date movie copy was acquired by the video store
MOVIE_COPY	DATE_SOLD	Date movie copy was sold (null if movie has not been sold)
MOVIE_COPY	MEDIA_FORMAT	Recording format of the movie copy (DVD or VHS)
MOVIE_COPY	MOVIE_ID	Part of primary key—foreign key to MOVIE table
MOVIE_GENRE	MOVIE_GENRE_CODE	Primary key—a code used to place movies into categories such as Comedy, Drama, Action-Adventure, and so forth
MOVIE_GENRE	MOVIE_GENRE_DESCRIPTION	Text description of a movie category (see MOVIE_GENRE_CODE)
MOVIE_LANGUAGE	LANGUAGE_CODE	Part of primary key—foreign key to LANGUAGE table
MOVIE_LANGUAGE	MOVIE_ID	Part of primary key—foreign key to MOVIE table
MOVIE_RENTAL	COPY_NUMBER	Part of primary key—foreign key to MOVIE_COPY table

Table 1-2   Video Store Database Table Columns *(Continued)*

Table Name	Column Name	Description
MOVIE_RENTAL	DUE_DATE	The date a rented movie is due to be returned to the store
MOVIE_RENTAL	LATE_OR_LOSS_FEE	Fee charged (if any) because the movie copy was returned late or was permanently lost
MOVIE_RENTAL	MOVIE_ID	Part of primary key—foreign key to MOVIE_COPY table
MOVIE_RENTAL	RENTAL_FEE	Fee charged for the rental (adjusted for any coupons or discounts)
MOVIE_RENTAL	RETURNED_DATE	Date movie copy was returned (null until movie is checked in as returned)
MOVIE_RENTAL	TRANSACTION_ID	Part of primary key—foreign key to CUSTOMER_TRANSACTION table
MPAA_RATING	MPAA_RATING_CODE	Primary key—movie rating code supplied by Motion Picture Association of America (MPAA), including G, PG, PG-13, R, NC-17, and NR (not rated)
MPAA_RATING	MPAA_RATING_DESCRIPTION	Text description of rating, as supplied by the MPAA
PERSON	BIRTH_DATE	The person's date of birth
PERSON	DEATH_DATE	The person's date of death (if person reported as deceased)
PERSON	PERSON_ADDRESS_1	First line of the person's street address

Table 1-2   Video Store Database Table Columns *(Continued)*

Table Name	Column Name	Description
PERSON	PERSON_ADDRESS_2	Optional second line of the person's street address
PERSON	PERSON_ADDRESS_CITY	The municipality for the person's mailing address
PERSON	PERSON_ADDRESS_ COUNTRY	The ISO abbreviation for the country for the person's mailing address
PERSON	PERSON_ADDRESS_ POSTAL_CODE	The postal code (ZIP code in the U.S.) for the person's mailing address
PERSON	PERSON_ADDRESS_STATE_ PROV	The state or province for the person's mailing address
PERSON	PERSON_FAMILY_NAME	The last name of the person
PERSON	PERSON_GIVEN_NAME	The first name of the person
PERSON	PERSON_ID	Primary key— sequential number assigned to each person who has an affiliation with the video store
PERSON	PERSON_MIDDLE_NAME	The middle name (or initial) of the person
PERSON	PERSON_PHONE	The person's primary phone number

Table 1-2   Video Store Database Table Columns *(Continued)*

Downloading the SQL for the Sample Database

A script file containing the SQL standard CREATE statements to create all the video store sample database tables and indexes used in the examples throughout this book, along with the INSERT statements to populate the tables with the sample data that was used in the examples, is available for download from the

www.osborne.com website. I strongly encourage you to create the sample database and run the examples as you read this book. Just follow these simple steps:

1. Use your web browser to go to www.osborne.com.
2. Click the "free code" link near the upper left-hand corner of the page.
3. Scroll down until you find the link for "SQL Demystified" and click it.
4. The download should start automatically—your browser will ask you where you wish to save the file.

In an ideal world, SQL that complies with the ISO/ANSI standard would run on any database that supports SQL. While that is not quite the case, the good news is that very few (if any) modifications have to be made for the most popular DBMSs on the market today. For some DBMSs, such as MySQL, no modifications are necessary. For Oracle and Microsoft SQL Server, the required modifications appear in the topics that follow. For other DBMSs, consult the vendor's documentation for information on supported data types, particularly date and time data types.

Modifications Required for Oracle

The Oracle default date format is DD-MON-RR, which is a two-digit day, a three-letter month, and a two-digit year with the century assumed based on a 50-year window. For example, January 15, 2005 would display as 15-JAN-05 in the Oracle default format. The SQL INSERT statements in the appendix and all the examples in this book use MM/DD/YYYY as the date format, with January 15, 2005 written as 01/15/2005. There are two ways to overcome this difference:

- **Change the date format**   While possible to do, it is not wise to change the default date format permanently for the database. However, it is very simple to change the format for your session just after you connect to the Oracle database. All you have to do is run this command in your Oracle SQL client (SQL*Plus or iSQL*Plus) before you run any statements that include dates:

```
ALTER SESSION SET NLS_DATE_FORMAT='MM/DD/YYYY';
```

- **Alter all date strings**   This is a more tedious solution that involves editing the SQL statements and changing all dates in MM/DD/YYYY format to DD-MON-RR format.

Modifications Required for Microsoft SQL Server

For Microsoft SQL Server, the following modifications are required:

- **Change DATE to DATETIME**   Microsoft SQL Server does not recognize DATE as a data type. Therefore, all references to DATE in the CREATE TABLE statements must be changed to DATETIME.

- **For iSQL, put statements in batches**   The iSQL client expects SQL statements to be run in batches with the keyword **go** written on a line by itself at the end of every batch. While most SQL clients run statements as soon as they encounter the semicolon that marks the end of each statement, iSQL waits for the keyword **go**. The number of statements in a batch is purely up to you, but if you put too many in a batch, problems are more difficult to resolve. Just add the keyword on a line by itself periodically throughout the SQL statements, and make sure you also have one at the very end.

Quiz

Choose the correct responses to each of the multiple-choice questions. Note that there may be more than one correct response to each question.

1. SQL is
    a. A language invented by Dr. E. F. Codd
    b. A language used to communicate with relational databases
    c. A language used to define Entity Relationship Diagrams
    d. Used to define and modify database objects
    e. Used to define web pages

2. A database is
    a. A named data structure such as a table, view, or index
    b. Software provided by the database vendor
    c. A collection of interrelated data items that are managed as a single unit
    d. Defined in the same way by all software vendors
    e. Implemented differently by different vendors

3. A database object is

   a. A named data structure such as a table, view, or index

   b. A structure such as a table, view, or index

   c. Software provided by the database vendor

   d. A collection of interrelated data items that are managed as a single unit

   e. A collection of related records that are stored as a single unit

4. A database management system is

   a. A structure such as a table, view, or index

   b. A collection of interrelated data items that are managed as a single unit

   c. Software provided by the database vendor

   d. Often abbreviated as DBMS

   e. A named data structure such as a table, view, or index

5. Examples of RDBMSs include

   a. INGRES

   b. MySQL

   c. PostgreSQL

   d. Oracle Database

   e. Microsoft SQL Server

6. Basic services provided by the DBMS include

   a. Support of a query language

   b. Generation of Entity Relationship Diagrams

   c. Security mechanisms to prevent unauthorized data access and modification

   d. Moving data to and from the physical files as needed

   e. Storage of data in tabular form

7. Components of a relational database include

   a. Relationships

   b. Tables

   c. User views

   d. ERDs

   e. Constraints

8. In an ERD, maximum cardinality is shown with

    a. A circle drawn on the relationship line

    b. A vertical line drawn across the relationship line

    c. A "crow's foot" on an end of the relationship line

    d. No symbol on the end of the relationship line

    e. The notation "<pk>" above the relationship line

9. Types of database constraints include

    a. NOT NULL

    b. Relationship

    c. Primary key

    d. CHECK

    e. Unique

10. Functions of views include

    a. Documenting relationships between tables

    b. Improving query performance

    c. Hiding columns users need not see

    d. Hiding rows users need not see

    e. Exposing complex database operations

11. Normalization is intended to solve the following problems:

    a. Insert anomaly

    b. Slow performance

    c. Creation anomaly

    d. Delete anomaly

    e. Update anomaly

12. The normalization process

    a. Starts with tables to help designers discover the user views

    b. Was developed by Dr. E. F. Codd

    c. Was developed by Oracle

    d. Is systematically applied to each user view

    e. Is easily mastered

13. A unique identifier
    a. Must be identified before a view can be normalized
    b. May be composed of only one attribute
    c. May be formed by inventing a new attribute
    d. May be composed of zero, one, or many attributes
    e. May be composed of concatenated attributes

14. First normal form resolves anomalies caused by
    a. Partial dependency on the primary key
    b. Repeating groups
    c. Transitive dependency
    d. Multivalued attributes
    e. One-to-many relationships

15. Second normal form resolves anomalies caused by
    a. Partial dependency on the primary key
    b. Repeating groups
    c. Transitive dependency
    d. Multivalued attributes
    e. One-to-many relationships

16. Third normal form resolves anomalies caused by
    a. Partial dependency on the primary key
    b. Repeating groups
    c. Transitive dependency
    d. Multivalued attributes
    e. One-to-many relationships

17. To be in third normal form, a relation
    a. Must be in first normal form
    b. Must be in second normal form
    c. Must have a unique identifier
    d. Must have no transitive dependencies
    e. Must have no repeating groups or multivalued attributes

18. When transforming an unnormalized relation to first normal form

    a. Attributes depending on only part of the key are removed

    b. Multivalued attributes are moved to a new relation

    c. Attributes that are transitively dependent are removed

    d. Repeating groups are moved to other relations

    e. The unique identifier of the original relation is copied to the new relation

19. Partial dependency issues

    a. Are resolved by second normal form

    b. Are resolved by third normal form

    c. Can only occur in relations with concatenated primary keys

    d. Occur when a non-key attribute depends on part of the primary key

    e. Occur when a non-key attribute depends on another non-key attribute

20. Transitive dependency issues

    a. Are resolved by second normal form

    b. Are resolved by third normal form

    c. Can only occur in relations with concatenated primary keys

    d. Occur when a non-key attribute depends on part of the primary key

    e. Occur when a non-key attribute depends on another non-key attribute

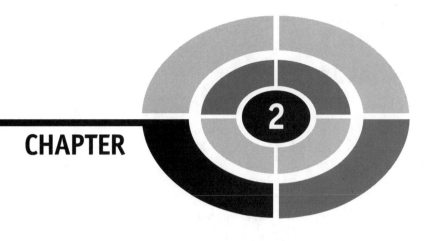

CHAPTER

2

SQL Concepts

This chapter introduces SQL, which will be expanded upon throughout the remainder of this book. SQL has become the universal language for relational databases and nearly every DBMS in modern use supports it. There is little doubt that this wide acceptance is the result of the time and effort that went into the development of language features and standards, making SQL highly portable across different RDBMS products.

Your learning experience with SQL will be greatly enhanced if you actively use SQL and a relational database to try the examples in this book as you read. Moreover, you'll learn even more if you experiment with your own variations of the examples. The video store database used throughout this book can be implemented on a relational database of your choice. Instructions for downloading the SQL statements that define the tables and load them with sample data appear toward the end of Chapter 1.

What Is SQL?

SQL (Structured Query Language) is a standard language used to communicate with a relational database. The name may be pronounced either as the letters S-Q-L or as the word "sequel." A *query* is simply a request that is sent to the database for which the database sends some form of response back to the sender. SQL is the most common language used to form database queries. SQL is considered a *nonprocedural* or *declarative* language, which means that you tell the computer the results you want without telling it how to achieve them. For example, if you want the average of a column of numbers, you simply use the AVG function to ask for it. There is no need to count how many numbers are in the column and to divide by that count—the SQL language processor in the DBMS handles all of that for you. SQL functions are presented in detail in Chapter 4.

It is important to understand that SQL is *not* a procedural language like C, Pascal, Basic, FORTRAN, COBOL, or Ada. *A procedural* language uses a series of statements that are executed in sequence. Procedural languages also include statements that can alter the execution sequence by branching to other parts of the procedure or looping back through some set of statements in the procedure. Many RDBMS vendors have procedural extensions to their basic SQL language, such as Oracle's PL/SQL (Procedural Language/SQL) or Microsoft's Transact-SQL, but keep in mind that these are extensions to SQL that form new languages—the SQL in them is still nonprocedural. SQL should also not be confused with object-oriented programming languages such as Java and C++. Simply stated, SQL is a language for managing and maintaining relational databases, not a language suitable for general programming of applications, such as order entry and payroll systems.

SQL is often used in conjunction with the procedural and object-oriented languages mentioned earlier to handle storing and retrieving data, with statements in the more general programming language used for other programming tasks, such as presenting data on a web page and responding to user input from the keyboard and mouse. When an interaction with the database is required, procedural language statements form the SQL statement, send it to the RDBMS for processing, and receive the results from the RDBMS and process them appropriately.

Connecting to the Database

When using SQL on a personal computer with a personal copy of a DBMS such as Microsoft Access or Oracle Personal Edition, all of the database components are running on one computer system. However, this arrangement isn't adequate for databases that need to be shared by multiple users. Therefore, it is much more common for the database to be deployed in a client/server arrangement as shown in Figure 2-1.

In a client/server arrangement:

- The DBMS software runs on a *server*, which is a shared computer system. For the purposes of this definition, a mainframe computer system can be considered a large server.

- The files that physically comprise the database are stored on disks that are connected to the database server.

- Users accessing the database use workstations called *clients* to access the database. The client must have a network connection to the database, which can be a private network deployed in a home or office or a public network such as the Internet.

- Software provided by the DBMS vendor runs on the client workstation to provide the user with the ability to enter SQL statements, submit them to the DBMS for processing, and view the results returned by the DBMS. This software is generically known as the *SQL client*.

It should be noted that nothing stops someone from installing the SQL client software on the same computer system as the DBMS itself. In fact, application

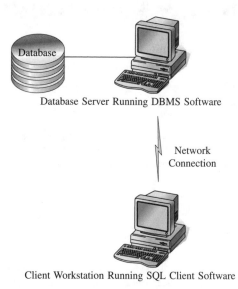

Database Server Running DBMS Software

Network
Connection

Client Workstation Running SQL Client Software

Figure 2-1   SQL client connection to the database

developers using DBMSs such as MySQL, Microsoft SQL Server, and Oracle commonly do this because it is so convenient to have the entire environment on a single computer system, such as a laptop. However, the moment shared access by multiple users is required, it is more convenient and efficient to have a single copy of the DBMS on a shared server and to have only the SQL client installed on each user's workstation.

SQL clients are categorized by the user interface on the client workstation, with three basic types: command-line, graphical, and web-based. A *command-line* interface is based solely on textual input and output, with commands entered from the keyboard and responses to the commands displayed as text messages. The main benefit of command-line interfaces is that they can run on just about any operating system. As an example of a command-line SQL client, Figure 2-2 shows Oracle SQL*Plus (one of Oracle's SQL clients) running in a Microsoft Windows command window. A *graphical user interface (GUI)* runs under some sort of windowing system, such as the X Window System, Mac OS, or Microsoft Windows, and displays data and command options using graphical features such as icons, buttons, and dialog boxes. Figure 2-3 shows Oracle SQL*Plus running as a GUI application on Microsoft Windows. A *web-based* interface runs on the database server, using a web browser on the client workstation to interact with the database user. Technically, a web-based SQL client isn't a client application at all because there is no

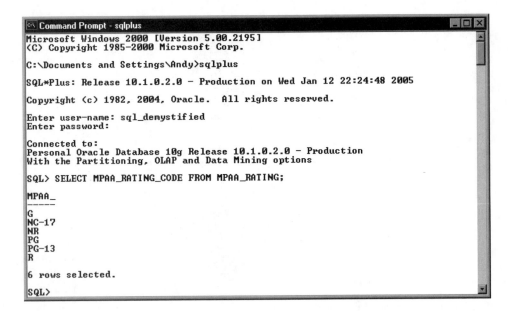

Figure 2-2   Oracle SQL*Plus running in a Microsoft Windows command window.

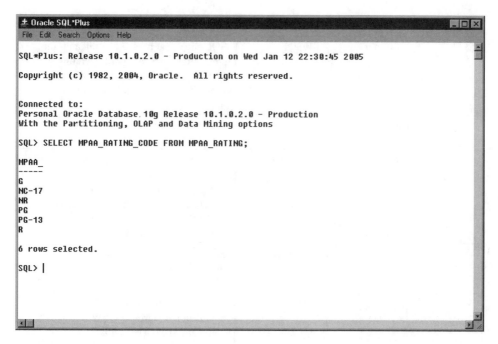

```
± Oracle SQL*Plus                                                    _ □ ×
File  Edit  Search  Options  Help

SQL*Plus: Release 10.1.0.2.0 - Production on Wed Jan 12 22:30:45 2005

Copyright (c) 1982, 2004, Oracle.  All rights reserved.


Connected to:
Personal Oracle Database 10g Release 10.1.0.2.0 - Production
With the Partitioning, OLAP and Data Mining options

SQL> SELECT MPAA_RATING_CODE FROM MPAA_RATING;

MPAA_
-----
G
NC-17
NR
PG
PG-13
R

6 rows selected.

SQL> |
```

Figure 2-3   Oracle SQL*Plus running as a Microsoft Windows application

DBMS vendor–specific software running on the client workstation. However, there are almost always DBMS vendor–supplied components that are silently download-ed by the web browser to assist it in the graphical presentation of the web form used for entering SQL statements and displaying results. Figure 2-4 shows the Oracle iSQL*Plus client running in the Mozilla Firefox browser.

The following table lists SQL client software from various DBMS vendors. There isn't space in this book to cover all the details about every SQL client that you might use, so please consult your DBMS vendor's documentation for informa-tion on installing and using the SQL client(s) available for your DBMS.

Vendor	DBMS	SQL Client	Description
Microsoft	Access	None	Microsoft Access is a personal use database, so the SQL client is integrated into the DBMS, all of which runs locally on the user's workstation.
Microsoft	SQL Server	iSQL	SQL client that runs as a command-line application in a Microsoft Windows command shell.
Microsoft	SQL Server	Query Analyzer	SQL client that runs as a Microsoft Windows application.

Vendor	DBMS	SQL Client	Description
MySQL	MySQL	MySQL	SQL client that runs as a command-line application on a variety of operating systems, including Microsoft Windows, Linux, Mac OS X, and various Unix implementations.
Oracle	Oracle	iSQL*Plus	Web-based SQL client—supported in versions from Oracle 9*i* and up.
Oracle	Oracle	SQL*Plus	SQL client that runs either as a Microsoft Windows application or as a command-line application on a variety of operating systems, including Microsoft Windows, Linux, Mac OS X, various Unix implementations, and others.
Oracle	Oracle	SQL Worksheet	SQL client written in Java—available in Oracle 8*i* and 9*i* but replaced by iSQL*Plus in Oracle 10*g*.
Sybase	Sybase	iSQL	SQL client that runs as a command-line application in a Microsoft Windows command shell. The similarity to Microsoft SQL Server is no accident—the earliest versions of Microsoft SQL Server were based on the Sybase DBMS.

A Brief History of SQL

In the later 1970s, a group of IBM researchers developed an experimental relational database called System/R, based on Dr. E. F. Codd's work. A language called SEQUEL (Structured English Query Language) was included in System/R to manipulate and retrieve data. The acronym "SEQUEL" was later condensed to the abbreviation "SQL" when it was discovered that the word "SEQUEL" was a trademark held by the Hawker-Siddeley Aircraft Company of the U.K.

Although IBM had the first implementation of SQL, two other products, with various names for their query languages, beat IBM to the marketplace with the first commercial relational database products: Relational Software's Oracle and Relational Technology's INGRES. IBM released SQL/DS in 1982, with the query language now named SQL (Structured Query Language). Although *structured programming* was the mantra of the day in the 1980s, the "structured" in the name SQL has nothing to do with structured programming since SQL isn't a procedural programming language. However, it is entirely possible that the marketing spin on

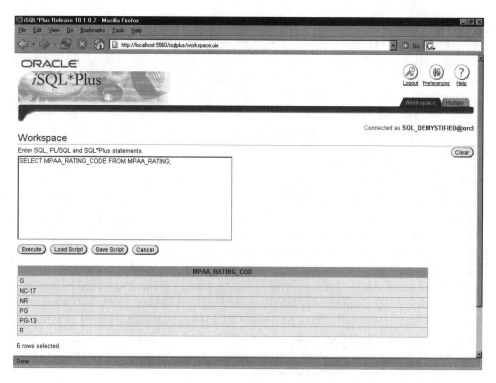

Figure 2-4   Oracle iSQL*Plus running in the Mozilla Firefox browser

structured programming helped bolster the name "SQL" over the names coined by other vendors of the day for their data query languages.

SQL standards committees were formed by ANSI (American National Standards Institute) in 1986 and ISO (International Organization for Standardization) in 1987. Fortunately, the committees from the two organizations worked together to develop a common, worldwide SQL standard. Two years later, the first standard specification, known as SQL-89, was published. The standard was expanded three years later into SQL-92, which weighed in at roughly 600 pages. The third generation was called SQL-99, or SQL3. Most RDBMS products are built to the SQL-92 (now called SQL2) standard. SQL3 includes many of the object features required for SQL to operate on an object-relational database, as well as language extensions to make SQL computationally complete (adding looping, branching, and case constructs). The most recent generation, known as SQL:2003, introduces XML-related features and other enhancements. Only a few vendors have implemented significant components of the SQL3 and SQL:2003 standards. While DBMS vendors have teams of people devoted to standards compliance, most people who write SQL are

not well versed in them. This is largely because the standards are not freely available. The SQL:2003 standard may be purchased from ISO (www.iso.org) or ANSI (webstore.ansi.org). For those on a budget, a late draft is available from Whitemarsh Information Systems Corporation (www.wiscorp.com/SQLStandards.html).

Standards are important because they promote *portability*, which is the ease with which software can be made to run ("ported") to other platforms. In the case of SQL, portability across RDBMS products from different vendors was poor until the vendors started complying with published standards. Nevertheless, nearly every vendor has added extensions to their "dialect" of SQL, partly because they wanted to differentiate their products and partly because market demands pressed them into implementing features before there were standards for them. One case in point is support for the DATE and TIMESTAMP data types. Dates are highly important in business data processing, but the developers of the original RDBMS products were computer scientists and academics, not business computing specialists, so such a need was unanticipated. As a result, the early SQL dialects did not have any special support for dates. As commercial products emerged, vendors responded to pressure from their biggest customers by hurriedly adding support for dates. Unfortunately, this led to each doing so in their own way. Whenever you migrate SQL statements from one vendor to another, beware of the SQL dialect differences. SQL is highly compatible and portable across vendor products, but complete database systems can seldom be moved without some adjustments.

SQL Syntax Conventions

This section presents the general syntax conventions used in forming SQL statements. However, keep in mind that there are a lot of vendor extensions and variations. For simplicity, the term *implementation* is used to refer to each version of SQL from each vendor (that is, Oracle 9*i*, Oracle 10*g*, Microsoft SQL Server 7, Microsoft SQL Server 2000, and Microsoft SQL Server 2005 all contain different *implementations* of SQL).

SQL syntax conventions will be easier to understand using a simple example. This statement lists the Movie ID and Movie Title for every movie in the video store that has a rating of PG:

```
SELECT MOVIE_ID, MOVIE_TITLE
  FROM MOVIE
 WHERE MPAA_RATING_CODE = 'PG';
```

The basic conventions are

- Each statement begins with a command, usually in the form of a single word, which is almost always an action verb. In this example, the statement starts with the SELECT command, which is described in detail in Chapter 4.

- Each statement ends with a delimiter, which is usually a semicolon (;). Some implementations allow the delimiter to be changed to some other character. Moreover, some implementations such as Oracle's will not execute an SQL statement that is missing the ending delimiter, while other implementations consider the ending delimiter optional.

- Statements are formed in a similar manner to English sentences, with one or more spaces used to separate language elements. A *language element*, similar to a word in an English sentence, is any keyword (SELECT, FROM, WHERE), database object name (MOVIE, MOVIE_ID, MOVIE_TITLE), operator (=), or constant ('PG') that may appear in a statement.

- Statements are written in a free-form style, which means there are no strict rules about the position of language elements on a line or where a statement may be broken to a new line. However, it is generally not a good idea to split any single language element across multiple lines. This statement is logically identical to the one shown at the beginning of this topic, but isn't as easy to read and understand:

```
SELECT MOVIE_ID,MOVIE_NAME FROM MOVIE WHERE
MPAA_RATING_CODE='PG';
```

- Statements are organized into a series of clauses, and usually clauses must appear in a particular sequence when they are present (many clauses are optional). In our example, there are three clauses, each beginning with a keyword (SELECT, FROM, WHERE).

- SQL language elements may be written in upper- or lowercase or mixed case. However, in most implementations, and per the ANSI/ISO standards, all lowercase characters are automatically shifted to uppercase for processing. This is not to say that data can never be in lowercase but rather that commands and database object names (tables, columns, etc.) must be in uppercase. Notable exceptions are Microsoft SQL Server and Sybase, both of which allow the database to operate in "case-sensitive mode" wherein object names written in different cases are treated as different names. In MySQL, object name case sensitivity is tied to whether or not the underlying operating system has case-sensitive names or not.

- Commas are used to separate items in a list. In our example, two column names were provided in a comma-separated list (MOVIE_ID, MOVIE_ TITLE). Spaces following each comma are completely optional—you can include no spaces, or as many as you want.

- Character strings that appear in SQL statements must be enclosed in single quotes (some SQL implementations also allow double quotes). Numeric constants are never enclosed in quotes. If a quote needs to appear within the character string, two single quotes next to each other take care of it. For example, if you wanted to find the movie *Sophie's Choice* in the database, you would write the WHERE clause like this:

```
WHERE MOVIE_NAME = 'Sophie''s Choice'
```

- Database object names are formed using *only* letters, numbers, and the underscore character. Underscores are typically used as separators between words to improve readability. As previously mentioned, some implementations allow case-sensitive names such as PersonMiddleName, a style often called "camelcase," but this is not a good practice if the SQL is to be portable to other implementations. After all, a name like "PERSONMIDDLENAME" is not very easy to read.

- Each SQL implementation has a defined set of *reserved words*, which are words that have specific meaning to the SQL query processor in the DBMS and therefore may not be used in other contexts, such as for the name of database objects. This restriction is to avoid misinterpretation of SQL statements by the DBMS. As you might guess, the list of reserved words varies significantly from one SQL implementation to another, so it is wise to consult the documentation for the implementation you are using to become familiar with them.

- A single-line comment is started with two consecutive hyphens (--). The two hyphens can be at the beginning of a line, in which case the entire line becomes a comment, or elsewhere in the line, in which case the remainder of the line is treated as a comment. For example:

```
--   This is a single line comment in SQL.
```

- A multiline comment begins with the combination of a slash and an asterisk (/*), and continues until the reverse combination (*/) is encountered. Be careful to end comments correctly, or many lines of SQL that you carefully wrote will be treated as comments by the RDBMS. Here is an example of a multiline comment:

```
/*   This is a multi-line comment.
     It continues until the ending combination of
     characters appears.   */
```

SQL Statement Categories

SQL statements are divided into categories based on the function that they serve. Some experts consider these categories to be either separate languages or sublanguages. However, in SQL they all have the same basic syntax and rules, so I consider them to be categories of statements within a single language. The categories, each of which is described in a subsequent section, are

- Data Definition Language (DDL)
- Data Query Language (DQL)
- Data Manipulation Language (DML)
- Data Control Language (DCL)
- Transaction Control Commands

Data Definition Language (DDL)

Data Definition Language (DDL) includes SQL statements that allow the database user to create and modify the structure of database objects, such as tables, views, and indexes. SQL statements that use the commands CREATE, ALTER, and DROP are considered part of DDL. It is important to understand that DDL statements affect the containers that hold the data in the database rather than the data itself. So there are DDL statements to create, drop, and alter tables, but none of these statements provide the ability to create or modify rows of data in those tables. DDL statements are presented in Chapter 3.

Data Query Language (DQL)

Data Query Language (DQL) includes SQL statements that retrieve data from the database. Although it's a very important part of SQL, DQL consists of statements that use only one command: SELECT. DQL is presented in Chapters 4, 5, and 6. Some vendors and authors lump DQL in with DML when they categorize SQL statements.

Data Manipulation Language (DML)

Data Manipulation Language (DML) includes SQL statements that allow the database user to add data to the database (in the form of rows in tables), remove data from the database, and modify existing data in the database. SQL statements that

use the commands INSERT, UPDATE, and DELETE are considered part of DML. DML is presented in Chapter 7.

Data Control Language (DCL)

Data Control Language (DCL) includes SQL statements that allow administrators to control access to the data within the database and the use of various DBMS system privileges, such as the ability to start up or shut down the database. SQL statements that use the commands GRANT and ALTER are considered part of DCL. DCL is presented in Chapter 8.

Transaction Control Commands

A *database transaction* is a set of commands that a database user wishes to treat as an "all or nothing" unit of work, meaning the entire transaction must either succeed or fail. The commands that control database transactions do not precisely conform to the syntax of SQL statements, but they do have a profound effect on the behavior of the SQL statements included in transactions. Transaction control commands are presented in Chapter 9.

Quiz

Choose the correct responses to each of the multiple-choice questions. Note that there may be more than one correct response to each question.

1. SQL
   a. May be pronounced as the letters S-Q-L
   b. May be pronounced as the word "sequel"
   c. May be used to render web pages
   d. May be used to communicate with any database
   e. May be used to communicate with relational databases

2. SQL is
   a. An object-oriented language
   b. A procedural language
   c. A nonprocedural language

d. A declarative language

e. A standard language

3. Procedural extensions to SQL include

a. Java

b. Oracle PL/SQL

c. C++

d. Microsoft Transact-SQL

e. FORTRAN

4. In a client/server arrangement

a. The DBMS software runs on the server

b. The DBMS software runs on the client

c. The SQL client software runs on the client

d. The SQL client software may run on the server

e. The database resides on disks connected to the client

5. A command-line SQL client

a. Requires a windowing system

b. Runs on a wide variety of clients

c. Requires a web browser on the client

d. Displays data and command options using graphical features

e. Displays responses to commands as text messages

6. A GUI SQL client

a. Requires a windowing system

b. Runs on a wide variety of clients

c. Requires a web browser on the client

d. Displays data and command options using graphical features

e. Displays responses to commands as text messages

7. A web-based SQL client

a. Requires a windowing system

b. Runs on a wide variety of clients

c. Requires a web browser on the client

d. Displays data and command options using graphical features

e. Displays responses to commands as text messages

8. SQL clients offered by Oracle are

    a. iSQL

    b. Query Analyzer

    c. iSQL*Plus

    d. SQL*Plus

    e. SQL Worksheet

9. SQL clients offered by Microsoft are

    a. iSQL

    b. Query Analyzer

    c. iSQL*Plus

    d. SQL*Plus

    e. SQL Worksheet

10. SQL was first developed

    a. By IBM

    b. By ANSI

    c. In 1982

    d. In the 1970s

    e. Based on ANSI standards

11. SQL standards include

    a. SQL-88

    b. SQL-89

    c. SQL-92

    d. SQL-99

    e. SQL:2003

12. Vendor extensions to SQL

    a. Make SQL more portable

    b. Make SQL less portable

    c. Help differentiate vendor products

    d. Were based on market demands

    e. Are compatible across vendor implementations

13. SQL statements
    a. Begin with a command keyword
    b. End with a command keyword
    c. Begin with a delimiter such as a semicolon
    d. End with a delimiter such as a semicolon
    e. Begin with a left parenthesis

14. SQL language elements include
    a. Keywords
    b. Database object names
    c. Operators
    d. Constraints
    e. Constants

15. SQL language elements are separated with
    a. Commas
    b. Exactly one space
    c. One or more spaces
    d. New lines
    e. Underscores

16. Database object names may include
    a. Parentheses
    b. Underscores
    c. Numbers
    d. Letters
    e. Commas

17. SQL statements may be divided into the following categories:
    a. Data Definition Language (DDL)
    b. Data Selection Language (DSL)
    c. Data Replication Language (DRL)
    d. Data Control Language (DCL)
    e. Data Manipulation Language (DML)

18. Data Definition Language (DDL) includes the following statements:
    a. SELECT
    b. INSERT
    c. CREATE
    d. ALTER
    e. DELETE

19. Data Query Language (DQL) includes the following statements:
    a. SELECT
    b. INSERT
    c. CREATE
    d. ALTER
    e. DELETE

20. Data Manipulation Language (DML) includes the following statements:
    a. SELECT
    b. INSERT
    c. CREATE
    d. ALTER
    e. DELETE

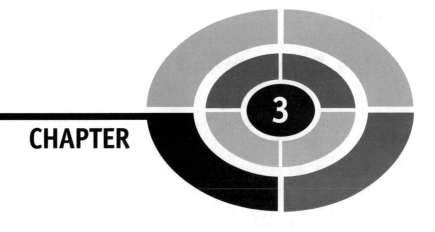

CHAPTER

3

Defining Database Objects Using SQL

This chapter introduces the SQL statements that are used to define and manage the database objects in a relational database. As already mentioned, the CREATE, ALTER, and DROP statements comprise a category of the SQL language called Data Definition Language (DDL). DDL is presented first because you have to create the database objects before you can put any data into the database. However, if you would rather learn another category of SQL such as DQL or DML first, the chapters are written so that you can skip ahead and come back to this chapter at a later time.

Syntax Conventions Used in This Chapter

SQL DDL statements have more options than other SQL statements. For this reason, I have adopted the following conventions for presenting DDL statement syntax in this chapter:

- SQL keywords and reserved words are shown in uppercase type, such as CREATE TABLE.

- Information you are expected to supply when writing the statement is shown in italics, such as *column_name*.

- Optional items are enclosed in square brackets, such as [WITH TIME ZONE].

- Choices from a list of possible items are separated by a vertical bar (the logical symbol for "or"), such as TABLE | VIEW | INDEX. You will sometimes see a list of optional choices, such as [NULL | NOT NULL].

- Group items that are explained or broken down further (usually following a description of a major statement type) are enclosed between a "less than" symbol and a "greater than" symbol, such as <column_specification>.

- An item that may be repeated is followed by an ellipse, such as [,<table_constraint>...].

- All other symbols, particularly commas and parentheses, are part of the required SQL syntax and therefore must be included as written.

Data Types

Before we explore the DDL statements themselves, you need to understand a bit more about how data is stored in table columns. As you will recall, a *column* is the smallest named unit of data that can be referenced in a relational database. Each column must be assigned a unique name and a data type. A *data type* is a category for the format of a particular column. Data types provide several valuable benefits:

- Restricting the data in the column to characters that make sense for the data type (for example, all numeric digits, or only valid calendar dates).

- Providing a set of behaviors useful to the data user. For example, if you subtract a number from another number, you get a number as a result; but if you subtract a date from another date, you get the difference, in days, between the two dates as a result.

- Assisting the RDBMS in efficiently storing the column data. For example, numbers can often be stored in an internal numeric format that saves space, compared with merely storing the numeric digits as a string of characters.

SQL supports three categories of data types: predefined types, constructed types, and user-defined types. *Predefined data types* are those that are supplied as a native part of the RDBMS by the vendor. *Constructed data types*, also known as *collection types*, hold arrays or sets of predefined data types, usually for the purpose of representing object-oriented data constructs in the RDMS. *User-defined data types*, in those RDBMSs that provide them, allow the database user to define their own data types, tailored to specific purposes.

In the remainder of this section, the SQL:2003 standard predefined data types are presented, followed by discussions of variations among today's most popular RDBMS products. Constructed data types and the creation of user-defined data types are a bit too advanced for an introductory book like this one.

SQL:2003 Standard Data Types

One of the biggest challenges to SQL portability across different vendor implementations is dealing with the enormous variation in supported data types. Many vendors went off on their own, prior to the adoption of standards, in response to customer demands. Most modern SQL implementations support all or most of the SQL:2003 standard data types, as presented here.

Most people find it convenient to group the SQL data types by the general class of data that they support. As you might guess, these classifications can be subject to debate, and in fact, the SQL:2003 standard defines some data types as belonging to more than one group. To avoid unnecessary confusion, I have listed each data type in only one group, with each group described in a separate topic. For each data type, there is a description, followed by the SQL syntax for it, and an example or two. Many of the data types are used in the video store sample database SQL if you want to see more examples.

Character Data Types

Character data types hold strings of characters, where a character can be any letter, number, or other symbol allowed by the computer system hosting the database. In general, it is a good practice to use character data types for numeric strings that will never be used in arithmetic operations or sorted in numeric order because they are more flexible than numeric data types. For example, it is usually best to store phone

numbers, ZIP codes, social security numbers, and the like as character data types. The standard character data types are

- **Fixed-length character** A character string of finite length. A length is always included to denote the size of the character string being stored. Shorter strings are padded with spaces on the right-hand end so that all strings in a column of this data type are exactly the same number of characters in length. The SQL syntax is

```
CHARACTER(length)  |  CHAR(length)
Example: SOCIAL_SECURITY_NUMBER  CHAR(9)
```

- **National character** A variation of CHARACTER that is stored in a particular national character set. This data type is intended to handle translations of character strings into various national languages. The SQL syntax is

```
NATIONAL CHARACTER(length)  |  NCHAR(length)
Example: MOVIE_TITLE  NCHAR(100)
```

- **Variable character** A character string of variable length. A length is always included to denote the *maximum* size of the character string being stored. This is a great space saver for strings that naturally vary in length, such as names and addresses. However, there is some overhead because the RDBMS must store the actual length of the string with the string itself (usually adding 1 byte to the physical size of the string) and must do a little extra work to calculate the length before storing the string. The SQL syntax is

```
CHARACTER VARYING(maximum_length)  |  VARCHAR(maximum_length)
Example: CUSTOMER_NAME  VARCHAR(125)
```

- **National variable character** A variation of variable character that is stored in a particular national character set. Like NCHAR, this data type is intended to handle translations of character strings into various national languages. The SQL syntax is

```
NATIONAL CHARACTER VARYING(maximum_length)  |  NVARCHAR(maximum_length)
Example: MOVIE_TITLE  NVARCHAR(100)
```

Numeric Data Types

As the name suggests, numeric data types hold *only* numbers. They are most useful for attributes that will be used in calculations. As a general rule, most database designers use numeric types only when the attribute will be used in mathematical calculations, such as prices, quantities, and tax rates. Character strings, while horribly inefficient for calculations, offer greater flexibility in SQL queries, so character types are preferred for numeric strings that will never be used in calculations, such as employee numbers, phone numbers, and product numbers. A common exception, however, is primary key columns where the values are automatically generated by the DBMS—these must always be numeric data types because the DBMS must increment the last value used for each new table row.

All numeric types have a *precision* (number of digits). Some numeric types also have a *scale* (the number of digits to the right of the decimal point). Integers and numeric types that include a scale are called *exact numeric* types, while real numbers that do not include a scale (basically floating point numbers) are called *approximate numeric* types.

The standard numeric types are

- **Numeric**   An exact numeric type that includes a precision and scale. The SQL syntax is

  ```
  NUMERIC(precision,scale)
  Example: EMPLOYEE_HOURLY_RATE   NUMERIC(5,2)
  ```

- **Decimal**   An exact numeric type that includes a precision and scale. However, the precision actually used by the DBMS will be equal to or greater than the precision specified. This is a subtle difference compared with NUMERIC, intended to allow the DBMS type to be mapped to a data type native to the platform on which the DBMS runs, which likely has predefined precision and scale. (A *platform* is a combination of an operating system and computer hardware, such as Windows XP on Intel, Linux on Intel, or Solaris on Sun.) The SQL syntax is

  ```
  DECIMAL(precision,scale)
  Example: EMPLOYEE_HOURLY_RATE   DECIMAL(5,2)
  ```

- **Integer**   An exact numeric type that includes only a precision, written as INTEGER or INT. Integers do not have decimal places, so a scale is not necessary because it is understood to be zero. The standard does not specify the smallest and largest data values allowed by the integer data type, so you need to check the upper limit in your DBMS documentation. The SQL syntax is

  ```
  INTEGER(precision) | INT(precision)
  Example: CUSTOMER_ACCOUNT_ID   INTEGER
  ```

- **Small integer**   A variation of the integer type, written as SMALLINT, that holds smaller numbers and therefore takes less space. The standard only specifies that the precision of SMALLINT be less than or equal to

the precision of INT, so you need to check your DBMS documentation for details. The SQL syntax is

```
SMALLINT(precision)
Example: CUSTOMER_ACCOUNT_ID   SMALLINT
```

- **Big integer**   A variation of the integer type, written as BIGINT, that holds larger numbers and therefore takes more space. The standard only specifies that the precision of BIGINT be greater than or equal to the precision of INT, so again you need to check your DBMS documentation for details. The SQL syntax is

```
BIGINT(precision)
Example: CUSTOMER_ACCOUNT_ID   BIGINT
```

- **Float**   An approximate numeric type implemented with precision greater than or equal to the specified precision. The precision specification is optional. On supported platforms, FLOAT is usually implemented using floating-point numbers. The SQL syntax is

```
FLOAT[(precision)]
Examples: INTEREST_RATE   FLOAT(16)
          INTEREST_RATE   FLOAT
```

- **Real**   An approximate numeric type with an implementation-defined precision. You need to check the DBMS documentation for details. The SQL syntax is

```
REAL
Example: INTEREST_RATE   REAL
```

- **Double precision**   An approximate numeric type with an implementation-defined precision that is greater than the implementation-defined precision for REAL. Again, check the DBMS documentation for details. The SQL syntax is

```
DOUBLE PRECISION | DOUBLE
Example: INTEREST_RATE   DOUBLE PRECISION
```

Temporal Data Types

As the name suggests, *temporal data types* (also called *datetime types*) store data that measures time in some way. As mentioned earlier, standards for these data types lagged behind commercial databases, so most DBMSs do not completely conform to the standard. I strongly recommend that you read up on these in your DBMS documentation before attempting to use them.

Temporal data types are composed of the following components, called *fields* in the standard:

Field Name (SQL Keyword)	Definition
YEAR	Two-digit or four-digit calendar year
MONTH	Month within the year
DAY	Day within the month
HOUR	Hour within the day
MINUTE	Minute within the hour
SECOND	Second within the minute
TIMEZONE_HOUR	Hour value of time zone displacement. For example, Pacific Standard Time has a displacement of +8 hours from UTC (Coordinated Universal Time).
TIMEZONE_MINUTE	Minute value of time zone displacement. While usually zero, there are some odd time zones around the world with half-hour offsets.

The TIMEZONE_HOUR and TIMEZONE_MINUTE fields are included in any temporal data type where the optional WITH TIMEZONE keyword is specified. The temporal data types are

- **Date**   A date containing the YEAR, MONTH, and DAY fields. The SQL syntax is

  ```
  DATE [WITH TIMEZONE]
  Example: DATE_ENROLLED   DATE
  ```

- **Time**   A time containing the HOUR, MINUTE, and SECOND fields. The SQL syntax is

  ```
  TIME [WITH TIMEZONE]
  Example: TIME_ENROLLED   TIME
  ```

- **Timestamp**   A combined date and time containing the YEAR, MONTH, DAY, HOUR, MINUTE, and SECOND fields. The SQL syntax is

  ```
  TIMESTAMP [WITH TIMEZONE]
  Example: DATE_TIME_ENROLLED   TIMESTAMP
  ```

- **Interval**   An interval of time containing the fields specified with an *interval qualifier*, which is essentially the *precision* of the interval. The SQL syntax is

  ```
  INTERVAL start_field TO end_field | INTERVAL field
  Examples: MEMBERSHIP_DURATION INTERVAL YEAR TO DAY
            TIME_WORKED         INTERVAL HOUR TO MINUTE
            RENTAL_DAYS         INTERVAL DAY
  ```

Large Object Types

Large objects allow for storage of data that is considerably larger than the data supported by the data types covered thus far, often several megabytes in size. The handling of large objects is an advanced topic that is beyond the scope of this book, so they are listed here without any syntax details. For now, you only need to know that the DBMSs that support these types usually store the actual data separately from the table that references it, and that data can be moved in and out of the large object in pieces, such as a few kilobytes at a time. All large objects are variable in length by definition. Consult your DBMS documentation for any special SQL syntax associated with large object types.

- **Character large object** A character large object, written in SQL as CLOB.
- **National character large object** A character large object that is stored in a particular national language, written in SQL as NCLOB.
- **Binary large object** A large object that holds binary data such as an image or sound clip, written in SQL as BLOB.

Another Data Type

There is one standard data type that does not fall into any of the previous categories:

- **Boolean** Stores a logical *true* or *false*. SQL syntax is

```
BOOLEAN
Example: PREFERRED_CUSTOMER  BOOLEAN
```

Vendor Data Type Extensions and Differences

Vendor variances from and extensions to published standards are an unfortunate fact of life. This section highlights the main differences between popular vendor SQL implementations and the SQL:2003 standard. You will see enormous differences in the way standard data types are implemented and in vendor extensions to the standard. This section is not intended to be a comprehensive reference, so as always, you should consult the documentation provided with your particular implementation.

Microsoft Access

Microsoft Access is the least standards-compliant of today's popular databases. The data types supported by Microsoft Access are

- **Text**   Equivalent to the VARCHAR standard data type, holding up to 255 characters.

- **Memo**   Holds large character strings up to 65,535 characters, but defined without a size.

- **Number**   Equivalent to the NUMERIC standard data type, but the precision and scale are set using a Field Size pull-down menu. Integers can be defined by setting the Decimal Places parameter to zero (0).

- **Date/Time**   Roughly equivalent to the TIMESTAMP standard and capable of storing any valid date and time between the years 100 and 9999.

- **Currency**   A numeric data type that is the equivalent of NUMERIC(19, 4), which is a number with 15 digits to the left of the decimal point and up to 4 digits to the right of the decimal point.

- **AutoNumber**   A 4-byte or 16-byte field (depending on the Field Size setting) that is automatically incremented by 1 whenever a new row is inserted into the table.

- **Yes/No**   Roughly equivalent to the BOOLEAN standard data type. However, Microsoft Access permits this data type to be formatted as Yes/ No, On/Off, or True/False.

- **OLE Object**   Similar to the BLOB standard data type, this type stores a Microsoft OLE object that can be up to 1GB (gigabyte) in size.

- **Hyperlink**   A specialized data type that can hold an Internet web address.

- **Lookup wizard**   A specialized data type that creates a link from a column in the current table to the contents of a column in another table. This data type is intended for dynamically linking tables when creating forms in Microsoft Access.

Microsoft SQL Server

Microsoft SQL Server's Transact-SQL supports the following standard data types:

- **BIGINT**   Whole numbers from -2^{63} through $2^{63} - 1$.

- **CHARACTER (CHAR)**   Fixed-length character up to 8000 characters.

- **DECIMAL**   Fixed precision and scale from $-10^{38} + 1$ through $10^{38} - 1$.

- **FLOAT**   Floating-point numbers in the range -1.79×10^{308} through -2.23×10^{-308}, 0, or in the range 2.23×10^{-308} through 1.79×10^{308}.

- **INTEGER**   Whole numbers from -2^{31} through $2^{31} - 1$.

- **NCHAR**   Fixed-length Unicode data up to 4000 characters. *Unicode* is a 16-bit character set standard for encoding data, designed and maintained by the nonprofit consortium Unicode, Inc.

- **NUMERIC**   Implemented the same as DECIMAL.

- **NVARCHAR**   Variable-length Unicode data up to 4000 characters.

- **REAL**   Floating-point numbers in the range -3.40×10^{38} through -1.18×10^{-38}, 0, or in the range 1.18×10^{-38} through 3.40×10^{38}.

- **SMALLINT**   Whole numbers from −32,768 through 32,767.

- **VARCHAR**   Variable-length character data up to 8000 characters.

Microsoft SQL Server offers the following extensions to the standard data types:

- **BINARY**   Fixed-length binary data with a maximum length of 8000 bytes.

- **BIT**   Integer data with a value of either 0 or 1.

- **DATETIME**   Date and time from January 1, 1753, through December 31, 9999, with an accuracy of three-hundredths of a second (3.33 milliseconds).

- **IMAGE**   Variable-length binary data with a maximum length of $2^{31} - 1$ bytes. Starting with SQL Server 2005, Microsoft recommends using VARBINARY(MAX) instead of IMAGE.

- **MONEY**   Monetary data values from -2^{63} through $2^{63} - 1$ with accuracy to a ten-thousandth of a monetary unit.

- **NTEXT**   Variable-length Unicode data with a maximum length of $2^{30} - 1$. Starting with SQL Server 2005, Microsoft recommends using NVARCHAR(MAX) instead of IMAGE.

- **SMALLDATETIME**   Date and time from January 1, 1900 through June 6, 2079, with an accuracy of one minute.

- **SMALLMONEY**   Monetary data values from −214,748.3648 through 214,748.3647 with accuracy to a ten-thousandth of a monetary unit.

- **TEXT**   Variable-length character data with a maximum length of $2^{31} - 1$ characters. Starting with SQL Server 2005, Microsoft recommends using VARCHAR(MAX) instead of TEXT.

- **TIMESTAMP**   A database-wide unique number that is updated every time a row is updated. Note that this is in ***direct conflict*** with the standard TIMESTAMP data type.

- **TINYINT**   Whole numbers from 0 through 255.

- **UNIQUEIDENTIFIER** A globally unique identifier (GUID).
- **VARBINARY** Variable-length binary data with a maximum length of 8000 bytes.

Oracle

Oracle SQL supports the following standard data types:

- **BLOB** Binary large object up to a maximum size of (4GB − 1) × (database block size).
- **CHAR** Fixed-length character data up to a maximum size of 2000 bytes.
- **CLOB** A character large object up to a maximum size of (4GB − 1) × (database block size).
- **DATE** Functions like the standard DATE data type, but it is technically more like the standard DATETIME data type because it can store both date and time. Supported dates in the range from January 1, 4712 BC through December 31, 9999 AD. An optional time in hours, minutes, and seconds may also be included. When omitted, the time component is stored as zeros, which is equivalent to midnight.
- **DECIMAL** Implemented as NUMBER(*precision, scale*).
- **DOUBLE PRECISION** Implemented as NUMBER.
- **FLOAT** Implemented as NUMBER.
- **INTEGER** Implemented as NUMBER(38).
- **INTERVAL** A time interval, but only INTERVAL YEAR TO MONTH and INTERVAL DAY TO SECOND are supported.
- **NCHAR** Fixed-length character data in a national language up to a maximum length of 2000 bytes.
- **NCLOB** Fixed-length character data in a national language up to a maximum size of (4GB − 1) × (database block size).
- **NUMERIC** Implemented as NUMBER(*precision, scale*).
- **NVARCHAR** Variable character data in a national language up to a maximum length of 4000 bytes.
- **REAL** Implemented as NUMBER.
- **SMALLINT** Implemented as NUMBER(38).

- **TIMESTAMP**   Date and time in year, month, day, hour, minute, and second, but unlike the SQL:2003 standard, the precision is specified in fractional seconds.
- **VARCHAR**   Variable character data up to a maximum length of 4000 characters.

Oracle SQL offers the following extensions to the standard data types:

- **BFILE**   A locator to a large binary file stored outside the database.
- **LONG**   Variable-length character data up to 2GB in size. This data type is no longer recommended by Oracle because CLOB replaces it.
- **LONG RAW**   Binary data with a maximum size of 2GB. This data type is no longer recommended by Oracle because BLOB replaces it.
- **NUMBER**   Numeric data with a precision from 1 through 38 and a precision from −84 through 127. Equivalent to the standard NUMERIC type.
- **NVARCHAR2**   Identical to NVARCHAR in all Oracle releases through 10*g* but recommended by Oracle over NVARCHAR because Oracle may someday change the implementation of NVARCHAR.
- **RAW**   Binary data with a maximum size of 2000 bytes. This data type is no longer recommended by Oracle because BLOB replaces it.
- **ROWID**   Base 64 string representing the unique address of a row in its table.
- **UROWID**   Base 64 string representing the logical address of a row in an index-organized table.
- **VARCHAR2**   Identical to VARCHAR in Oracle releases 7 through 10*g* but recommended by Oracle over VARCHAR because Oracle may someday change the implementation of VARCHAR.

IBM DB2 Universal Database

The IBM DB2 Universal Database (UDB) supports the following standard data types:

- **BLOB**   A binary large object with a maximum length of 2,147,483,647 bytes.
- **CHAR**   Fixed-length character data with a maximum length of 254 characters.

- **CLOB**   Character large object data with a maximum length of 2,147,483,647 bytes.

- **DATE**   A date containing the YEAR, MONTH, and DAY fields. The year may range from 0001 through 9999, and the day must be valid for the particular year and month.

- **DECIMAL**   A packed decimal or zoned decimal number with an implicit decimal point. Values range from $-10^{31} + 1$ through $10^{31} - 1$.

- **DOUBLE PRECISION (DOUBLE)**   A double-precision floating-point number (approximate data type) that can be zero or in the range -7.2×10^{75} through -5.4×10^{-79} or in the range $+5.4 \times 10^{-79}$ through $+7.2 \times 10^{75}$.

- **INTEGER**   An integer number in the range $-2{,}147{,}483{,}648$ through 2,147,483,647.

- **NUMERIC**   Implemented the same as DECIMAL.

- **REAL**   A single-precision floating-point number (approximate data type) that can be zero or in the range -3.4×10^{38} through -1.17×10^{-37} or in the range $+1.17 \times 10^{-37}$ through $+3.4 \times 10^{38}$.

- **SMALLINT**   An integer number in the range $-32{,}768$ through 32,767.

- **TIME**   A time containing the HOUR, MINUTE, and SECOND fields using a 24-hour clock.

- **TIMESTAMP**   A combined date and time containing the YEAR, MONTH, DAY, HOUR, MINUTE, and SECOND fields. The year may range from 0001 through 9999, and the day must be valid for the particular year and month. The time component uses a 24-hour clock.

- **VARCHAR**   Variable-length character data with a maximum length of 32,672 characters.

The IBM DB2 Universal Database offers the following extensions to the standard data types:

- **DBCLOB**   Similar to an NCLOB, a double-byte character large object with a maximum length of 1,073,741,823 characters.

- **GRAPHIC**   A fixed-length double-byte character string with a maximum length of 127 characters.

- **VARGRAPHIC**   A variable-length double-byte character string with a maximum length of 16,336 characters.

MySQL

MySQL supports the following standard data types:

- **BOOLEAN**   Implemented as TINYINT(1).
- **SMALLINT**   A small integer in the range −32768 through 32767 signed, or 0 through 65,535 unsigned.
- **INTEGER (INT)**   An integer in the range −2,147,483,648 through 2,147,483,647 signed, or 0 through 4,294,967,295 unsigned.
- **BIGINT**   A large integer in the range −9,223,372,036,854,775,808 through 9,223,372,036,854,775,807 signed, or 0 through 18,446,744,073, 709,551,615 unsigned.
- **FLOAT**   A floating-point number with a precision of 0 through 24. Allowable values are −3.402823466 × 10^{38} through −1.175494351 × 10^{−38}, 0, and 1.175494351 × 10^{−38} through 3.402823466×10^{+38}.
- **DOUBLE PRECISION (DOUBLE)**   A floating-point number with a precision of 25 through 53. Allowable values are −1.7976931348623157 × 10^{308} through −2.2250738585072014×10^{−308}, 0, or 2.2250738585072014 × 10^{−308} through 1.7976931348623157 × 10^{308}.
- **DECIMAL (DEC)**   A number, stored as a character string. The range of values is the same as DOUBLE PRECISION.
- **DATE**   A date, displayed in YYYY-MM-DD format, with the valid range for the year being 1000 through 9999.
- **TIMESTAMP**   A combination of date and time with the range of values from 1970-01−01 00:00:00 through part of the year 2037. MySQL stores this data type as the number of seconds since midnight on January 1, 1970, which is the same way the so-called Unix *epoch* date is stored.
- **TIME**   Time stored in an HH:MM:SS format. The valid range for hours is −838 through +838.
- **CHAR**   A fixed-length character string with a maximum length of 255 characters.
- **NATIONAL CHAR (NCHAR)**   A fixed-length string in a national language with a maximum length of 255 characters.
- **VARCHAR**   A variable-length character string with a maximum length of 65,535 characters.
- **NATIONAL VARCHAR (NVARCHAR)**   A variable-length character string in a national language with a maximum length of 255 characters.

MySQL offers the following extensions to the standard data types:

- **TINYINT**   A small integer in the range −128 through +127 signed or 0 to 255 unsigned.

- **MEDIUMINT**   A medium-size integer in the range −8,388,608 through 8,388,607 signed or 0 through 16,777,215 unsigned.

- **BIT**   Implemented as TINYINT(1).

- **DATETIME**   A combined date and time stored with a year in the range 1000 through 9999 and the time in 24-hour format.

- **YEAR**   A year stored in a two-digit or four-digit format. In the two-digit format, valid values are 70 through 69, representing 1970 through 2069. In the four-digit format, valid values are 1901 through 2155 and 0000.

- **CHAR BINARY (BINARY)**   A fixed-length binary string with a maximum length of 255 bytes.

- **VARCHAR BINARY (VARBINARY)**   A variable-length binary string with a maximum length of 65,535 bytes.

- **TINYBLOB, TINYTEXT**   A binary or character string with a maximum length of 255 bytes.

- **BLOB, TEXT**   A binary or character string with a maximum length of 65,535 bytes.

- **MEDIUMBLOB, MEDIUMTEXT**   A binary or character string with a maximum length of 16,777,215 bytes.

- **LONGBLOB, LONGTEXT**   A binary or character with a maximum length of 4,294,967,295 bytes.

- **ENUM**   An enumerated list, which is a string column that may contain one of the values specified in the list of values in the column definition.

- **SET**   A set list, which is a string column that may contain any of a number of values specified in the list of values in the column definition.

PostgreSQL

PostgreSQL supports the following standard data types:

- **SMALLINT**   A small integer in the range −32768 through +32767.

- **INTEGER**   An integer in the range −2,147,483,648 through +2,147,483,647.

- **BIGINT**   A large integer in the range −9,223,372,036,854,775,808 through 9,223,372,036,854,775,807.
- **DECIMAL**   An exact variable-length number with no size limits.
- **NUMERIC**   An exact variable-length number with no size limits.
- **REAL**   An approximate number with 6 decimal places of precision.
- **DOUBLE PRECISION**   An approximate number with 15 decimal places of precision.
- **CHARACTER VARYING (VARCHAR)**   A variable-length character string with a user-defined limit, and a maximum size of about 1GB.
- **CHARACTER (CHAR)**   A fixed-length character string with a maximum size of about 1GB.
- **TIMESTAMP**   A combined date and time with a date range of 4713 BC through 32767 AD and time precision down to 1 microsecond. An optional TIMEZONE may be included.
- **INTERVAL**   A time interval in the range of −178,000,000 through +178,000,000 years with time precision down to 1 microsecond.
- **TIME**   A time of day with precision down to 1 microsecond. An optional TIMEZONE may be included.
- **BOOLEAN**   A logical true or false with various allowable values for both the true and false states.

PostgreSQL offers the following extensions to the standard data types:

- **SERIAL**   An automatically incremented integer in the range 1 through 2,147,483,647.
- **BIGSERIAL**   An automatically incremented integer in the range 1 through 9,223,372,036,854,775,807.
- **MONEY**   A currency amount in the range −21,474,836.48 through +21,474,836.47.
- **TEXT**   A variable-length character string of unlimited length but with a maximum storage size of about 1GB.
- **BYTEA**   A variable-length binary string.
- **Geometric Types**   A set of data types that can be used to represent two-dimensional objects, including POINT, LINE, LSEG, BOX, PATH, POLYGON, and CIRCLE.

- **Network Address Types**   A set of data types that can be used to store IPv4, IPv6, and MAC addresses.

- **BIT**   A fixed-length string of binary 1's and 0's.

- **BIT VARYING**   A variable-length string of binary 1's and 0's.

- **Arrays**   An array of any built-in or user-defined data type.

- **Composite Types**   User-defined data types composed of other data types.

- **Object Identifier Types**   A series of data types used to identify objects internally in the database.

NULL Values and Three-Valued Logic

In defining columns in database tables, you have the option of specifying whether null values are permitted for the column. A *null value* in a relational database is a special code that can be placed in a column that indicates that the value for that column in that row is unknown. A null value is not the same as a blank, an empty string, or a zero—it is indeed a special code that has no other meaning in the database.

A uniform way to treat null values is an ANSI/ISO standard for relational databases. However, there has been considerable debate over the usefulness of the option, largely because the database cannot tell you *why* the value is unknown. For example, if you leave the value for the MPAA Rating Code null for a movie in our video store's MOVIE table, you don't know whether it is unknown because the movie hasn't been rated yet, the MPAA Rating system does not apply to the movie for some reason, or the movie has been rated but you just don't know what the rating is. The other dilemma is that null values are not equal to anything, including other null values, which introduces three-valued logic into database searches. With nulls in use, a search can return a condition *true* (the column value matches the search criteria), *false* (the column value does not match the search criteria), or *unknown* (the column value is null). The developers who write the application programs have to handle null values as a special case.

In Microsoft Access, the NOT NULL constraint is controlled by the Required option on the table design panel. In SQL DDL, you simply include the keyword NULL or NOT NULL with the column definition (just to the right of the column's data type). Watch out for defaults! In Oracle, DB2, and most other relational databases, if you skip the specification, the default is NULL, which means that the column may contain null values. However, in Microsoft SQL Server and Sybase Adaptive Server, it is just the opposite: if you skip the specification, the default is NOT NULL, meaning the column *may not* contain null values.

Data Definition Language (DDL) Statements

Data Definition Language (DDL) statements define the database objects but do not insert or update any data stored within those objects (DML statements serve that function). In SQL, there are three basic commands with DDL:

- **CREATE**   Creates a new database object of the type named in the statement. Because the syntax is so widely varied, CREATE DATABASE, CREATE TABLE, CREATE INDEX, and CREATE VIEW are presented in separate topics.

- **ALTER**   Changes the definition of an existing database object of the type named in the statement. ALTER TABLE is presented in this chapter because it is so commonly used. Consult your DBMS documentation for proprietary uses of the ALTER statement such as ALTER DATABASE, ALTER SYSTEM, ALTER USER, ALTER SESSION, and so forth.

- **DROP**   Drops (destroys) an existing database object of the type named in the statement.

The CREATE DATABASE Statement

As mentioned in Chapter 1, the definition of a database varies quite a bit from one vendor implementation to another. In general, however, most DBMSs require that you create a database before you can create any other database objects. The general syntax for the CREATE DATABASE statement is

```
CREATE DATABASE database_name [vendor_specific_options];
```

In the Oracle DBMS, the CREATE USER statement creates a schema within the current database that is roughly equivalent to what most other DBMSs call a database.

The SQL standard also provides for a CREATE SCHEMA statement that allows for the creation of groupings of database objects for easier administration, but you will find considerable variation in implementation across vendors, mostly because different vendors have physically implemented their databases in very different ways.

The CREATE TABLE Statement

The CREATE TABLE statement is one of the most fundamental in SQL. The relational paradigm requires all stored data to be anchored in a table, so the ability to

store anything in the database always starts with the creation of a table. The basic
syntax for the CREATE TABLE statement is

```
CREATE TABLE table_name
  ( <column_definition>
  [,<column_definition> ...]
  [,<table_constraint] ... );
```

This looks really simple, and except for some tedium involved in forming column definitions, the CREATE TABLE statement is really simple. Each statement
includes a table name and a comma-separated list of one or more column definitions enclosed in a pair of parentheses. The table name must be unique within the
database and must adhere to SQL syntax conventions as described in Chapter 2.
A table must have at least one column, which makes logical sense when you think
about it. Some vendor implementations provide for physical storage attributes such
as space allocation in the CREATE TABLE statement, so do check your DBMS
documentation to learn more. Column definitions are discussed next, followed by a
discussion of table constraints.

Column Definition in SQL DDL

The basic syntax used to define table columns is

```
<column_definition>:
  column_name  data_type
  [DEFAULT expression]
  [NULL | NOT NULL]
  [<column_constraint>]
```

As an example, here is the DDL for creating the CUSTOMER_ACCOUNT table
for our sample video store database:

```
CREATE TABLE CUSTOMER_ACCOUNT (
CUSTOMER_ACCOUNT_ID   INTEGER                NOT NULL,
CUSTOMER_HOLD_INDIC   CHAR(1)  DEFAULT 'N' NOT NULL
   CHECK (CUSTOMER_HOLD_INDIC IN ('Y','N')),
DATE_ENROLLED         DATE                   NOT NULL,
DATE_TERMINATED       DATE                   NULL,
CUSTOMER_DEPOSIT_AMOUNT NUMERIC(5,2)         NULL,
CREDIT_CARD_ON_FILE_INDIC CHAR(1)            NOT NULL
   CHECK (CREDIT_CARD_ON_FILE_INDIC IN 'Y','N')),
CHILD_RENTAL_ALLOWED_INDIC CHAR(1)           NOT NULL
   CHECK (CHILD_RENTAL_ALLOWED_INDIC IN ('Y','N')),
   PRIMARY KEY (CUSTOMER_ACCOUNT_ID));
```

Let's have a look at the components of a column definition:

- **Column Name**   The column name must be unique within the table and must conform to SQL syntax conventions as described in Chapter 2.
- **Data Type**   The data type must be a valid data type for the DBMS implementation as described earlier in this chapter.
- **Column Constraints**   This is discussed in the next topic.

Column Constraints

Column constraints restrict (constrain) the values allowed in the table column in some way. (Constraints were introduced in Chapter 1.) Technically, the DEFAULT and NULL | NOT NULL clauses are special forms of column constraints, but they are not always implemented in the same way as other column constraints within the DBMS. A column constraint may only reference one column of a table, but there is an easy workaround because any column constraint may be rewritten as a table constraint. (Table constraints are covered later in this chapter.) Column constraints can take any of the following forms:

- **DEFAULT clause**   An expression that is applied to a column value when a new row is inserted into the table that does not provide a value for the column. The expression can be any valid expression that SQL can understand, such as a constant, an SQL function, or another syntax that yields a proper data value for the column when evaluated by the SQL engine in the DBMS. For example, notice the specification of DEFAULT 'N' on the CUSTOMER_HOLD_INDIC column shown in the CUSTOMER_ACCOUNT table. This default will ensure that a newly inserted Customer Account will always get a value of 'N' (not on hold) when the statement inserting the new row either provides no value for the column or specifies the keyword DEFAULT for the column value. Another common use for the default clause is to set dates such as transaction dates to the current date as new rows are inserted. However, the syntax for assigning the current date varies so much across vendor DBMS implementations that I have avoided using it in the sample video store DDL. Here is the SQL syntax and an example of a column with a DEFAULT clause:

```
DEFAULT (expression)
Example:
CUSTOMER_HOLD_INDIC  CHAR(1)  DEFAULT 'N' NOT NULL
```

- **NULL | NOT NULL constraint**   As discussed earlier in this chapter, a specification of NULL allows null values in a column, while a specification of NOT NULL prohibits null values in the column. *Be careful of defaults.* If you omit this clause in a Microsoft SQL Server or Sybase database, NOT NULL will be assumed by the DBMS, but if you omit the clause in most other DBMSs, such as Oracle, DB2, MySQL, and PostgreSQL, the behavior is *just the opposite*: NULL will be assumed. A NOT NULL constraint can also be written as a CHECK constraint (as shown next) that specifies a condition of IS NOT NULL. Here is the SQL syntax and some examples:

```
NULL | NOT NULL
Examples:
DATE_ENROLLED      DATE    NOT NULL
DATE_TERMINATED    DATE    NULL
```

- **CHECK Constraint**   A check constraint can be used to enforce any business rule that can be applied to a single column of a table. The condition included in the constraint must always be true whenever the column data in the table is changed or the DBMS rejects the change and displays an error message. An important restriction is that the condition in a column constraint cannot reference any other column. Note in the CUSTOMER_ACCOUNT table example that there are three columns (CUSTOMER_HOLD_INDIC, CREDIT_CARD_ON_FILE_INDIC, and CHILD_RENTAL_ALLOWED_INDIC) that have a CHECK constraint that allows only the values 'Y' and 'N' in the column data. Column constraints may be given an optional name following the CONSTRAINT keyword, which is a good practice because constraint names usually appear in any error message displayed when the constraint is violated. Here is the syntax of a CHECK constraint and an example:

```
[CONSTRAINT constraint_name] CHECK (condition)
Example:
CREDIT_CARD_ON_FILE_INDIC  CHAR(1)  NOT NULL
   CHECK (CREDIT_CARD_ON_FILE_INDIC IN 'Y','N'))
```

As already mentioned, a NOT NULL clause like the one on the CUSTOMER_ ACCOUNT_ID column can also be written as a CHECK constraint instead. Here is the way the column definition would look with a check constraint that includes the optional constraint name:

```
CUSTOMER_ACCOUNT_ID  INTEGER
  CONSTRAINT CK_CUST_ACCT_ID CHECK (ACCOUNT_ID IS NOT NULL)
```

- **UNIQUE constraint**   A unique constraint on a column guarantees unique values for that column within the table, usually with the assistance of an index that is automatically created by the DBMS. Here is the syntax and an example for a column unique constraint:

```
[CONSTRAINT constraint_name] UNIQUE
Example:
CUSTOMER_ACCOUNT_ID  INTEGER  NOT NULL UNIQUE
```

- **PRIMARY KEY constraint**   A primary key constraint on a column declares the column as the primary key of the table, which requires that the column data contain no null values and contain unique values within the table. As with a unique constraint, most DBMSs automatically create an index to assist in checking for unique column data values. Here is the syntax and an example for a column primary key constraint:

```
[CONSTRAINT constraint_name] PRIMARY KEY
Example:
CUSTOMER_ACCOUNT_ID  INTEGER  NOT NULL PRIMARY KEY
```

- **Referential (FOREIGN KEY) constraint**   A referential constraint on a column (sometimes called a foreign key constraint) defines the relationship between a foreign key and a primary key so that the DBMS may guarantee that the foreign key value, when not null, always references an existing primary key value. The syntax for a column referential constraint is

```
[CONSTRAINT constraint_name]
   REFERENCES table_name(column_name)
   [ON DELETE CASCADE | ON DELETE SET NULL]
Example:
MPAA_RATING_CODE  CHAR(5)  NOT NULL
   REFERENCES MPAA_RATING (MPAA_RATING_CODE)
```

The optional ON DELETE clause tells the DBMS what to do if the referenced parent table row (the row that contains the primary key) is deleted, with the option to either delete all the rows containing the foreign key value (CASCADE) or to set all the foreign key values to null (SET NULL). Keep in mind that most but not all DBMS implementations support the ON DELETE clause.

Table Constraints

As already mentioned, any column constraint can be written instead as a table constraint, meaning the clause that defines the constraint appears after all the column definitions in the CREATE TABLE statement instead of in the midst of a column definition. The main advantage of table constraints over column constraints is that table constraints can reference more than one column. The meaning of each type of constraint has already been covered (in the column constraints topic), so only the general syntax and an example are shown here. The examples all use the CUSTOMER_ACCOUNT table, but some of them have been altered in order to demonstrate key points.

- **CHECK constraint**

```
[CONSTRAINT constraint_name] CHECK (condition)
Example:
CONSTRAINT CK_CUSTOMER_DEPOSIT_AMOUNT
    CHECK (CUSTOMER_DEPOSIT_AMOUNT >= 0 OR
            CUSTOMER_DEPOSIT_AMOUNT IS NULL)
```

  This check constraint prevents a negative amount from being stored in the CUSTOMER_DEPOSIT_AMOUNT column. Notice the OR in the expression that also allows null values in the column. If this were not included, any attempt to store a null value would fail because a null value is not greater than or equal to zero.

- **UNIQUE constraint**

```
[CONSTRAINT constraint_name] UNIQUE (column_name [,column_name...])
Example:
CONSTRAINT UK_CUST_ACCT_DATE_ENROLLED
    UNIQUE (CUSTOMER_ACCOUNT_ID, DATE_ENROLLED)
```

  This constraint specifies that the combination of CUSTOMER_ACCOUNT_ ID and DATE_ENROLLED be unique among all rows in the CUSTOMER_ ACCOUNT table. However, CUSTOMER_ACCOUNT_ID is already unique all by itself, so adding this constraint doesn't make much sense. I included it here only to illustrate a unique constraint that involves more than one column.

- **PRIMARY KEY constraint**

```
[CONSTRAINT constraint_name]
    PRIMARY KEY (column_name [,column_name...])
Example:
CONSTRAINT PK_CUSTOMER_ACCOUNT
    PRIMARY KEY (CUSTOMER_ACCOUNT_ID)
```

  This is the same as the primary definition in the CUSTOMER_ACCOUNT table example you have been using in this topic, except that I added a constraint name to it.

- **Referential (FOREIGN KEY) constraint**

```
[CONSTRAINT constraint_name]
   FOREIGN KEY (column_name [,column_name...])
   REFERENCES table_name (column_name [,column_name...])
   [ON DELETE CASCADE | ON DELETE SET NULL]
```

Notice that unlike the column constraint form of referential constraint, this one can reference multiple columns. As designed, the CUSTOMER_ACCOUNT table has no foreign key columns, but let's consider an alternate design. Some database designers frown upon the use of CHECK constraints to control column values because the database design must be changed in order to add or remove values. Suppose, for example, an enhancement to the video store's system requires a new value of 'E' (exempt) for the CREDIT_CARD_ON_FILE_INDIC column. You can change the CHECK constraint to allow the new table, but if you had put all the codes and descriptions in a table (often called a "code," "reference," or "lookup" table), all you would have to do is insert a row into the table for the new code value and you'd be ready to go. This flexibility is exactly why the video store database design contains tables for things like the MPAA_RATING_CODE—when the MPAA changes their rating system, you can simply adjust the data in the code table accordingly. Code tables are also a nice source for populating the pull-down lists of values for application components such as web forms.

Assuming that a table called CARD_ON_FILE_TYPE has been created with a primary key of CARD_ON_FILE_CODE, here is the referential constraint that defines CREDIT_CARD_ON_FILE_INDIC as a foreign key:

```
CONSTRAINT FK_CARD_ON_FILE_INDIC
   FOREIGN KEY (CREDIT_CARD_ON_FILE_INDIC)
   REFERENCES CARD_ON_FILE_TYPE (CARD_ON_FILE_CODE)
```

As you can see, there isn't always one "correct" database design but several alternatives from which to choose. Said another way, database design is not an exact science. It is generally considered a best practice to name a foreign key the same as the corresponding primary key column, but as you can see from this example, SQL will let you give them different names if you want or need to.

The CREATE INDEX Statement

The CREATE INDEX statement is a lot simpler than the CREATE TABLE statement that we just explored. Here is the basic syntax:

```
CREATE [UNIQUE] INDEX index_name ON table_name
  (column_name [ASC | DESC] [, column_name [ASC |DESC]...]);
```

- The optional UNIQUE keyword defines the index as unique, meaning that no two rows in the table can have the exact same combination of column values. You may be wondering why you would do this when defining a unique constraint would do the same thing. The answer is that it's a matter of personal style and choice. Some designers don't want the DBMS automatically creating an index for them (as happens with unique constraints), because creating the index themselves gives them more control. Other designers would much rather have the DBMS do the work for them, not only because it's less work, but also because it leads to fewer errors and greater consistency.

- The optional ASC keyword creates the index in ascending order on the column, while DESC creates the index in descending order on the column. When neither is specified, the default is ascending order.

- An index must have at least one column, but there is no practical upper limit on the number of columns.

Indexes are powerful tools because they allow the DBMS to find data much more quickly, much like using the index in the back of a book to quickly find a topic of interest. Moreover, indexes on foreign key columns can dramatically improve join performance. However, indexes take storage space and they must be maintained— every time a column value referenced by an index is changed, the index must also be changed. The DBMS automatically maintains the index, but the maintenance activity consumes resources on the computer system.

The CREATE VIEW Statement

As mentioned in Chapter 1, views offer some great benefits to database users by tailoring data to suit individual requirements and hiding complexity. Views have very little overhead when created correctly, and they store no data. In essence, a view is a stored SQL query that can be referenced in SQL DML and DQL statements as if it were a real table. Some like to think of views as "virtual tables" because they behave like tables (with some restrictions) but don't physically exist as tables. The general syntax for the CREATE VIEW statement is

```
CREATE [OR REPLACE] VIEW view_name AS sql_query;
```

- The optional OR REPLACE keyword eliminates the need for you to drop an existing view before re-creating it. When OR REPLACE is specified, if the view already exists, it is replaced, and if it does not already exist, the new view is simply added to the database.

- The view name must conform to the same naming rules as tables and other database objects. As you will learn in Chapter 4, SQL queries name the objects from which they select data but not the object type. This means that view names must be unique among all tables and views in the database. Said another way, view names and table names must come from the same *namespace*, meaning the same domain of names.

- The SQL query included in the view definition can be any valid SQL SELECT statement. You will learn about this essential statement in Chapter 4. Creating views is a natural progression—you work with the SQL query, making changes and rerunning it until you get the results exactly the way you want them. Then, you simply add the CREATE VIEW statement in front of the query that you have worked out and run the statement to permanently store the query in the database as a view. It's a very productive (and enjoyable) way to work with databases.

The ALTER TABLE Statement

Once a table has been created, just about anything that was specified in the CREATE TABLE statement can be changed using the ALTER TABLE statement. In recent years, DBMS vendors have offered ever-increasing flexibility in changing the definition of tables in place (that is, without having to drop and recreate them). Much of this is out of necessity because of 7×24 uptime requirements (databases that can never be taken out of service) and rapid data growth rates, yielding tables so large that it's not practical to drop and re-create them.

Another area where personal style and preference come into play is the use of the ALTER TABLE statement. Many database administrators prefer to keep their CREATE TABLE statements neat and simple, and thus they refrain from defining constraints in the CREATE TABLE statement. Instead, they add ALTER TABLE statements after the CREATE TABLE statement to add all the constraints to the table (primary key, foreign key, unique, check, and so forth). The downside of this approach is that it requires a lot more typing. On the other hand, the CREATE TABLE statement is a lot easier to understand without constraints, and writing constraints independently makes it a lot easier to reuse the statements should you need to drop and re-create constraints.

While there is a bit of variation across DBMS implementations, here is a list of the types of changes usually supported by the ALTER TABLE statement, along with the general syntax for each type:

- Adding a column to a table. The column definition is exactly the same syntax as the one used in the CREATE TABLE statement.

```
ALTER TABLE table_name
  ADD ( <column_definition>
      [,<column_definition> ...];
Example:
ALTER TABLE CUSTOMER_ACCOUNT
  ADD (CUSTOMER_HOLD_DATE  DATE   NULL,
       HOLD_PLACED_BY       VARCHAR(50));
```

- Changing the definition of a column. Most DBMSs won't let you decrease column precision if there is data in the table, and very few will let you change the data type of an existing column. However, the ability to increase the precision of a column, add or change a column default, or change between NULL and NOT NULL is typically supported. Changing unnamed column constraints can be problematic, which is another good reason to name all your constraints.

```
ALTER TABLE table_name
  MODIFY [COLUMN] (column_definition)
                  [,<column_definition> ...];
Example:
ALTER TABLE CUSTOMER_ACCOUNT
  MODIFY (CUSTOMER_DEPOSIT_AMOUNT  NUMERIC(7,2)
          DEFAULT 0  NOT NULL);
```

NOTE: *Microsoft SQL Server, DB2, and PostgreSQL use the keyword ALTER COLUMN instead of MODIFY COLUMN. However, MySQL and Oracle use the MODIFY keyword as shown. Also note that most DBMSs will not permit you to change a column to NOT NULL if there are existing rows in the table that have null values in that column—you have to change the null values to some other value first. The UPDATE statement required to modify column data values is covered in Chapter 7.*

- Adding a new constraint. The constraint definition is identical to a table constraint definition that could appear in a CREATE TABLE statement.

```
ALTER TABLE table_name
ADD CONSTRAINT <constraint_definition>;
```

```
Example:
ALTER TABLE CUSTOMER_ACCOUNT
 ADD CONSTRAINT CK_CUSTOMER_DEPOSIT_AMOUNT
    CHECK (CUSTOMER_DEPOSIT_AMOUNT >= 0 OR
           CUSTOMER_DEPOSIT_AMOUNT IS NULL);
```

- Dropping the primary key of the table. If the primary key is referenced by any referential constraints, those must be dropped first.

```
ALTER TABLE table_name DROP PRIMARY KEY;
```

- Renaming a column. Of the databases surveyed, only Oracle (version 8.0 or higher) supports this syntax. However, Microsoft SQL Server has a stored procedure called sp_rename that provides a way to rename database columns, tables, and other database objects.

```
ALTER TABLE table_name
   RENAME old_column_name TO new_column_name;
```

The DROP Statement

The DROP statement is the simplest of the DDL statements. The basic syntax is

```
DROP <object_type> object_name [<drop_options>]
```

- The object type names the type of object to be dropped, such as INDEX, TABLE, or VIEW.
- The drop options are DBMS-specific. In particular, if a table is referenced by any referential constraints, the DBMS will generally prevent you from dropping it. However, several DBMSs provide a "cascade" option that tells the DBMS to drop any referential constraints that get in the way of dropping the table. Unfortunately, the syntax is not consistent across vendors—PostgreSQL and MySQL use the keyword CASCADE for this purpose, but Oracle requires the keyword CASCADE CONSTRAINTS.

  Here are a few examples. Beware: once you drop something, *it's gone*— there is no "undo" command in relational databases, and SQL doesn't ask "Are you sure?"

```
DROP TABLE CUSTOMER_ACCOUNT;
DROP TABLE CUSTOMER_ACCOUNT CASCADE CONSTRAINTS; (Oracle)
DROP TABLE CUSTOMER_ACCOUNT CASCADE;   (MySQL / PostgreSQL)
DROP INDEX IX_MOVIE_TITLE;
```

Quiz

Choose the correct responses to each of the multiple-choice questions. Note that there may be more than one *correct response* to each question.

1. The benefits of data types are
   a. They conform to published standards
   b. They provide a set of behaviors useful to database users
   c. They provide data independence
   d. They restrict column data to characters that make sense
   e. They assist the DBMS in efficiently storing column data

2. Character data types
   a. Are more flexible than numeric data types
   b. Support both fixed- and variable-length column data
   c. Always require specification of the precision and scale
   d. Cause columns to be padded with length out to the maximum length
   e. Can store strings in national language formats

3. Numeric data types
   a. Are more flexible than character data types
   b. Restrict column values to numbers and related symbols such as commas and dollar signs
   c. Always require specification of precision and scale
   d. Store either exact or approximate values
   e. Are well suited to use in calculations

4. Standard numeric types include
   a. INTEGER
   b. NUMBER
   c. FLOAT
   d. BOOLEAN
   e. INTERVAL

5. Standard temporal data types include

   a. DATETIME

   b. DATE

   c. TIMESTAMP

   d. TIMEZONE

   e. TIME

6. NULL values

   a. Can be used to represent missing or unknown data values

   b. Are the same as blanks (spaces)

   c. Are equal to other NULL values

   d. Are not equal to other NULL values

   e. Are always allowed by default

7. DDL statements include

   a. CREATE

   b. ALTER

   c. DELETE

   d. INSERT

   e. UPDATE

8. The CREATE DATABASE statement

   a. Works exactly the same way in all relational DBMSs

   b. Always specifies the database name

   c. Always specifies the database owner's name

   d. May include vendor-specific parameters

   e. Works the same as the CREATE SCHEMA statement

9. The column definition in the CREATE TABLE statement may include

   a. The table name

   b. The column name

   c. A table constraint

   d. A DEFAULT clause

   e. A NULL or NOT NULL clause

10. A table column name

   a. Must be specified in the CREATE TABLE statement

   b. Must be unique within the database

   c. Must be unique within the table

   d. May only be named in one index

   e. Must be specified in the ALTER TABLE statement

11. A column constraint

   a. May reference one or more columns

   b. May be included in either a CREATE TABLE or ALTER TABLE statement

   c. Uses syntax that is identical or nearly identical to a table constraint of the same type

   d. Can be used anywhere a table constraint can be used

   e. Has syntax that varies little from one constraint type to another

12. The correct syntax for a DEFAULT clause is

   a. DEFAULT (*precision,scale*)

   b. DEFAULT [NULL | NOT NULL]

   c. DEFAULT (*expression*)

   d. DEFAULT (*column_name*) REFERENCES *table_name* (*column_name*)

   e. DEFAULT [UNIQUE | PRIMARY KEY]

13. The correct syntax for a NOT NULL constraint is

   a. *column_name data_type* IS NOT NULL

   b. *column_name data_type* NOT NULL

   c. DEFAULT [NULL | NOT NULL]

   d. CREATE NOT NULL INDEX ON *column_name*

   e. *column_name* REFERENCES NOT NULL

14. The correct syntax for a UNIQUE CONSTRAINT is

   a. [CONSTRAINT *constraint_name*] UNIQUE (*column_name*)

   b. [CONSTRAINT *constraint_name*] UNIQUE (*table_name*)

   c. DEFAULT UNIQUE (*column_name*)

   d. *column_name* REFERENCES UNIQUE *table_name*

   e. DEFAULT [UNIQUE | PRIMARY KEY]

15. The correct syntax for a REFERENTIAL CONSTRAINT is

    a. [CONSTRAINT *constraint_name*] REFERENCES *index_name*

    b. [CONSTRAINT *constraint_name*] REFERENCES *table_name*

    c. FOREIGN KEY *column_name* REFERENCES *table_name* (*column_name*)

    d. REFERENCES *table_name* (*column_name*)

    e. *column_name* REFERENCES UNIQUE *table_name*

16. The CREATE INDEX statement

    a. Is used to create unique and primary key constraints

    b. May include the keyword UNIQUE

    c. Must reference two or more column names

    d. May include the ASC or DSC keyword for any column

    e. May specify ascending or descending for one or more columns

17. The CREATE VIEW statement

    a. Stores a query in the database

    b. May include an optional CASCADE keyword

    c. May include an optional OR REPLACE keyword

    d. Must contain a valid DML command

    e. Must contain a valid SELECT statement

18. Valid uses of the ALTER TABLE statement include

    a. Adding columns

    b. Changing column precision or length

    c. Renaming a table

    d. Dropping a primary key constraint

    e. Adding a primary key constraint

19. An ALTER TABLE statement cannot be used to

    a. Change a column's data type to a numeric type if the column contains non-numeric data

    b. Rename a column

    c. Change a NULL constraint to NOT NULL for a column that contains NULL values

d. Drop a foreign key constraint when the constraint references a primary key

    e. Drop a primary key constraint if there are foreign keys referencing the primary key

20. The DROP statement can be used to drop a

    a. Referential constraint

    b. Index

    c. Table

    d. Table column

    e. View

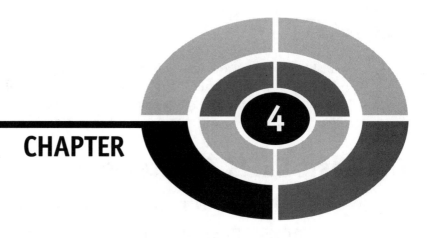

Retrieving Data Using Data Query Language (DQL)

The SQL Data Query Language (DQL) includes only one command, but it's a very important one: SELECT. The SELECT command is used to retrieve data from the database (without modifying it) so that it can be processed by an application program or simply displayed for an individual. It is undoubtedly the most commonly used SQL command. Many database users use the term "SELECT statement" when referring to SQL statements that use the SELECT command. The result of a SELECT statement, which is called a *result set*, is always returned in the form of

a table (that is, in rows and columns). Keep in mind that SQL is a nonprocedural language, so you specify the result that you want (that is, the way you want the result set to be returned) rather than how to achieve it.

The Basic SELECT Statement

The most basic SELECT statement contains two clauses:

- **SELECT [DISTINCT]**   Lists the columns that are to be returned in the result set, separated by commas. The asterisk symbol (*) may be used in place of a column list in order to select all columns in a table or view. This is a useful feature for quickly listing data, but it should be avoided in statements that will be reused because it compromises logical data independence—any new column added to the table or view will be automatically selected the next time the statement is run, and this may not be a desirable result. The keyword DISTINCT may be added after the SELECT keyword to eliminate any duplicate rows in the query results.

- **FROM**   Lists the tables or views from which data is to be selected. A *synonym*, which is an alias for a table or view that is defined in the database, may be used in place of the real name for the table or view.

Actually, the FROM clause isn't quite as straightforward as it sounds. Most relational DBMSs provide functions that return system level data that does not reside in a table or view, such as the current date and time, which is provided in Oracle by the CURRENT_DATE function, and in Microsoft SQL Server by the getdate() function. Moreover, in Microsoft SQL Server, it is permissible to omit the FROM clause in a SELECT statement if none of the data being retrieved comes from a table or view. In most, if not all, other SQL implementations, the FROM clause is mandatory. Oracle has an unusual feature—it provides a dummy table called DUAL that can be used when none of the columns in the SELECT statement comes from a real table or view.

The following example selects the MOVIE_GENRE, MPAA_RATING_CODE, and MOVIE_TITLE columns from the MOVIE table. There are 20 movies in the sample MOVIE table, but only the first four are shown here.

```
SELECT MOVIE_GENRE_CODE, MPAA_RATING_CODE, MOVIE_TITLE
  FROM MOVIE;
```

```
MOVIE_GENRE_CODE MPAA_RATING_CODE MOVIE_TITLE
---------------- ---------------- ----------------------
Drama            R                Mystic River
ActAd            R                The Last Samurai
Comdy            PG-13            Something's Gotta Give
ActAd            PG-13            The Italian Job
...              ...              ...
(20 row(s) affected)
```

Note the following:

- The result set shown was generated by Microsoft SQL Server. If you try it with a different DBMS, the format might be a little different.

- The rows in the result set are in no particular order. You will learn how to specify the order in which you want rows returned in the next section.

- All rows in the MOVIE table were returned because we did not tell the DBMS to limit the rows. You'll learn how to do this in an upcoming topic.

- The last line of the result set is a message telling you that the statement ran successfully, which is sometimes called feedback. The message shown here came from Microsoft SQL Server. Other DBMSs use different message formats. For example, Oracle would have displayed "20 rows selected." instead.

- You may have noticed that the data in the MOVIE_GENRE column isn't always clear. It's easy to see the meaning of "Drama" and "Comdy" (Comedy), but "ActAd" (Action/Adventure) is mighty cryptic. These are codes for movie categories, and the MOVIE_GENRE_CODE column in the MOVIE table is a foreign key to the MOVIE_GENRE table. As an alternative design, I could have simply numbered the categories, but when there are a relatively small number of values, I prefer codes that are easier for humans to remember, often called mnemonic values. In Chapter 5 you will learn how to combine columns from multiple tables in a single SELECT statement, called *joining* tables, which in this example would allow us to replace the MOVIE_GENRE_CODE column with the MOVIE_GENRE_ DESCRIPTION from the MOVIE_GENRE table, yielding a much more user-friendly result set.

- I have indented the line containing the FROM clause so it aligns nicely with the line above it. This is not at all necessary, but formatting SQL in this way is a nice practice because it makes your SQL easier to read.

Column Name Aliases

You may have noticed in the result set of the previous query that the column names from the table automatically appear as the column headers in the result set. However, it doesn't have to be this way because the SQL statement provides a convenient way to give the columns aliases. The aliases then become the column names in the result set. One word of caution, however—the aliases do not exist until after the SQL statement has run, so they cannot be used in most other parts of the SQL statement. A column alias is assigned by placing the keyword "AS" after the column name in the SELECT list (with at least one space before and after it), followed by the name you wish to assign to the column in the result set. Many DBMSs will allow you to omit the "AS" keyword, simply leaving a space between the column name and alias name—the SQL engine knows it's an alias instead of the next column name because commas are used to separate column names in the SELECT list. In essence, the alias renames the column but only in the result set. Here is the same SQL statement I used before, with MOVIE_GENRE_CODE renamed to GENRE and MPAA_RATING_CODE renamed to RATING. As before, only the first four rows are displayed here:

```
SELECT MOVIE_GENRE_CODE AS GENRE,
       MPAA_RATING_CODE AS RATING, MOVIE_TITLE
  FROM MOVIE;

GENRE RATING MOVIE_TITLE
----- ------ -------------------------
Drama R      Mystic River
ActAd R      The Last Samurai
Comdy PG-13  Something's Gotta Give
ActAd PG-13  The Italian Job
```

Sorting Results

Query results are often more useful if we specify a sequence for the returned rows that makes sense to the person or application program that will be using the information. There is no guarantee as to the sequence of the rows in the result set *unless* the desired sequence is specified in the query. In SQL, this is done by adding an ORDER BY clause to the SELECT statement, with a list of one or more columns that will be used to order the rows in ascending or descending sequence according to the data values in the columns. Also note the following points:

- Ascending sequence is the default for each column, but the keyword ASC may be added after the column name for ascending sequence, and DESC may be added for descending sequence.

- The column(s) named in the ORDER BY list do not have to be included in the query result set (that is, the SELECT list). However, it is better human engineering if you do.

- The SQL engine in the DBMS will figure out the best way to sequence the columns. In general, sorting data is an expensive process in terms of computer resources, so most DBMSs will use an index to access the rows in the desired sequence, assuming one exists, and only do an actual sort as a last resort.

- You *can* use column alias names in the ORDER BY clause, but when you do so, you are forcing the SQL engine in the DBMS to sort the result set after the query has been run. An index on the column(s) on which you are sorting the data cannot be used because that index references the column names and not the aliases. The point here is that the SQL engine has more flexibility in how it goes about putting the result set in the requested sequence if you always use column names in the ORDER BY clause.

- Instead of column names, the relative position of the columns in the results may be listed. For example, ORDER BY 1,2 would order the results in ascending sequence by the first two columns in the result set. The number provided has no correlation with the column position in the source table or view, however. This option is frowned upon in formal SQL because someone changing the query at a later time might shuffle columns around in the SELECT list and not realize that, in doing so, they are changing the columns used for sorting results.

In the case of the prior SELECT statement, let's assume that presenting the rows in ascending order by MPAA Rating and Movie Genre Code would be useful. From a human engineering perspective, it's best to place those columns first in the query results and in the same order as the ORDER BY column list (at least in languages that are read left to right). This makes the row ordering readily apparent to the reader. The revised SELECT statement and query results follow. All 20 rows in the MOVIE table are listed so you can see the sequencing. However, some movie titles were shortened so that each row fits on one line on the printed page. In typical SQL clients, rows that are too long wrap to a new line for display, but I have avoided that here because wrapped lines are so difficult to read.

```
SELECT MPAA_RATING_CODE AS RATING,
     MOVIE_GENRE_CODE AS GENRE, MOVIE_TITLE
```

```
FROM MOVIE
ORDER BY MPAA_RATING_CODE, MOVIE_GENRE_CODE;

RATING GENRE MOVIE_TITLE
------ ----- --------------------------------------------------
PG-13  ActAd The Italian Job
PG-13  ActAd Pirates of the Caribbean: The Curse of the
PG-13  ActAd Master and Commander: The Far Side of the
PG-13  ActAd The Day After Tomorrow
PG-13  Comdy 50 First Dates
PG-13  Comdy Matchstick Men
PG-13  Comdy The School of Rock
PG-13  Comdy Something's Gotta Give
PG-13  Drama Big Fish
PG-13  Rmce  Two Weeks Notice
PG-13  Rmce  13 Going on 30
R      ActAd Man on Fire
R      ActAd Kill Bill: Vol. 1
R      ActAd The Last Samurai
R      Drama Mystic River
R      Drama Lost in Translation
R      Drama Road to Perdition
R      Drama Cold Mountain
R      Drama Monster
R      Forgn Das Boot

(20 row(s) affected)
```

Note that in the result set, all rows for the same value of MPAA Rating Code (RATING column) appear together, and within each MPAA Rating the rows are ordered by the Movie Genre Code (GENRE column). Most IT (Information Technology) professionals would say that the result set is ordered by Genre *within* Rating. Just for fun, let's order the rows by Genre *descending* within Rating *ascending*. Here is the revised SELECT statement and the corresponding result set (from an Oracle database this time, using the SQL*Plus client, so you can see the differences in the formatting of the result set):

```
SELECT MPAA_RATING_CODE AS RATING,
       MOVIE_GENRE_CODE AS GENRE, MOVIE_TITLE
  FROM MOVIE
 ORDER BY MPAA_RATING_CODE ASC, MOVIE_GENRE_CODE DESC
```

```
RATIN GENRE MOVIE_TITLE
----- ----- ----------------------------------------
PG-13 Rmce  Two Weeks Notice
PG-13 Rmce  13 Going on 30
PG-13 Drama Big Fish
PG-13 Comdy Something's Gotta Give
PG-13 Comdy 50 First Dates
PG-13 Comdy The School of Rock
PG-13 Comdy Matchstick Men
PG-13 ActAd The Italian Job
PG-13 ActAd Master and Commander: The Far Side of the
PG-13 ActAd Pirates of the Caribbean: The Curse of the
PG-13 ActAd The Day After Tomorrow
R     Forgn Das Boot
R     Drama Mystic River
R     Drama Cold Mountain
R     Drama Road to Perdition
R     Drama Lost in Translation
R     Drama Monster
R     ActAd The Last Samurai
R     ActAd Man on Fire
R     ActAd Kill Bill: Vol. 1

20 rows selected.
```

Did you notice the following differences?

- As specified, Genre is sorted in descending order within Rating.

- Oracle displayed "RATIN" instead of "RATING" as the column header in the result set. The column alias really is "RATING", but Oracle's SQL*Plus automatically shortens column headers if they are longer than the longest data value in the column's data (a trait I have never particularly liked). The good news is that this behavior can be changed with some formatting commands that come with SQL*Plus, which we won't go into here. The *better* news is that Oracle's latest SQL Client, iSQL*Plus, doesn't behave this way at all. However, the real lesson here is that there is a wide variation in the behavior of the various databases and SQL clients, and you have to be ready to deal with those differences.

- The completion message at the end of the result set is "20 rows selected." instead of "(20 row(s) affected)".

Using the WHERE Clause to Filter Rows

SQL uses the WHERE clause for the selection of rows to display. As you have already seen, a query without a WHERE clause yields a result set that contains all the rows in the table(s) or view(s) referenced in the FROM clause. When a WHERE clause is included, the rules of Boolean algebra, named for logician George Boole, are used to evaluate the WHERE clause for each row of data. Only rows for which the WHERE clause evaluates as a logical "true" are displayed in the query results.

As you will see in the examples that follow, individual tests of conditions must evaluate as "true," "false," or "unknown." Actually, the "unknown" result is not part of Boolean algebra at all—it comes from the use of null values in relational databases. See "IS NULL" in the "Logical Operators" section a bit later in this chapter.

Comparison Operators

Comparison operators are used in the WHERE clause to compare two values, yielding a logical "true" or "false" as a result. The two values being compared may be constants supplied in the WHERE clause, column values from the database, or a combination of the two. The comparison operators that can be used in WHERE clauses are shown in the following table:

Operator	Description
=	Equal to
<	Less than
<=	Less than or equal to
>	Greater than
>=	Greater than or equal to
!=	Not equal to
<>	Not equal to (ANSI standard)

Here are some examples:

- List all movies with an MPAA Rating of PG-13.

```
SELECT MPAA_RATING_CODE AS RATING,
       MOVIE_TITLE
  FROM MOVIE
 WHERE MPAA_RATING_CODE = 'PG-13'
 ORDER BY MOVIE_TITLE;
```

```
RATING MOVIE_TITLE
------ -------------------------------------------------
PG-13  13 Going on 30
PG-13  50 First Dates
PG-13  Big Fish
PG-13  Master and Commander: The Far Side of the World
PG-13  Matchstick Men
PG-13  Pirates of the Caribbean: The Curse of the Black
PG-13  Something's Gotta Give
PG-13  The Day After Tomorrow
PG-13  The Italian Job
PG-13  The School of Rock
PG-13  Two Weeks Notice

11 rows selected.
```

- List all movies with an MPAA Rating other than PG-13. Notice that there
  are 20 rows in the MOVIE table, and the DBMS found 11 of them matching
  on PG-13, so it seems logical that it would find the other 9 that are not equal
  to "PG-13." However, if there were a null value in the column, that row
  would not appear in the results of either of these queries. It will seem odd to
  you at first, but a null value isn't equal to PG-13 and it isn't "not equal" to
  PG-13—it's just null. You'll see more on null values in an upcoming topic.

```
SELECT MPAA_RATING_CODE AS RATING,
       MOVIE_TITLE
  FROM MOVIE
 WHERE MPAA_RATING_CODE <> 'PG-13'
 ORDER BY MOVIE_TITLE;

RATING MOVIE_TITLE
------ -------------------------------------------------
R      Cold Mountain
R      Das Boot
R      Kill Bill: Vol. 1
R      Lost in Translation
R      Man on Fire
R      Monster
R      Mystic River
R      Road to Perdition
R      The Last Samurai

9 rows selected.
```

- List all movies with a DVD Retail Price under 19.99, in descending order by price.

```
SELECT RETAIL_PRICE_DVD, MOVIE_TITLE
  FROM MOVIE
 WHERE RETAIL_PRICE_DVD < 19.99
 ORDER BY RETAIL_PRICE_DVD DESC;


RETAIL_PRICE_DVD MOVIE_TITLE
---------------- ------------------------------------
           19.97 Matchstick Men
           19.96 Mystic River
           19.96 The Last Samurai
           19.94 Big Fish
           19.94 50 First Dates
           19.94 Das Boot
           14.99 Road to Perdition
           14.98 Lost in Translation
           14.97 Two Weeks Notice

9 rows selected.
```

- List all movies with a DVD Retail Price of 19.99 or less. Notice that one title with a price of exactly 19.99 appears in the results of this query, but it was not in the results of the previous example.

```
SELECT RETAIL_PRICE_DVD, MOVIE_TITLE
  FROM MOVIE
 WHERE RETAIL_PRICE_DVD <= 19.99
 ORDER BY RETAIL_PRICE_DVD DESC;


RETAIL_PRICE_DVD MOVIE_TITLE
---------------- ------------------------------------
           19.99 The Italian Job
           19.97 Matchstick Men
           19.96 Mystic River
           19.96 The Last Samurai
           19.94 Big Fish
           19.94 Das Boot
           19.94 50 First Dates
           14.99 Road to Perdition
           14.98 Lost in Translation
           14.97 Two Weeks Notice

10 rows selected.
```

- List all movies with a DVD Retail Price of 25.00 or more, sorting in ascending order by price.

```
SELECT RETAIL_PRICE_DVD, MOVIE_TITLE
   FROM MOVIE
  WHERE RETAIL_PRICE_DVD >= 25.00
  ORDER BY RETAIL_PRICE_DVD ASC;

RETAIL_PRICE_DVD MOVIE_TITLE
---------------- -----------------------------------------
           28.95 13 Going on 30
           29.98 Man on Fire
           29.98 The Day After Tomorrow
           29.99 Something's Gotta Give
           29.99 Kill Bill: Vol. 1
           29.99 Cold Mountain
           29.99 Monster
           29.99 The School of Rock
           29.99 Pirates of the Caribbean: The Curse of
           39.99 Master and Commander: The Far Side of

10 rows selected.
```

Conjunctive Operators

Sometimes multiple conditions are necessary in order to narrow the query result set. When multiple conditions are used, they must be logically combined in the WHERE clause, and this is the job of *conjunctive operators*. These operators are

- **AND**   The WHERE clause evaluates to "true" if *all* of the conditions connected with the AND operator are true.

- **OR**   The WHERE clause evaluates to "true" if *any* of the conditions connected with the OR operator are true.

Things get complicated if AND and OR operators are mixed in the same WHERE clause. The AND operator is a higher precedence and therefore is evaluated before any OR operators. However, you can do yourself a big favor by *always* using parentheses to control the evaluation of a WHERE clause that mixes the two conjunctive operators. Conditions inside parentheses are always evaluated first, and making the evaluation you intend explicitly clear in the statement not only helps you, but also anyone else who might read your SQL statement at a later time.

Here are some examples using conjunctive operators:

- List all movies that are rated PG-13 *and* have a DVD retail price of 19.99 or less, in ascending sequence by price.

```
SELECT MPAA_RATING_CODE AS RATING,
       RETAIL_PRICE_DVD AS PRICE,
       MOVIE_TITLE
  FROM MOVIE
 WHERE MPAA_RATING_CODE = 'PG-13'
   AND RETAIL_PRICE_DVD <= 19.99
 ORDER BY RETAIL_PRICE_DVD;


RATING       PRICE MOVIE_TITLE
------  ---------- -------------------------------------
PG-13        14.97 Two Weeks Notice
PG-13        19.94 Big Fish
PG-13        19.94 50 First Dates
PG-13        19.97 Matchstick Men
PG-13        19.99 The Italian Job

5 rows selected.
```

- List all movies that are rated PG-13 *or* have a DVD retail price of 19.99 or less, in ascending sequence by price. You should get more rows in this result set because all PG-13 movies will be listed regardless of price, and all movies with a price of 19.99 or less will be listed regardless of their rating.

```
SELECT MPAA_RATING_CODE AS RATING,
       RETAIL_PRICE_DVD AS PRICE,
       MOVIE_TITLE
  FROM MOVIE
 WHERE MPAA_RATING_CODE = 'PG-13'
    OR RETAIL_PRICE_DVD <= 19.99
 ORDER BY MPAA_RATING_CODE, RETAIL_PRICE_DVD;


RATING       PRICE MOVIE_TITLE
------  ---------- -------------------------------------
PG-13        14.97 Two Weeks Notice
R            14.98 Lost in Translation
R            14.99 Road to Perdition
PG-13        19.94 Big Fish
R            19.94 Das Boot
PG-13        19.94 50 First Dates
```

```
R               19.96 Mystic River
R               19.96 The Last Samurai
PG-13           19.97 Matchstick Men
PG-13           19.99 The Italian Job
PG-13           28.95 13 Going on 30
PG-13           29.98 The Day After Tomorrow
PG-13           29.99 Something's Gotta Give
PG-13           29.99 The School of Rock
PG-13           29.99 Pirates of the Caribbean: The Curse of
PG-13           39.99 Master and Commander: The Far Side of
```

```
16 rows selected.
```

- List all movies that are rated PG-13 and are either in the drama or action-adventure genre. While the intent may seem clear in the previous sentence, if the WHERE clause is written exactly as stated and without parentheses, you get incorrect results. The problem is that AND is evaluated before OR, which means that you will get all the movies with genre ActAd regardless of their rating. Here is the statement written that way and the unintended result set:

```sql
SELECT MOVIE_GENRE_CODE AS GENRE,
       MPAA_RATING_CODE AS RATING,
       MOVIE_TITLE
  FROM MOVIE
 WHERE MOVIE_GENRE_CODE = 'ActAd'
    OR MOVIE_GENRE_CODE = 'Drama'
   AND MPAA_RATING_CODE = 'PG-13'
 ORDER BY MOVIE_GENRE_CODE, MPAA_RATING_CODE;
```

```
GENRE RATING MOVIE_TITLE
----- ------ ---------------------------------------
ActAd PG-13  The Italian Job
ActAd PG-13  Pirates of the Caribbean: The Curse of
ActAd PG-13  The Day After Tomorrow
ActAd PG-13  Master and Commander: The Far Side of
ActAd R      The Last Samurai
ActAd R      Man on Fire
ActAd R      Kill Bill: Vol. 1
Drama PG-13  Big Fish
```

```
8 rows selected.
```

- Let's add parentheses so all the movies are PG-13 and either Action-Adventure or Drama. Here is the corrected statement and the results (which are now as intended):

```
SELECT MOVIE_GENRE_CODE AS GENRE,
       MPAA_RATING_CODE AS RATING,
       MOVIE_TITLE
  FROM MOVIE
 WHERE (MOVIE_GENRE_CODE = 'ActAd'
    OR  MOVIE_GENRE_CODE = 'Drama')
   AND MPAA_RATING_CODE = 'PG-13'
 ORDER BY MOVIE_GENRE_CODE, MPAA_RATING_CODE;
GENRE RATING MOVIE_TITLE
----- ------ ------------------------------------
ActAd PG-13  The Italian Job
ActAd PG-13  Pirates of the Caribbean: The Curse of
ActAd PG-13  Master and Commander: The Far Side of
ActAd PG-13  The Day After Tomorrow
Drama PG-13  Big Fish

5 rows selected.
```

Logical Operators

Logical operators use keywords instead of symbols when forming comparisons. The logical operators available in most SQL implementations are presented in topics that follow. The keyword NOT can be added to any of them to logically reverse the comparison.

IS NULL

The IS NULL operator is used to determine if a value is null. It is important to remember that null values in the database are not equal to anything else, including another null value. This is why a condition such as "= NULL" is always incorrect—nothing is ever equal to a null value. Here are some examples:

- Find all active customer accounts, which are those where the DATE_TERMINATED column contains a null value:

```
SELECT CUSTOMER_ACCOUNT_ID
  FROM CUSTOMER_ACCOUNT
 WHERE DATE_TERMINATED IS NULL;
```

```
CUSTOMER_ACCOUNT_ID
-------------------
                  1
                  2
                  3
                  4
                  5
                  7
                  8
                  9
```

```
8 rows selected.
```

- Find all inactive customer accounts, which are those where the DATE_
  TERMINATED column contains a value *other* than null:

```
SELECT CUSTOMER_ACCOUNT_ID
  FROM CUSTOMER_ACCOUNT
 WHERE DATE_TERMINATED IS NOT NULL;
```

```
CUSTOMER_ACCOUNT_ID
-------------------
                  6
```

```
1 row selected.
```

BETWEEN

The BETWEEN operator is used to determine if a value falls within a range. The range is specified using a minimum value and a maximum value, and the range is *inclusive*, which means that the minimum and maximum values are included in the range. This is a nice shorthand way of writing a range condition that is also easier to read and understand. For instance, the condition "WHERE MOVIE_ID BETWEEN 7 AND 9" is the same as the condition "WHERE MOVIE_ID >= 7 AND MOVIE_ID <= 9". Here are some examples:

- Find all movies with a RETAIL_PRICE_DVD between 14.99 and 19.99.
  Notice that movies with a price of exactly 14.99 or 19.99 are included in
  the result set.

```
SELECT MOVIE_TITLE, RETAIL_PRICE_DVD
  FROM MOVIE
 WHERE RETAIL_PRICE_DVD BETWEEN 14.99 AND 19.99
 ORDER BY RETAIL_PRICE_DVD;
```

```
MOVIE_TITLE              RETAIL_PRICE_DVD
-------------------      ----------------
Road to Perdition                  14.99
Big Fish                           19.94
Das Boot                           19.94
50 First Dates                     19.94
Mystic River                       19.96
The Last Samurai                   19.96
Matchstick Men                     19.97
The Italian Job                    19.99

8 rows selected.
```

- List all movies with a RETAIL_PRICE_DVD that is *not* between 14.99 and 19.99. Notice that movies with a price of exactly 14.99 and 19.99 are not included, and only those with a price less than 14.99 or greater than 19.99 are selected.

```
SELECT MOVIE_TITLE, RETAIL_PRICE_DVD
  FROM MOVIE
 WHERE RETAIL_PRICE_DVD NOT BETWEEN 14.99 AND 19.99
 ORDER BY RETAIL_PRICE_DVD;
```

```
MOVIE_TITLE              RETAIL_PRICE_DVD
-------------------      ----------------
Two Weeks Notice                   14.97
Lost in Translation                14.98
13 Going on 30                     28.95
Man on Fire                        29.98
The Day After Tomorr               29.98
Something's Gotta Gi               29.99
Cold Mountain                      29.99
Monster                            29.99
The School of Rock                 29.99
Kill Bill: Vol. 1                  29.99
Pirates of the Carib               29.99
Master and Commander               39.99

12 rows selected.
```

- List customer accounts opened during January 2005. Note that logical operators work on date columns just as well as they do on numeric and character format columns:

```
SELECT CUSTOMER_ACCOUNT_ID, DATE_ENROLLED
  FROM CUSTOMER_ACCOUNT
 WHERE DATE_ENROLLED BETWEEN '2005/01/01'
                         AND '2005/01/31';


CUSTOMER_ACCOUNT_ID DATE_ENROLLED
------------------- -------------
                  1 2005-01-01
                  2 2005-01-18


2 rows selected.
```

NOTE: *In Oracle, the default date format must be changed in order for this example to work correctly. This statement will change the date format for the current database session to the format used in the example:*

```
ALTER SESSION SET NLS_DATE_FORMAT='YYYY/MM/DD'
```

LIKE

The LIKE operator is used to compare a character value to a pattern, returning a logical "true" if the character value matches the pattern, and "false" if not. Two wildcard characters may be used in the pattern:

- **Underscore (_)**   The underscore character (_) may be used as a positional wildcard, meaning it matches any character in that position of the character string being evaluated.

- **Percent (%)**   The percent sign (%) may be used as a nonpositional wildcard, meaning it matches any number of characters for any length.

   Note that Microsoft Access has a similar feature, but the question mark (?) is used as the positional wildcard, and the asterisk (*) as the nonpositional wildcard (these match the conventions used in DOS and Visual Basic).

Here are some sample patterns to help you visualize the use of patterns containing wildcards:

Pattern	Interpretation
%Now	Matches any character string that ends with "Now".
Now%	Matches any character string that begins with "Now".
%Now%	Matches any character string that contains "Now" (whether at the beginning, the end, or in the middle).
N_w	Matches any character string containing exactly three characters, where the first character is "N" and the last character is "w".
%N_w%	Matches any character string that contains the character "N" followed by any character, followed by the character "w", whether at the beginning, end, or in the middle of the string.

Keep in mind that data in relational databases is *always* case sensitive. A lowercase letter in the data will *not* match with an uppercase letter in a LIKE clause pattern, and vice versa. However, the UPPER and LOWER functions introduced a little later in this chapter can be used to shift the case of the data coming from the database to make matching mixed case data a little easier.

Here is an example using the LIKE operator:

- List all movie titles that contain the character string "on":

```
SELECT MOVIE_TITLE
  FROM MOVIE
 WHERE MOVIE_TITLE LIKE '%on%';

MOVIE_TITLE
--------------------
13 Going on 30
Lost in Translation
Man on Fire
Monster
Road to Perdition

5 rows selected.
```

Perhaps that isn't quite what you wanted. If you had intended to find titles that contained only the word "on" instead of the letters "on" when they appear as part of a word, you should have placed spaces in the pattern, like this:

```
SELECT MOVIE_TITLE
  FROM MOVIE
 WHERE MOVIE_TITLE LIKE '% on %';

MOVIE_TITLE
--------------------
13 Going on 30
Man on Fire

2 rows selected.
```

IN

The IN operator is used to determine if a value falls within a list of values. The list of values may be provided as literal values, using a comma-separated list that is enclosed in parentheses, or may be selected from the database using a *subselect*, which is a query within a query. Subselects are covered in detail in Chapter 5. Here are some examples using the IN operator:

- List all movies that have a MOVIE_GENRE_CODE of Drama, Forgn or Rmce. Obviously, this query could be written with three equal conditions separated with the OR logical operator, but look how much easier it is to write using the IN operator:

```
SELECT MOVIE_GENRE_CODE AS GENRE, MOVIE_TITLE
  FROM MOVIE
 WHERE MOVIE_GENRE_CODE IN ('Drama','Forgn','Rmce')
 ORDER BY MOVIE_GENRE_CODE, MOVIE_TITLE;

GENRE MOVIE_TITLE
----- --------------------
Drama Big Fish
Drama Cold Mountain
Drama Lost in Translation
Drama Monster
Drama Mystic River
Drama Road to Perdition
Forgn Das Boot
Rmce  13 Going on 30
Rmce  Two Weeks Notice

9 rows selected.
```

- List all movies where the description of the movie genre contains the word "and". This requires a subselect to find the values of MOVIE_GENRE_ CODE that have the word "and" in their description. Then the IN operator is used to find movies that have one of the codes selected in the subselect. Subselects are covered in more detail in Chapter 5. For now, just keep in mind that the inner select (the one in parentheses) is executed first and the result set from the inner select is used as the list of values by the IN operator in the outer select. Note that while several genres have descriptions that contain the word "and", only one of these categories (Action and Adventure, or "ActAd") currently has movies in the video store. Of course, this is not a bad thing at all because this query can be run at a later time when the inventory might contain those additional genres.

```
SELECT MOVIE_GENRE_CODE AS GENRE, MOVIE_TITLE
  FROM MOVIE
 WHERE MOVIE_GENRE_CODE IN
    (SELECT MOVIE_GENRE_CODE
       FROM MOVIE_GENRE
      WHERE MOVIE_GENRE_DESCRIPTION LIKE '% and %')
 ORDER BY MOVIE_GENRE_CODE, MOVIE_TITLE;


GENRE MOVIE_TITLE
----- --------------------------------------------
ActAd Kill Bill: Vol. 1
ActAd Man on Fire
ActAd Master and Commander: The Far Side of the
ActAd Pirates of the Caribbean: The Curse of the
ActAd The Day After Tomorrow
ActAd The Italian Job
ActAd The Last Samurai

7 rows selected.
```

EXISTS

The EXISTS operator is used to determine if a subselect has any rows in it. If there are no rows in the subselect's result set, a logical "false" is set; if the result set has one or more rows in it, a logical "true" is set. Again, subselects are covered in more detail in Chapter 5, but here is an example using EXISTS so you can see how it works:

- The store manager has heard that the movie *The Last Samurai* rents well in both DVD and VHS formats, and she wants to be sure there is a

VHS copy in the store's inventory. The MOVIE_COPY table has a row
for each copy of a movie in the inventory, so you can use a subselect to
find out if there are VHS copies of the movie in inventory. The EXISTS
operator is most often used in conjunction with a more complicated form
of subquery call a *correlated subquery*, where a data value from the outer
select (the MOVIE_ID in this case) is matched against rows in the inner
query. If you find the syntax in this example confusing, don't be overly
concerned because we'll revisit it in Chapter 5. For now, just know that
the subselect will return a row if the movie has a VHS copy in stock and
will return no rows if not. By the way, this same query could also be
written using the IN operator or using a *join*, which matches rows in the
two tables. Joins are also covered in Chapter 5.

```
SELECT MOVIE_ID, MOVIE_TITLE
  FROM MOVIE m
 WHERE MOVIE_TITLE = 'The Last Samurai'
   AND EXISTS
   (SELECT MOVIE_ID
      FROM MOVIE_COPY c
    WHERE m.MOVIE_ID = c.MOVIE_ID);


  MOVIE_ID MOVIE_TITLE
---------- ------------------
         2 The Last Samurai

1 row selected.
```

- If you reverse the logic using a NOT EXISTS, you can list the movie title
  only if there is *not* a VHS copy in the inventory.

```
SELECT MOVIE_ID, MOVIE_TITLE
  FROM MOVIE m
 WHERE MOVIE_TITLE = 'The Last Samurai'
   AND NOT EXISTS
   (SELECT MOVIE_ID
      FROM MOVIE_COPY c
    WHERE m.MOVIE_ID = c.MOVIE_ID);

no rows selected
```

Arithmetic Operators

Arithmetic operators perform mathematical calculations in SQL—just as you would in a spreadsheet formula or in a programming language such as Java or C. The four arithmetic operators are as follows:

Operator	Description
+	Addition
−	Subtraction
*	Multiplication
/	Division

As with the conjunctive operators, if you mix arithmetic operators in the same SQL statement without using parentheses, there is a precedence that determines the order in which the operators are evaluated. Thankfully, the precedence in SQL is the same one we use in regular mathematics. In grade school, I learned the phrase "*P*lease *M*y *D*ear *A*unt *S*ally" to remind me that the order of precedence is *p*arentheses, *m*ultiplication, *d*ivision, *a*ddition, and *s*ubtraction. However, it's *always* best to use parentheses so that neither you nor anyone who reads your SQL statement has to remember the order of precedence. Here are some examples using arithmetic operators:

- How much would it cost to buy both the VHS and DVD copies of *The Last Samurai*? Notice that I am using an alias name for the column in the result set. If I didn't do this, the SQL engine would be forced to generate a name for the column since the column value in the result set comes from a function instead of a column. Generated names are usually not easy to read, so I recommend you always give an alias name to any calculated column.

```
SELECT RETAIL_PRICE_VHS + RETAIL_PRICE_DVD AS COST
  FROM MOVIE
 WHERE MOVIE_TITLE = 'The Last Samurai';

     COST
----------
    35.91
```

- How much would the same purchase cost if I had a coupon for $5 off? Although not technically necessary, I added parentheses because they make the statement more readable.

```
SELECT (RETAIL_PRICE_VHS + RETAIL_PRICE_DVD) - 5 AS COST
  FROM MOVIE
 WHERE MOVIE_TITLE = 'The Last Samurai';

      COST
----------
     30.91
```

- If the tax rate is 8.25 percent (0.0825), what would be the sales tax on the purchase? Assume that tax is calculated on the entire sale price (that is, before any coupons are subtracted). The parentheses in this statement are essential to getting a correct result—you must make sure the addition is done *before* the multiplication. You might also notice that I omitted the spaces before and after the addition operator (+). While more difficult to read this way, SQL does not require that arithmetic operators have spaces around them.

```
SELECT (RETAIL_PRICE_VHS+RETAIL_PRICE_DVD) * 0.0825 AS TAX
  FROM MOVIE
 WHERE MOVIE_TITLE = 'The Last Samurai';

       TAX
----------
    2.8728
```

You may have noticed that the result has more than two decimal places, which doesn't match the precision of U.S. currency (dollars and cents). However, you have not learned how to round numbers yet. Rounding can be done using an SQL *function*, which I discuss in the "Basic SQL Functions" section, so you'll soon know how to round.

- What is the average cost of a copy of *The Last Samurai*? You'll determine this by adding the DVD and VHS prices and dividing by 2. Again, the parentheses are essential to achieving a correct result. You may notice that this result could also benefit from rounding.

```
SELECT (RETAIL_PRICE_VHS + RETAIL_PRICE_DVD) / 2 AS AVG_COST
  FROM MOVIE
 WHERE MOVIE_TITLE = 'The Last Samurai'

   AVG_COST
----------
    17.955
```

Basic SQL Functions

A *function* is a special type of program that returns a single value each time it is invoked. The term comes from the mathematical concept of a function. In SQL, functions always require an expression, which often includes the name of a column. Functions are most often used in the column list of the SELECT statement and are invoked for each row processed by the query and therefore return a single value for each row that appears in the result set. Sometimes the term *column function* is used to remind you that the function is being applied to a table or view column. A number of functions are provided by the DBMS vendor, and in most SQL implementations, you can write your own using a special language that comes with the DBMS, such as PL/SQL for Oracle, or Transact SQL for Microsoft SQL Server and Sybase Adaptive Server.

Functions can be categorized in many ways, but most people categorize them by the type of work that they perform. The most common functions are described here, but as always, check your DBMS documentation—it's likely that it provides more functions than the ones covered in this book. The categories used in this book are character, mathematical, conversion, and aggregate, and each category has its own sections.

Character Functions

Character functions are so named because they handle character data.

String Concatenation

The *string concatenation* function puts multiple character strings together to form a single column value in the query results. The standard string concatenation function in SQL is invoked with two vertical bars (||), but there are exceptions, such as Microsoft SQL Server, which uses the plus sign (+) to concatenate strings. Here are some examples of string concatenation:

- The video store wishes to send a mailing to each customer that addresses them as "Valuable Customer" plus their first (given) and last (family) names. The names are stored in the PERSON table. Note that you can mix and match literal strings (including spaces) and column data any way you wish. Here is the solution in Oracle:

```
SELECT 'Valuable Customer ' || PERSON_GIVEN_NAME ||
       ' ' || PERSON_FAMILY_NAME AS CUSTOMER_SALUTATION
FROM PERSON;
```

```
CUSTOMER_SALUTATION
-----------------------------------------
Valuable Customer Austin Alexander
Valuable Customer Tin Chung
Valuable Customer Cassandra Alvarado
Valuable Customer Raul Alvarado
Valuable Customer Klaus Schmidt
Valuable Customer Katarina Schmidt
Valuable Customer Karl Schmidt
Valuable Customer Toshiro Yamada
Valuable Customer Beverly Baker
Valuable Customer Gerald Bernstein
Valuable Customer Rose Bernstein
Valuable Customer Steven Bernstein
Valuable Customer Linda Campos
Valuable Customer Jorge Jimenez
Valuable Customer Liyi Huang


15 rows selected.
```

- Here is the same solution, modified to work in Microsoft SQL Server (result set omitted since it is essentially the same as the previous):

```
SELECT 'Valuable Customer ' + PERSON_GIVEN_NAME +
       ' ' + PERSON_FAMILY_NAME AS CUSTOMER_SALUTATION
  FROM PERSON;
```

UPPER

The UPPER function shifts letters in a character string into uppercase letters. Numbers and special characters are left just as they were. Here are some examples:

- List the comedy movies (MOVIE_GENRE_CODE = 'Comdy') with the titles in uppercase text. Note that a column alias is used to make sure the column name MOVIE_TITLE appears in the result set.

```
SELECT UPPER(MOVIE_TITLE) AS MOVIE_TITLE
  FROM MOVIE
 WHERE MOVIE_GENRE_CODE = 'Comdy';


MOVIE_TITLE
-------------------------
SOMETHING'S GOTTA GIVE
50 FIRST DATES
```

```
MATCHSTICK MEN
THE SCHOOL OF ROCK

4 rows selected.
```

- The UPPER function is also often used in WHERE conditions. Suppose you can't remember whether the MOVIE_GENRE_CODE was stored in upper- or lowercase or mixed case. If you shift it all to uppercase in the WHERE condition, you can get a correct result anyway.

```
SELECT UPPER(MOVIE_TITLE) AS MOVIE_TITLE
  FROM MOVIE
 WHERE UPPER(MOVIE_GENRE_CODE) = 'COMDY';


MOVIE_TITLE
-------------------------
50 FIRST DATES
MATCHSTICK MEN
SOMETHING'S GOTTA GIVE
THE SCHOOL OF ROCK

4 rows selected.
```

Be cautious when using SQL functions in WHERE conditions. Under most circumstances, a column with a function applied to it cannot be matched by an index. So, for large tables, using functions in WHERE conditions can lead to truly memorable performance problems. Did you notice that the order of the rows in the result set changed when the UPPER function was used in the WHERE clause? I used Oracle for the preceding queries, so your results with another DBMS may vary. But why did it happen? First, there was no ORDER BY clause, so the DBMS is not required to return the rows in any particular order. Second, it used an index to find the rows in the first example and simply scanned the table in the second example; obviously, the index isn't in the same order as the rows in the table. The lesson here is to *always* specify an ORDER BY if the order of rows in the result set matters to you.

LOWER

The LOWER function does just the opposite of the UPPER function—it shifts any letters in the character string to lowercase letters. Here are the same examples using the LOWER function:

- List the comedy movies (MOVIE_GENRE_CODE = 'Comdy') with the titles in lowercase text. Note that a column alias is used to make sure the column name MOVIE_TITLE appears in the result set.

```
SELECT LOWER(MOVIE_TITLE) AS MOVIE_TITLE
  FROM MOVIE
 WHERE MOVIE_GENRE_CODE = 'Comdy';

MOVIE_TITLE
-------------------------
something's gotta give
50 first dates
matchstick men
the school of rock

4 rows selected.
```

- As with the UPPER function, you can use the LOWER function in a WHERE clause when you aren't sure about the case of the text you are trying to match. List movies that have the word "of" in the title, regardless of whether it is capitalized or not. Note the combined use of the LIKE operator and LOWER function. Also note that you must handle special cases where the word "of" could be the first word or last word in the title (that is, where it might not have a space before it or after it). These cases don't actually exist in the sample database, but they could, and you cannot simply use LIKE '%of%' or you might select a title because it had a word like 'often' in it. The lesson here is that you have to know something about what *might* be in the data in order to write SQL that will *always* produce the expected result.

```
SELECT MOVIE_TITLE
  FROM MOVIE
 WHERE LOWER(MOVIE_TITLE) LIKE '% of %'
    OR LOWER(MOVIE_TITLE) LIKE 'of%'
    OR LOWER(MOVIE_TITLE) LIKE '% of';

MOVIE_TITLE
----------------------------------------------------------
Master and Commander: The Far Side of the World
Pirates of the Caribbean: The Curse of the Black Pearl
The School of Rock

3 rows selected.
```

SUBSTR

The SUBSTR function appears in most SQL implementations, but it sometimes has a somewhat different name. For example, the function is named SUBSTRING in Microsoft SQL Server, Sybase Adaptive Server, and MySQL, while the name SUBSTR is used in Oracle and DB2. It returns a portion of a string as determined by the parameters, which provide the name of the column, first (starting) position of the column data to be returned, and the number of characters (length) to be returned. And, while it's an unusual use of SUBSTR, a literal string can be provided instead of a column name. The general form of the function is shown first, followed by an example:

```
SUBSTR (COLUMN_NAME, starting_position, length)
```

- Some people have full middle names in the PERSON table, while others have only a first initial. List the full name of each person whose last name begins with the letter "B" in the form of a single string that contains the given (first) name, middle initial, and family (last) name.

Here is the solution using Oracle:

```
SELECT PERSON_GIVEN_NAME || ' ' ||
       SUBSTR(PERSON_MIDDLE_NAME, 1, 1) || '. ' ||
       PERSON_FAMILY_NAME AS FULL_NAME
  FROM PERSON
 WHERE SUBSTR(PERSON_FAMILY_NAME, 1, 1) = 'B'

FULL_NAME
--------------------
Beverly V. Baker
Gerald M. Bernstein
Rose B. Bernstein
Steven R. Bernstein

4 rows selected.
```

Note the use of SUBSTR in the WHERE clause to filter out people with a family name that doesn't begin with "B". By now you should be able to think of other ways to do this, including the LIKE operator.

Here is the Microsoft SQL Server version of the previous example:

```
SELECT PERSON_GIVEN_NAME + ' ' +
       SUBSTRING(PERSON_MIDDLE_NAME, 1, 1) + '. ' +
       PERSON_FAMILY_NAME AS FULL_NAME
  FROM PERSON
 WHERE SUBSTRING(PERSON_FAMILY_NAME, 1, 1) = 'B'
```

```
FULL_NAME
---------------------
Beverly V. Baker
Gerald M. Bernstein
Rose B. Bernstein
Steven R. Bernstein

(4 row(s) affected)
```

LENGTH

The LENGTH function returns the length of a character string. However, Microsoft SQL Server and Sybase Adaptive Server use the name LEN for their version of the function. Here are some examples:

- List the length of the movie title for the movie with a MOVIE_ID of 1. Assume an Oracle, DB2, or MySQL database.

```
SELECT MOVIE_TITLE, LENGTH(MOVIE_TITLE) AS LENGTH
  FROM MOVIE
 WHERE MOVIE_ID = 1;


MOVIE_TITLE          LENGTH
------------------ ----------
Mystic River             12
```

- List all movie titles that are shorter than 10 characters in length. Assume a Microsoft SQL Server database.

```
SELECT MOVIE_TITLE, LEN(MOVIE_TITLE) AS LENGTH
  FROM MOVIE
 WHERE LEN(MOVIE_TITLE) < 10;


MOVIE_TITLE    LENGTH
------------ ----------
Big Fish          8
Das Boot          8
Monster           7
```

Mathematical Functions

Mathematical functions manipulate numeric values according to mathematical rules. The ROUND function is presented in detail, including an example, followed by a table that lists other mathematical functions that are commonly found in

SQL implementations. As always, check your DBMS documentation for a specific list of supported mathematical functions.

ROUND

The ROUND function rounds off a number to the specified number of decimal places. The number is provided as the first expression and the number of decimal places as the second. The general format of the ROUND function is shown next, followed by an example adapted from earlier in the chapter.

```
ROUND (numeric_expression,number_of_decimal_places)
```

- What is the average cost of a copy of *The Last Samurai*, rounded to the nearest penny?

```
SELECT ROUND((RETAIL_PRICE_VHS + RETAIL_PRICE_DVD) / 2, 2)
       AS AVG_COST
  FROM MOVIE
 WHERE MOVIE_TITLE = 'The Last Samurai';


  AVG_COST
----------
     17.96
```

Other Mathematical Functions

The table that follows lists the most commonly found mathematical functions. The general syntax for all of them is the same:

```
FUNCTION_NAME(expression)
```

Function	Description
ABS	Absolute value of the given number
COS	Trigonometric cosine of the given angle (in radians)
EXP	Exponential value of the given number
POWER	Raise number to a power (both number and power are parameters)
SIN	Trigonometric sine of the given angle (in radians)
TAN	Trigonometric tangent of the given angle (in radians)

Conversion Functions

Conversion functions convert data from one data type to another.

CAST

The CAST function converts data from one data type to another. Note, however, that it is not yet supported by DB2. Here is the general syntax of the CAST function, followed by an example:

```
CAST (expression AS data_type)
```

- List the DVD price of *The Last Samurai* with a leading dollar sign. The numeric value must be converted to (cast as) a character string so that you can concatenate it with a literal containing a dollar sign. Note that for Microsoft SQL Server, the concatenation operator in the statement has to be changed from "||" to "+".

```
SELECT '$' || CAST(RETAIL_PRICE_DVD AS VARCHAR(6)) AS PRICE
  FROM MOVIE
 WHERE MOVIE_TITLE = 'The Last Samurai';


PRICE
-------
$19.96
```

CONVERT TO

Many DBMS implementations offer a CONVERT or CONVERT TO function. However, the CAST function is generally recommended instead because it is implemented in a more standard way across vendors.

Aggregate Functions and Grouping Rows

An *aggregate function* is a function that combines multiple rows of data together into a single row. The following table shows aggregate functions that are supported in most SQL implementations:

Function Name	Description
AVG	Calculates the average value for a column or expression.
COUNT	Counts the number of values found in a column. The DISTINCT keyword can be used to count the number of unique values instead of the total number of values (rows) in a column.
MAX	Finds the maximum value in a column.
MIN	Finds the minimum value in a column.
SUM	Sums (totals up) the values in a column.

Here are some examples:

- What is the average price of a DVD? Notice that the ROUND and AVG functions are nested so you get the result in dollars and cents.

```
SELECT ROUND(AVG(RETAIL_PRICE_DVD),2) AS AVG_PRICE
  FROM MOVIE;


AVG_PRICE
----------
    24.67
```

- How many movies are in the MOVIE table?

```
SELECT COUNT(*) AS NUM_MOVIES
  FROM MOVIE;


NUM_MOVIES
----------
        20
```

- How many different movie genres are represented in the MOVIE table? Notice the use of DISTINCT so the DBMS counts unique values of MOVIE_GENRE_CODE.

```
SELECT COUNT(DISTINCT(MOVIE_GENRE_CODE)) AS NUM_GENRES
  FROM MOVIE


NUM_GENRES
----------
         5
```

- What is the shortest and longest movie title? Notice the nesting of the LENGTH function with the MIN and MAX functions. This version works in Oracle, DB2, and MySQL (change LENGTH to LEN for Microsoft SQL Server and Sybase).

```
SELECT MIN(LENGTH(MOVIE_TITLE)) AS MIN_LENGTH,
       MAX(LENGTH(MOVIE_TITLE)) AS MAX_LENGTH
  FROM MOVIE;


MIN_LENGTH MAX_LENGTH
---------- ----------
         7         54
```

GROUP BY Clause

As you have seen, if you use an aggregate function by itself in a query, you get one row back for the entire query. This makes sense because there is no way for the RDBMS to know what other result you might want, unless you tell it, which is the very purpose of the GROUP BY clause. It tells the DBMS to form the rows selected by the query into *groups* based on the values of one or more columns and to apply the aggregate function(s) to each group, returning one row for each group in the result set. This is much like asking for subtotals by department instead of one grand total for an entire company, but as you have seen, aggregate functions can do much more than just add things up. By the way, the DBMS will sort the rows selected by the query on the columns listed in the GROUP BY clause (so it can group them easily), so the groups will be returned in ascending sequence unless you add an ORDER BY that specifies another sequence. Here is an example:

- List each movie genre code with the number of movies that are assigned to it.

```
SELECT MOVIE_GENRE_CODE AS GENRE, COUNT(*) AS COUNT
  FROM MOVIE
 GROUP BY MOVIE_GENRE_CODE;
```

GENRE	COUNT
ActAd	7
Comdy	4
Drama	6
Forgn	1
Rmce	2

What happens if you leave the GROUP BY clause out of this query? The DBMS returns an error message, and unfortunately, the error message is often quite cryptic. Most newcomers to SQL have difficulty understanding the problem, but without the GROUP BY clause, the query is illogical. The COUNT(*) function is an aggregate function, so without a GROUP BY, it returns a single row of data. However, the MOVIE_GENRE_CODE is a column and without being named in a GROUP BY, the query will return the value from every row in the table. Without the GROUP BY to correlate the two, the DBMS does not know what to do. No wonder some people call them "aggravating functions" instead of aggregate functions. But it really isn't that difficult. Just remember one rule: Whenever a query includes an aggregate function, then *every* column in the query results must either be formed using an aggregate function or be named in the GROUP BY clause.

Compound Query Operators

Sometimes it is useful to run multiple queries and to combine the results into a single result set.

UNION

The UNION operator appends all the rows in the result set of one query to that of another, but it also eliminates any duplicate rows, much like the DISTINCT keyword does. The operation is permitted only if the queries involved are *union compatible*, which means they have the same number of columns and the data types of the corresponding columns are compatible. Here is an example:

- List all the non-null values of rental fees or late-or-lost fees from the MOVIE_RENTAL table in a single column.

```
SELECT RENTAL_FEE AS FEE
  FROM MOVIE_RENTAL
 WHERE RENTAL_FEE IS NOT NULL
UNION
SELECT LATE_OR_LOSS_FEE AS FEE
  FROM MOVIE_RENTAL
 WHERE LATE_OR_LOSS_FEE IS NOT NULL;

       FEE
----------
         4
         6
      6.25
     29.98
     29.99
```

If you find this one difficult to visualize, just run the two queries independently, and then combine them to see the result. You'll find out that the second and third rows are rental fees that are found by the first query, while the first, fourth, and fifth rows are late-or-loss fees from the second query.

UNION ALL

UNION ALL works like UNION except that duplicate rows are *not* eliminated from the result set. If you repeat the previous example with UNION ALL, you will get a result set of 24 rows instead of 5 rows.

INTERSECT

The INTERSECT operator finds values selected by one query that also appear in the other query. Essentially, it finds the intersection of the values in the two result sets. However, only a few DBMS implementations (most notably Oracle and DB2) support it. You won't find it in Microsoft SQL Server or MySQL. Here is an example:

- Are any of the DVD prices the same as one of the VHS prices in the MOVIE table? The result set contains no rows, so the answer is no.

```
SELECT RENTAL_FEE AS FEE
  FROM MOVIE_RENTAL
 WHERE RENTAL_FEE IS NOT NULL
INTERSECT
SELECT LATE_OR_LOSS_FEE AS FEE
  FROM MOVIE_RENTAL
 WHERE LATE_OR_LOSS_FEE IS NOT NULL

no rows selected
```

EXCEPT

EXCEPT is the ANSI/ISO standard operator that finds the difference between two result sets, basically by returning values from the first query that are not included in the result set of the second query. Very few DBMS implementations have implemented this operator. In some implementations such as Oracle, it is named MINUS instead of EXCEPT.

Quiz

Choose the correct responses to each of the multiple-choice questions. Note that there may be more than one correct response to each question.

1. A SELECT without a WHERE clause
    a. Selects all columns in the table or view
    b. Results in an error message
    c. Selects all rows in the table or view
    d. Lists only the definition of the table or view
    e. Always outputs results to a log file

2. In SQL, row order in the query results

   a. Is specified by the SORTED BY clause

   b. May be either ascending or descending for any column

   c. Defaults to descending when sequence is not specified

   d. Is unpredictable unless specified in the query

   e. May only be specified for columns in the query result set

3. The BETWEEN operator

   a. Specifies a range of values that includes the end points

   b. Can be rewritten using the <= and NOT <= operators

   c. Can be rewritten using the <= and >= operators

   d. Selects rows added to a table during a time interval

   e. Is not included in the ISO/ANSI standard

4. The standard LIKE operator

   a. Uses question marks as nonpositional wildcards

   b. Uses underscores as positional wildcards

   c. Uses underscores as nonpositional wildcards

   d. Uses percent signs as positional wildcards

   e. Uses percent signs as nonpositional wildcards

5. An SQL statement containing an aggregate function

   a. May also contain calculated columns

   b. May also contain ordinary columns

   c. Must include an ORDER BY clause

   d. Must contain a GROUP BY clause

   e. May not include both GROUP BY and ORDER BY clauses

6. When AND and OR operators are mixed in the same WHERE clause

   a. The DBMS returns an error message

   b. The AND has a higher precedence than the OR

   c. The OR has a higher precedence than the AND

   d. Parentheses are mandatory

   e. Parentheses are optional

7. The proper syntax for eliminating null values in query results is

   a. = NULL

   b. NOT = NULL

   c. <> NULL

   d. IS NULL

   e. IS NOT NULL

8. Standard SQL string functions include

   a. UPPER

   b. MIDDLE

   c. LOWER

   d. SUBSTR

   e. EXISTS

9. Standard SQL mathematical functions include

   a. LENGTH

   b. ROUND

   c. CAST

   d. MIN

   e. ABS

10. The UNION operator

   a. Eliminates duplicate rows in the result set

   b. Includes duplicate rows in the result set

   c. Combines two queries into a single joined query

   d. Combines the result sets of two queries into a single result set

   e. Is named JOIN in some SQL implementations

Write the SQL statement for each of these problems.

11. Find all movies in the MOVIE table where the MPAA_RATING_CODE is a value other than "R".

12. List the title and price of all movies that have a RETAIL_PRICE_DVD that is at least 19.99 but no more than 29.99, sorted in ascending sequence by price.

13. List all movies that have a genre (MOVIE_GENRE_CODE) of Comdy and a rating (MPAA_RATING_CODE) of PG-13, along with movies that have a genre of Drama and a rating of R.

14. How many rentals (MOVIE_RENTAL table) have no value for the LATE_ OR_LOSS_FEE column?

15. How many people have a last name (PERSON_FAMILY_NAME) that includes the letter "a", in either uppercase or lowercase?

16. List all movie titles that contain the word "the" anywhere in the title, capitalized or not.

17. Use the SUM function to find the total of the RENTAL_FEE column in the MOVIE_RENTAL table.

18. List the first five characters of the last names (PERSON_FAMILY_NAME) from the PERSON table, but eliminate all duplicate values in the query results.

19. From the MOVIE table, list each genre (MOVIE_GENRE_CODE) with the average DVD price (RETAIL_PRICE_DVD) for that genre, rounded to two decimal places.

20. List each movie (MOVIE_ID) that has been rented (MOVIE_RENTAL table) with the total amount of money collected in rental fees (RENTAL_ FEE) and late-or-loss fees (LATE_OR_LOSS_FEE) for that movie. Hint: add RENTAL_FEE and LATE_OR_LOSS_FEE and then SUM that result for each value of MOVIE_ID. Some of the values for LATE_OR_LOSS_ FEE are null, so unless you use a function that replaces null values with another value (zero in this case), you will get null values in the result. In Oracle the function is called NVL, in Microsoft SQL Server it is called ISNULL, and in MySQL it is called IFNULL. (There doesn't appear to be an equivalent function in DB2.)

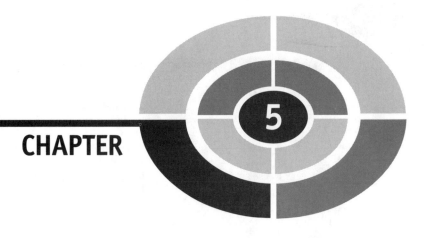

CHAPTER

5

Combining Data from Multiple Tables

In Chapter 4, we looked at SQL statements that select data from a single table. However, it's often very useful to combine data from multiple tables in a single query. For example, in the listing of three columns from the MOVIE table shown in Figure 5-1, notice the values displayed for the MOVIE_GENRE column. While some of the rows contain values that you could easily guess, such as "Drama," "Forgn," and "SciFi," others are not so obvious, such as "ActAd," "ChFam," and "Indep."

When I designed this database for the video store, I deliberately used codes instead of full descriptions for the movie genres in the MOVIE table. This is not only a good database design practice that follows the rules of normalization, but it also reduces the size of each row in the MOVIE table by using a five-character code in

MOVIE_ID	MOVIE_GENRE_CODE	MOVIE_TITLE
1	Drama	Mystic River
2	ActAd	The Last Samurai
3	Comdy	Something's Gotta Give
4	ActAd	The Italian Job
5	ActAd	Kill Bill: Vol. 1
6	ActAd	Pirates of the Caribbean: The Curse of the Black Pearl
7	Drama	Big Fish
8	ActAd	Man on Fire
9	ActAd	Master and Commander: The Far Side of the World
10	Drama	Lost in Translation
11	Rmce	Two Weeks Notice
12	Comdy	50 First Dates
13	Comdy	Matchstick Men
14	Drama	Cold Mountain
15	Drama	Road to Perdition
16	Comdy	The School of Rock
17	Rmce	13 Going on 30
18	Drama	Monster
19	ActAd	The Day After Tomorrow
20	Forgn	Das Boot

20 rows selected.

Figure 5-1   MOVIE table listing (three columns)

place of a description that could be 100 characters long. Moreover, as you will recall from the normalization discussion in Chapter 1, I have avoided the update anomaly—should a movie genre description change, I don't have to update that description for every movie that is assigned to that genre in the MOVIE table. During normalization, the genre description was moved to its own table, MOVIE_GENRE, with the MOVIE_GENRE_CODE remaining as a foreign key in the MOVIE table, which references the primary key column (same column name) in the MOVIE_GENRE table. While some designers prefer primary key values that have no real-world meaning because the values might have to change on occasion, I chose to use a mnemonic code for the genre code because it allows those who are very familiar with the data to understand the genre assigned to the movies without having to look them up in the MOVIE_GENRE table. Obviously, you cannot display the MOVIE table as shown in Figure 5-1 on the video store's web page—you need to obtain the full description of the movie genre from the MOVIE_GENRE table. That is the very point of this chapter: combining data from multiple tables in a single query. Figure 5-2 shows a listing of the MOVIE_GENRE table.

MOVIE_GENRE_CODE	MOVIE_GENRE_DESCRIPTION
ActAd	Action and Adventure
Anime	Anime and Animation
ChFam	Children and Family
Class	Classics
Comdy	Comedy
Doc	Documentary
Drama	Drama
Forgn	Foreign
Hor	Horror
Indep	Independent
Music	Music and Musicals
Rmce	Romance
SciFi	Science Fiction and Fantasy
Specl	Special Interest
Sport	Sports
Thril	Thrillers

16 rows selected.

Figure 5-2   MOVIE_GENRE table listing

Joins

A *join* is a relational database operation that combines columns from two or more tables into a single query result. A join occurs whenever the FROM clause in a SELECT statement lists more than one table name. Here is an example, but as you will see, it has a big problem:

```
SELECT MOVIE_ID, MOVIE_GENRE_DESCRIPTION AS GENRE, MOVIE_TITLE
  FROM MOVIE, MOVIE_GENRE
 ORDER BY MOVIE_ID;

  MOVIE_ID GENRE                MOVIE_TITLE
---------- -------------------- ------------------
         1 Action and Adventure Mystic River
         1 Anime and Animation  Mystic River
         1 Classics             Mystic River
         1 Documentary          Mystic River
         1 Foreign              Mystic River
         1 Independent          Mystic River
         1 Romance              Mystic River
         1 Special Interest     Mystic River
         1 Thrillers            Mystic River
```

```
1 Sports                 Mystic River
1 Science Fiction and    Mystic River
1 Music and Musicals     Mystic River
1 Horror                 Mystic River
1 Drama                  Mystic River
1 Comedy                 Mystic River
1 Children and Family    Mystic River
2 Action and Adventure   The Last Samurai
2 Thrillers              The Last Samurai
2 Sports                 The Last Samurai
2 Special Interest       The Last Samurai
2 Science Fiction and    The Last Samurai
2 Romance                The Last Samurai
2 Music and Musicals     The Last Samurai
2 Independent            The Last Samurai
2 Horror                 The Last Samurai
2 Anime and Animation    The Last Samurai
2 Children and Family    The Last Samurai
2 Documentary            The Last Samurai
2 Foreign                The Last Samurai
2 Drama                  The Last Samurai
2 Comedy                 The Last Samurai
2 Classics               The Last Samurai
...     ...                      ...
320 rows selected.
```

The result set from the query was truncated after the first two movie titles (32 rows). A total of 320 rows were selected. But since there are only 20 movies in the MOVIE table, how is this possible? The problem is that I told the database to join the two tables but I failed to tell it how to match rows between the two tables. The result is known as a *Cartesian product* (named for French philosopher and mathematician René Descartes), which in a relational database is a result set where each row in one table is joined with *every* row in another. In this case, each row in MOVIE has been joined with every row in MOVIE_GENRE to make it appear that each movie belongs to every genre, which is, of course, incorrect. There are 320 rows because there are 16 genres and 20 movies ($16 \times 20 = 320$). You can easily see the pattern in the result set—the first movie title is assigned to all 16 genres, then the second, and so forth.

The solution is to specify *how* to join the tables, specifically, which columns should be matched between the two tables to link them. Normally, this will be the primary key of one table and the foreign key of the other, but there can be exceptions. You may be wondering why SQL even allows a Cartesian product, but believe it or not, there are rare circumstances when one is required. Be careful—a Cartesian product of two 1000-row tables will return one million rows! The next topic shows you how to do a standard relational join, also known as an *equijoin*.

Equijoins

An *equijoin*, or *inner join*, is one where one or more columns in one table (typically the foreign key) are matched with similar columns in another table (typically the primary key) using the *equal* condition (that is, columns are considered to match when their data values are equal). You'll find this to be the most common form of join. However, the term *equijoin* is seldom used outside of academic circles, with the term *inner join* or *standard join* being much more common.

There are two ways to specify the columns to be matched: using the WHERE clause, or using the JOIN clause. The JOIN clause is a relatively new addition to standard SQL, so most old timers are more used to the WHERE clause method.

Joins Using the WHERE Clause

Using the WHERE clause to join tables is very much like using it to eliminate unwanted rows in the result set. However, there are some differences. First, you are comparing a column to another column in the WHERE condition instead of comparing a column value to a constant or expression. Second, when the columns in the two tables have the same name (which is a best practice), you must *qualify* the column names so the SQL engine can tell which of the two columns is being referenced. While your intention may seem obvious to you, the SQL engine is going to insist that you make *unambiguous* references to every column you mention in an SQL statement. By the way, this includes not only columns in the WHERE clause, but also elsewhere in the statement, including in the SELECT list. The simplest form of qualifier is the table name itself, with a period (dot) used to separate it from the column name. Following is an example of a join specified in the WHERE clause with table names used as qualifiers. Notice how it selects MOVIE_ID and MOVIE_TITLE from MOVIE and the corresponding genre (GENRE_DESCRIPTION) from MOVIE_GENRE.

```
SELECT MOVIE_ID, MOVIE_GENRE_DESCRIPTION AS GENRE,
       MOVIE_TITLE
  FROM MOVIE, MOVIE_GENRE
 WHERE MOVIE.MOVIE_GENRE_CODE= MOVIE_GENRE.MOVIE_GENRE_CODE
 ORDER BY MOVIE_ID;
```

```
MOVIE_ID GENRE                    MOVIE_TITLE
-------- ----------------------   ------------------------
       1 Drama                    Mystic River
       2 Action and Adventure     The Last Samurai
       3 Comedy                   Something's Gotta Give
       4 Action and Adventure     The Italian Job
       5 Action and Adventure     Kill Bill: Vol. 1
       6 Action and Adventure     Pirates of the Caribbean:
       7 Drama                    Big Fish
       8 Action and Adventure     Man on Fire
       9 Action and Adventure     Master and Commander: The
      10 Drama                    Lost in Translation
      11 Romance                  Two Weeks Notice
      12 Comedy                   50 First Dates
      13 Comedy                   Matchstick Men
      14 Drama                    Cold Mountain
      15 Drama                    Road to Perdition
      16 Comedy                   The School of Rock
      17 Romance                  13 Going on 30
      18 Drama                    Monster
      19 Action and Adventure     The Day After Tomorrow
      20 Foreign                  Das Boot
```

20 rows selected.

Using the full table name as a column qualifier can be tedious and time consuming, especially when table names can be 30 or more characters long in modern DBMSs. That's why a provision for table name aliases was included in SQL. They work much like the column name aliases available in the SELECT clause, except that the keyword "AS" is not used (in most SQL implementations)—just leave a space between the table name and its alias in the FROM list. While some people use mnemonics for table name aliases, it's more common to see sequential capital letters use (that is, "A," "B," "C," and so forth). Once you assign an alias to a table name in the FROM clause, you *must* use the alias instead of the table name throughout the SQL statement. Table name aliases in the SELECT clause will seem odd at first because you use the alias before you've actually defined it (the SELECT clause precedes the FROM clause), and you may find it easier to fill in the FROM clause before you fill in the column list in the SELECT clause as you write SQL statements.

The following example shows the statement we just looked at with aliases for the table names added. Although not necessary, table name aliases were also added to the column list in the SELECT and ORDER BY clauses so you can see how that looks.

```
SELECT A.MOVIE_ID, B.MOVIE_GENRE_DESCRIPTION AS GENRE,
       A.MOVIE_TITLE
  FROM MOVIE A, MOVIE_GENRE B
 WHERE A.MOVIE_GENRE_CODE = B.MOVIE_GENRE_CODE
 ORDER BY A.MOVIE_ID;
```

Joins Using the JOIN clause

As already mentioned, the JOIN clause is a newer addition to SQL, added in the SQL-92 standard, so the implementation you are using may not support it as yet, although most current SQL implementations do. The JOIN clause is written as a table reference in the FROM clause and essentially combines the table list in the FROM clause and the join conditions previously written in the WHERE clause into a single clause. Here is the general syntax of the JOIN clause for an inner join, followed by some examples.

```
table_name [INNER] JOIN table_name
  { ON condition | USING (column_name [,column_name]) }
```

Note the two options. The ON clause allows for specification of a condition just like the one in the WHERE clause in the prior example. The USING clause, on the other hand, simply lists the column names to be used for matching rows. However, the USING clause only works when the columns to be matched have identical names in both tables. Here are some examples:

- JOIN with the ON condition:

```
SELECT MOVIE_ID, MOVIE_GENRE_DESCRIPTION AS GENRE,
       MOVIE_TITLE
  FROM MOVIE JOIN MOVIE_GENRE ON
       MOVIE.MOVIE_GENRE_CODE = MOVIE_GENRE.MOVIE_GENRE_CODE
 ORDER BY MOVIE_ID;
```

- JOIN with table aliases instead of table names:

```
SELECT MOVIE_ID, MOVIE_GENRE_DESCRIPTION AS GENRE,
       MOVIE_TITLE
  FROM MOVIE A JOIN MOVIE_GENRE B ON
       A.MOVIE_GENRE_CODE = B.MOVIE_GENRE_CODE
 ORDER BY MOVIE_ID;
```

- JOIN with the USING keyword (instead of the ON condition). This is a very nice shorthand option when the columns in the two tables have the same name. However, it is a very new standard, so as of this writing, only Oracle and MySQL support this syntax (Microsoft SQL Server and DB2 do not).

```
SELECT MOVIE_ID, MOVIE_GENRE_DESCRIPTION AS GENRE,
       MOVIE_TITLE
  FROM MOVIE JOIN MOVIE_GENRE USING (MOVIE_GENRE_CODE)
 ORDER BY MOVIE_ID;
```

- JOIN with a multiple-column foreign key. This query lists movie copies from the MOVIE_COPY table that have not been sold (DATE_SOLD IS NULL) and which have been rented (join to the MOVIE_RENTAL table) and not yet returned (RETURNED_DATE IS NULL). Since this table has not been used in a previous example, you may want to refer to the overview of the Video Sample database that appears at the end of Chapter 1 to see how it fits into the database schema. Also, keep in mind that, as of this writing, only Oracle and MySQL support this syntax.

```
SELECT MOVIE_ID, COPY_NUMBER, DUE_DATE
   FROM MOVIE_COPY JOIN MOVIE_RENTAL
        USING (MOVIE_ID, COPY_NUMBER)
  WHERE DATE_SOLD IS NULL
    AND RETURNED_DATE IS NULL;


MOVIE_ID COPY_NUMBER DUE_DATE
--------- ----------- ----------
        2           2 02/27/2005
        3           2 03/04/2005
        5           1 02/27/2005
        5           2 02/19/2005
       10           1 03/04/2005
       17           1 03/04/2005

6 rows selected.
```

- Just to illustrate how much typing the JOIN clause saves, here is the prior query rewritten using join conditions in the WHERE clause. Note that you now must qualify all references to the MOVIE_ID and COPY_NUMBER columns to avoid ambiguous column references. This statement will give you exactly the same result as the previous example:

```
SELECT A.MOVIE_ID, A.COPY_NUMBER, DUE_DATE
   FROM MOVIE_COPY A, MOVIE_RENTAL B
  WHERE A.MOVIE_ID = B.MOVIE_ID
    AND A.COPY_NUMBER = B.COPY_NUMBER
    AND DATE_SOLD IS NULL
    AND RETURNED_DATE IS NULL;
```

Natural Joins

A *natural join* is based on all columns in the two tables that have matching column names. In essence, the equijoins you have already seen are also natural joins. However, the syntax for the natural join is much simpler because there is no need to name a condition or a column list—the columns to be used are understood. Note that, as of this writing, only Oracle and MySQL support this form of join syntax.

Some descriptions of the natural join that you might read elsewhere indicate that the column list being selected has something to do with the definition of a natural join. Actually, it doesn't—you can select whatever columns you wish, but like all SELECT statements, no two columns in the result set may have the same column name, so you have to rename any duplicate column names using a column alias.

Here is the join of MOVIE and MOVIE_GENRE, rewritten as a natural join:

```
SELECT MOVIE_ID, MOVIE_GENRE_DESCRIPTION AS GENRE,
       MOVIE_TITLE
  FROM MOVIE NATURAL JOIN MOVIE_GENRE
 ORDER BY MOVIE_ID;
```

By the way, joins can involve more than two tables. The following example shows a natural join that gets the MOVIE_ID from the MOVIE table, the MOVIE_GENRE_DESCRIPTION from the MOVIE_GENRE table, and the MPAA_RATING_DESCRIPTION from the MPAA_RATING table for the first five movies in the MOVIE table. Note the use of the WHERE clause to eliminate unwanted rows from the MOVIE table. The text for the RATING_DESC column was allowed to wrap to new lines in the query results because of its length. The example actually specifies two joins. The first JOIN clause directs the SQL engine to first join the MOVIE and MOVIE_GENRE tables, and the second JOIN clause directs it to take those joined rows (essentially an intermediate result set) and join them to the MPAA_RATING table.

```
SELECT MOVIE_ID, MOVIE_GENRE_DESCRIPTION AS GENRE,
       MPAA_RATING_CODE AS RATING,
       MPAA_RATING_DESCRIPTION AS RATING_DESC
  FROM MOVIE NATURAL JOIN MOVIE_GENRE
            NATURAL JOIN MPAA_RATING
 WHERE MOVIE_ID < 6
 ORDER BY MOVIE_ID;


MOVIE_ID  GENRE                   RATING RATING_DESC
--------- --------------------    ------ --------------------
        1 Drama                   R      Under 17 requires ac
                                         companying parent or
                                         adult guardian

        2 Action and Adventure    R      Under 17 requires ac
                                         companying parent or
                                         adult guardian
```

3	Comedy	PG-13	Parents strongly cau tioned
4	Action and Adventure	PG-13	Parents strongly cau tioned
5	Action and Adventure	R	Under 17 requires ac companying parent or adult guardian

```
5 rows selected.
```

Just in case you are using an SQL implementation that lacks support for natural joins, here is the previous query rewritten using the JOIN and ON keywords:

```
SELECT A.MOVIE_ID, B.MOVIE_GENRE_DESCRIPTION AS GENRE,
       C.MPAA_RATING_CODE AS RATING,
       C.MPAA_RATING_DESCRIPTION AS RATING_DESC
  FROM MOVIE A JOIN MOVIE_GENRE B ON
       A.MOVIE_GENRE_CODE = B.MOVIE_GENRE_CODE
            JOIN MPAA_RATING C ON
       A.MPAA_RATING_CODE = C.MPAA_RATING_CODE
 WHERE MOVIE_ID < 6
 ORDER BY MOVIE_ID;
```

Outer Joins

All of the joins we have looked at so far are exclusive joins (a term I like a lot better than *inner* joins), meaning that the only rows that appear in the result set are ones where a match was found in all the tables being joined. However, there are times when you want unmatched rows included in the query results. For example, what if the manager of the video store wanted a listing of all movie genres and any movie titles that are assigned to each one? It was business users in need of solutions to problems such as this one who demanded (and eventually got) a solution from the database vendors.

An *outer join* (which might be better named an *inclusive join*) includes un-matched rows from at least one of the tables in the query results. When there are unmatched rows, any data values selected from the table where a matching row was not found are set to null. There are basically three types:

- **Left outer join** Returns all rows in the left-hand table (the one named first, or leftmost in the JOIN clause) along with any rows in the right-hand table that can be matched.

- **Right outer join**   Returns all rows in the right-hand table (the one named second, or rightmost in the JOIN clause) along with any rows in the left-hand table that can be matched. Essentially, a left outer join may be rewritten as a right outer join simply by reversing the order of the table names and changing the keyword LEFT to RIGHT.

- **Full outer join**   Returns all rows from both tables. This join is the least likely to be supported by your SQL implementation because the standard syntax for it is newer than the other two. It is essential to understand that this is not the same as a Cartesian product, which joins *every* row in one table with *every* row in the other. A full outer join joins each row in one table with zero to many *matching* rows in the other table. In reality, you won't find an occasion to use a full outer join very often, but it can come in handy if there is a relationship between two tables that is optional in both directions.

The general syntax for an outer join is

```
table_name {RIGHT | LEFT| FULL} [OUTER] JOIN table_name
  { ON condition | USING (column_name [,column_name]) }
```

Here are some examples of outer joins:

- Listing of all movie genre descriptions, along with any movies that are assigned to each genre. Note the rows in the result set that have no value for MOVIE_TITLE—these are the movie genres that have no movies assigned to them. If your DBMS implementation does not support a join with the USING keyword, just change the statement so it uses the ON keyword as shown in the example following this one.

```
SELECT MOVIE_GENRE_DESCRIPTION AS GENRE,
       MOVIE_TITLE
  FROM MOVIE_GENRE LEFT OUTER JOIN MOVIE
       USING (MOVIE_GENRE_CODE);


GENRE                            MOVIE_TITLE
-----------------------------    ------------------------------
Action and Adventure             Kill Bill: Vol. 1
Action and Adventure             Man on Fire
Action and Adventure             Pirates of the Caribbean:
Action and Adventure             Master and Commander: The
Action and Adventure             The Day After Tomorrow
Action and Adventure             The Last Samurai
Action and Adventure             The Italian Job
```

```
Anime and Animation
Children and Family
Classics
Comedy                          50 First Dates
Comedy                          Matchstick Men
Comedy                          The School of Rock
Comedy                          Something's Gotta Give
Documentary
Drama                           Big Fish
Drama                           Road to Perdition
Drama                           Mystic River
Drama                           Monster
Drama                           Cold Mountain
Drama                           Lost in Translation
Foreign                         Das Boot
Horror
Independent
Music and Musicals
Romance                         13 Going on 30
Romance                         Two Weeks Notice
Science Fiction and Fantasy
Special Interest
Sports
Thrillers

31 rows selected.
```

- Previous query rewritten as a right outer join with an ON condition.

```
SELECT MOVIE_GENRE_DESCRIPTION AS GENRE,
       MOVIE_TITLE
  FROM MOVIE RIGHT OUTER JOIN MOVIE_GENRE
       ON MOVIE.MOVIE_GENRE_CODE =
          MOVIE_GENRE.MOVIE_GENRE_CODE;
```

- Previous query rewritten as a full outer join. Since each movie must have a genre code assigned, this will give exactly the same result as the right outer join just shown. However, if the movie genre code were optional, the full outer join would allow you to display genres that had no movie assigned as well as movies that had no genre assigned.

```
SELECT MOVIE_GENRE_DESCRIPTION AS GENRE,
       MOVIE_TITLE
  FROM MOVIE FULL OUTER JOIN MOVIE_GENRE
       ON MOVIE.MOVIE_GENRE_CODE =
          MOVIE_GENRE.MOVIE_GENRE_CODE;
```

- Listing of movie genre descriptions that have no movies assigned to them. There are other ways to do this, but this query uses the fact that unmatched rows come back as null values to select only genres with no matching movies. Since MOVIE_TITLE will always be null in the result set, there is no reason to select (and display) the column.

```
SELECT MOVIE_GENRE_DESCRIPTION AS GENRE
  FROM MOVIE RIGHT OUTER JOIN MOVIE_GENRE
       ON MOVIE.MOVIE_GENRE_CODE =
          MOVIE_GENRE.MOVIE_GENRE_CODE
 WHERE MOVIE_TITLE IS NULL;


GENRE
------------------------------
Anime and Animation
Children and Family
Classics
Documentary
Horror
Independent
Music and Musicals
Science Fiction and Fantasy
Special Interest
Sports
Thrillers

11 rows selected.
```

In answer to market demand from their customers, several relational database vendors introduced outer joins before the standard JOIN clause was agreed upon. The following topics present a few implementations of proprietary outer join syntax. These proprietary solutions are shown here only because you might run across them in legacy SQL. The standard JOIN clause should be used whenever possible because it's portable and easier to understand.

Oracle Outer Join Syntax

Oracle Corporation decided to use a plus sign enclosed by parentheses to define outer joins. The symbol "(+)" is placed in the WHERE clause on the side *opposite* from the table from which you want all rows returned (whether matched or not). Since the data from the other table (the one where only matching rows are returned) is filled with null values when no matching row is found, it may be easiest to re-member that the "(+)" symbol goes on the side of the WHERE clause where you

want nulls "added" when no matching row is found. Here is the previous example rewritten in Oracle's proprietary syntax:

```
SELECT MOVIE_GENRE_DESCRIPTION AS GENRE
  FROM MOVIE A, MOVIE_GENRE B
 WHERE A.MOVIE_GENRE_CODE(+) =
       B.MOVIE_GENRE_CODE
   AND MOVIE_TITLE IS NULL;
```

Microsoft SQL Server Outer Join Syntax

Microsoft SQL Server uses the operator "*=" in the WHERE condition for a left outer join and "=*" for a right outer join. In both cases, there cannot be a space between the asterisk and the equal sign. Here is the previous example rewritten in the SQL Server proprietary syntax (as a right outer join):

```
SELECT MOVIE_GENRE_DESCRIPTION AS GENRE
  FROM MOVIE A, MOVIE_GENRE B
 WHERE A.MOVIE_GENRE_CODE =*
       B.MOVIE_GENRE_CODE
   AND MOVIE_TITLE IS NULL;
```

Self Joins

A *self join* is a join of a table to itself. This will seem very odd at first, but sometimes there are relationships where the primary key and foreign key are in the same table. These are called *recursive relationships*, and there is one in the video store database. (You may want to refer back to Figure 1-8 in Chapter 1 at this point.) The EMPLOYEE table has a column called SUPERVISOR_PERSON_ID, which is a foreign key to PERSON_ID in the same table. It is used to link each employee to their supervisor, who is, of course, another employee, which means that the supervisor also has a row in the EMPLOYEE table. The following query shows three columns from the EMPLOYEE table, including the PERSON_ID and SUPERVISOR_PERSON_ID:

```
SELECT PERSON_ID, EMPLOYEE_HOURLY_RATE AS HOURLY_RATE,
       SUPERVISOR_PERSON_ID
  FROM EMPLOYEE;


PERSON_ID HOURLY_RATE SUPERVISOR_PERSON_ID
---------- ----------- --------------------
        1          15
        2        9.75                     1
       10        9.75                     1
```

This data shows that Employees 2 and 10 report to Employee 1, and that Employee 1 reports to no one—it's a good bet he or she is the owner or manager of the video store. It's no surprise that the supervisor earns a higher hourly rate than the people he or she supervises.

Now suppose the video store is required to produce a report showing the wage differential between supervisors and subordinates. The data here is small enough that such calculations could be done manually, but let's assume that you want to automate the report and distribute it to an entire chain of stores that use your database design. You can join each employee to their supervisor's row in the table to obtain the supervisor's hourly rate. Here is that query:

```
SELECT A.PERSON_ID, A.EMPLOYEE_HOURLY_RATE AS HOURLY_RATE,
       B.EMPLOYEE_HOURLY_RATE AS SUPV_HOURLY_RATE
  FROM EMPLOYEE A JOIN EMPLOYEE B
       ON A.SUPERVISOR_PERSON_ID = B.PERSON_ID;


PERSON_ID HOURLY_RATE SUPV_HOURLY_RATE
---------- ----------- ----------------
        2        9.75               15

       10        9.75               15
```

Note the following:

- The FROM clause has the EMPLOYEE table listed twice. The older style WHERE clause can also be used to invoke a self join. It would look like this:

```
SELECT A.PERSON_ID, A.EMPLOYEE_HOURLY_RATE AS HOURLY_RATE,
       B.EMPLOYEE_HOURLY_RATE AS SUPV_HOURLY_RATE
  FROM EMPLOYEE A, EMPLOYEE B
 WHERE A.SUPERVISOR_PERSON_ID = B.PERSON_ID
```

- The table names *must* include aliases because when you join a table to itself, *every* column name is ambiguous. You therefore need to qualify every column reference using the table alias.

- The supervisor (the row with PERSON_ID = 1) does not appear in the query results. Why not? If you answered that the query is an inner join, you got it. Employee 1 has no supervisor (the SUPERVISOR_PERSON_ID has a null value for PERSON_ID = 1), so the inner join fails to find a matching row, and as a result, the unmatched row drops out of the query results.

Here is the final query, including the calculation of the rate difference, and a join to the PERSON table to obtain the employee's name:

```
SELECT A.PERSON_ID, C.PERSON_GIVEN_NAME AS FIRST_NAME,
       C.PERSON_FAMILY_NAME AS LAST_NAME,
```

```
                B.EMPLOYEE_HOURLY_RATE - A.EMPLOYEE_HOURLY_RATE
                              AS RATE_DIFF
      FROM EMPLOYEE A JOIN EMPLOYEE B
           ON A.SUPERVISOR_PERSON_ID = B.PERSON_ID
        JOIN PERSON C
           ON A.PERSON_ID = C.PERSON_ID;


PERSON_ID FIRST_NAME  LAST_NAME    RATE_DIFF
--------- ----------- -----------  ----------
        2 Tin         Chung             5.25
       10 Gerald      Bernstein         5.25
```

Other Joins

Most joins are equijoins. However, it isn't always necessary to use the equal condition in matching rows to be joined. As a word of caution, however, there are more potential performance issues with joins that are not equijoins because indexes are less likely to be used by the DBMS when the conditional operator is other than "=".

One common use of the not equal (<>) operator in joins is searching for duplicate rows in a table. When joining a table to itself to detect duplicates, you always have to add a join condition to make sure you don't match a row to itself. Here is a query that looks for duplicate movie titles in the MOVIE table. Note the "not equal" (<>) comparison on the primary key column (MOVIE_ID) to prevent a row from being matched to itself:

```
SELECT A.MOVIE_ID, B.MOVIE_ID
  FROM MOVIE A JOIN MOVIE B
       ON A.MOVIE_ID <> B.MOVIE_ID
       AND A.MOVIE_TITLE = B.MOVIE_TITLE;
```

Cross Joins

A *cross join* is nothing more than standard syntax for a Cartesian product. As mentioned earlier, sometimes a Cartesian product is desirable, and it must have been those situations that motivated the standards committees to add this syntax to standard SQL. The query that appeared at the very beginning of this chapter (the one that joined the MOVIE and MOVIE_GENRE tables into a Cartesian product) can be written this way as a cross join:

```
SELECT MOVIE_ID, MOVIE_GENRE_DESCRIPTION AS GENRE, MOVIE_TITLE
  FROM MOVIE CROSS JOIN MOVIE_GENRE
 ORDER BY MOVIE_ID;
```

Subselects

A very powerful feature of SQL is the *subselect* (or *subquery*), which as the name implies, refers to a SELECT statement that contains a subordinate SELECT. Subselects are typically used in the WHERE clause as a way of limiting rows returned in the result set of the outer query. This can be a very flexible way of selecting data. However, they can be used in other ways, as you will see in the next section, "Inline Views."

An essential syntax rule is that the subselect must be enclosed in parentheses. Another important point to understand is that anything you can do using a subselect can also be done using a join. In fact, some SQL implementations automatically rewrite subselects as joins inside the SQL engine before running them, but unless you look at the internals of the SQL implementation, you as a database user will never know that happened.

Noncorrelated Subselects

A *noncorrelated subselect* is a subselect where the inner select makes no reference to the outer select that contains it. This means that the inner select can be run first, and the result set of the inner select used in the outer select. Here are some examples:

- Listing of all languages for which there are no movies in the video store inventory.

```
SELECT LANGUAGE_CODE, LANGUAGE_NAME
  FROM LANGUAGE
 WHERE LANGUAGE_CODE NOT IN
   (SELECT DISTINCT LANGUAGE_CODE
      FROM MOVIE_LANGUAGE)
 ORDER BY LANGUAGE_CODE


LANGUAGE_CODE LANGUAGE_NAME
------------- -------------
ja            Japanese
ko            Korean
nl            Dutch
ru            Russian
zh            Chinese
```

The inner select returns a list of language codes that appear on movies in the MOVIE_LANGUAGE table. The DISTINCT keyword removes any duplicate language codes from the result set, and in doing so, makes the

outer select much more efficient—the fewer the values that appear in an IN clause list, the more efficient the query. There are 40 rows in the MOVIE_ LANGUAGE table, and thus there would be 40 values in the IN list, but it is reduced to only 4 values by the DISTINCT keyword. Here is the inner select run by itself to help you visualize how it works:

```
SELECT DISTINCT LANGUAGE_CODE
  FROM MOVIE_LANGUAGE;

LANGUAGE_CODE
-------------
de           (German)
en           (English)
es           (Spanish)
fr           (French)
```

- The store manager is looking at the effect of a recent price increase and needs a list of transactions (TRANSACTION_IDs) where the customer paid more than the average fee (RENTAL_FEE) for a movie. Here is the query:

```
SELECT DISTINCT TRANSACTION_ID
  FROM MOVIE_RENTAL
 WHERE RENTAL_FEE >
   (SELECT AVG(RENTAL_FEE)
      FROM MOVIE_RENTAL)

TRANSACTION_ID
--------------
             9
            10
```

The inner query finds the average rental fee and then the outer query finds all rows in the MOVIE_RENTAL table with a RENTAL_FEE that exceeds the average. While IN and NOT IN are the most common operators used to connect subqueries to outer queries, in this case the subquery returns only one row; therefore you can use the greater than (>) operator for comparison. The DISTINCT eliminates any duplicate transaction IDs.

- The previous query result set would be more useful to the store manager if it included the transaction date. One way to accomplish this is to add a join to the CUSTOMER_TRANSACTION table in the outer select. However, since you just learned about subselects, let's do that with another subselect. This demonstrates that you can nest subselects when you need to. Here is the query:

```
SELECT TRANSACTION_ID, TRANSACTION_DATE AS TRANS_DATE
  FROM CUSTOMER_TRANSACTION
 WHERE TRANSACTION_ID IN
    (SELECT DISTINCT TRANSACTION_ID
       FROM MOVIE_RENTAL
      WHERE RENTAL_FEE >
        (SELECT AVG(RENTAL_FEE)
           FROM MOVIE_RENTAL))

TRANSACTION_ID TRANS_DATE
-------------- ----------
             9 03/01/2005
            10 03/01/2005
```

Correlated Subselects

A *correlated subselect* is a subselect where the inner select refers to values provided by the outer select. These are far less efficient than noncorrelated subselects because the inner query must be invoked for each row found by the outer query. Recall that with a noncorrelated subselect, the inner query is only run once. An example follows.

- The store wishes to mail a discount coupon to any customer who paid more than $15 in rental fees in any single rental transaction. Here is the query:

```
SELECT DISTINCT CUSTOMER_ACCOUNT_ID
  FROM CUSTOMER_TRANSACTION A
 WHERE 15 <
    (SELECT SUM(RENTAL_FEE)
       FROM MOVIE_RENTAL B
      WHERE A.TRANSACTION_ID = B.TRANSACTION_ID)

CUSTOMER_ACCOUNT_ID
-------------------
                  2
                  7
                  9
```

Note the alias assigned to the table names in the inner and outer queries and the use of them in the WHERE clause in the inner query. This is the hallmark of a correlated subselect. The outer select finds a distinct list of CUSTOMER_ACCOUNT_ID values in the CUSTOMER_TRANSACTION_TABLE. For each value found, the value is passed to the inner query, which is run to find the sum of rental fees for that transaction. If the sum of rental fees is greater than or equal to 15 (actually expressed

in the query as "if 15 is less than the sum of rental fees"), then the WHERE clause in the outer select evaluates to "true," and the corresponding CUSTOMER_ID is added to the result set.

Inline Views

A few SQL implementations, Oracle in particular, support using a subselect in the FROM clause of a query, a construct that is called an *inline view*. Essentially, this allows the result set of a subquery to be treated as if it were a predefined table or view. Here is an example:

- This query finds the maximum number of times any single movie has been rented:

```
SELECT MAX(RENTAL_COUNT) AS MAX_RENTAL_COUNT
   FROM
      (SELECT MOVIE_ID, COUNT(*) AS RENTAL_COUNT
         FROM MOVIE_RENTAL
       GROUP BY MOVIE_ID)
MAX_RENTAL_COUNT
- - - - - - - - - - - - - - -
               5
```

The inner query counts the number of rentals for each value of MOVIE_ID. The outer query then selects the maximum value of RENTAL_COUNT from the inner query, treated it as if it were a predefined view. There is no limit to what you can do with inline views—you can even join them to other views or tables.

Quiz

Choose the correct responses to each of the multiple-choice questions. Note that there may be more than one correct response to each question.

1. A subselect
   a. May be used to select values to be applied to WHERE clause conditions
   b. May be corrugated or noncorrugated
   c. Is a powerful way of calculating columns
   d. Must not be enclosed in parentheses
   e. Allows for the flexible selection of rows

2. A join without a WHERE clause or JOIN clause

    a. Results in an error message

    b. Returns no rows in the result set

    c. Performs an outer join

    d. Performs an inner join

    e. Results in a Cartesian product

3. An outer join

    a. May be written in Oracle SQL using a (+) symbol in the FROM clause

    b. May be written in Microsoft SQL Server using a *= or =* operator in the WHERE clause

    c. Returns all rows from only one of the two tables

    d. Returns all rows from one or both of the two tables

    e. Can be a left, right, or full outer join

4. A self join

    a. Can never result in a Cartesian product

    b. Can be either an inner or outer join

    c. Resolves recursive relationships

    d. May use a subselect to further limit rows

    e. Involves two different tables

5. A join

    a. Combines columns from two or more tables into a single query result

    b. Combines rows from multiple queries into a single query result

    c. Occurs whenever the FROM clause references more than one table

    d. Requires the use of a JOIN clause

    e. Requires a comma-separated table name list in the FROM clause

6. An equijoin

    a. Is also known as an outer join

    b. Is also known as an inner join

    c. Is also known as a self join

    d. Always matches rows using an equal (=) condition

    e. Always matches rows using a not equal (<>) condition

7. Column name qualifiers

   a. Resolve ambiguous column references

   b. May be a table name

   c. May be a number denoting the relative position of the table in the FROM list

   d. May be a column alias defined in the FROM clause

   e. May be a table alias defined in the FROM clause

8. A cross join is the same as

   a. A natural join

   b. A Cartesian product

   c. An outer join

   d. An inner join

   e. A self join

9. A JOIN clause with a USING keyword

   a. Cannot be used when the columns being matched have different names

   b. Cannot be used when the columns being matched have the same names

   c. Defines an inner join

   d. Defines an outer join

   e. Defines a self join

10. A correlated subselect

    a. Runs more efficiently than a noncorrelated subselect

    b. Runs less efficiently than a noncorrelated subselect

    c. Has a nested select that references column values from the outer select

    d. Has an outer select that references column values from the inner select

    e. Has a nested select that makes no reference to the column values in the outer select

Write SQL SELECT statements to solve the problems listed below.

11. List the name and Customer Account ID of any deceased person (DEATH_DATE that is NOT NULL) who is still listed on a Customer Account.

12. List the name of employees who are listed on a Customer Account. Use joins to determine which customers are employees and which employees have accounts.

13. Rewrite the previous query to use subselects instead of joins.

14. List the last name of each employee along with the last name of their supervisor.

15. List the count of the number of rentals by format (DVD vs. VHS).

16. List the Movie ID and Due Date of all movies that are currently out on rental (Returned Data in Movie Rental contains NULL values) and have not been purchased (Date Sold in Movie Copy contains NULL values).

17. List the Movie ID and Title of any movies that have never been rented.

18. Using subselects to filter rows, list the Movie Title of all movies where there is a VHS copy in the inventory (MEDIA_FORMAT = 'V', DATE_SOLD must be null) and yet there is no DVD copy in inventory (MEDIA_FORMAT = 'D').

19. Rewrite the previous query using a join instead of a subselect to find the VHS movie.

20. List any movie where there are multiple copies in inventory in the same format.

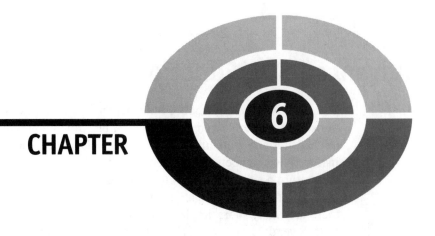

CHAPTER

6

Advanced Query Writing

Before we move on to Data Manipulation Language in Chapter 7, this chapter is intended to round out your knowledge of SQL queries by covering some advanced topics that were only brushed upon in Chapters 4 and 5. It covers the following topics:

- Advanced SQL functions, including character, mathematical, and date/time functions
- A description of how to take advantage of views
- A description of how to use SQL to generate SQL statements
- Information on the SQL CASE expression and its use in forming statements that have portions that are only executed under predefined conditions

Advanced SQL Functions

SQL functions were introduced in Chapter 4. The topics that follow describe functions that were not covered in Chapter 4 but which you will find useful. In addition to character and mathematical functions, selected date and time functions are also included. Remember that all SQL functions have a common characteristic in that they return a single value, so they are useful in several places in SQL statements, including the SELECT statement column list and WHERE clause. As a reminder, there are many more implementation-specific functions provided by the various DBMS vendors, so always check the vendor-supplied documentation for more useful functions.

Character Functions

Character functions operate on character data. This topic presents some commonly used functions in addition to those covered in Chapter 4. Except as noted, you will find the function supported by the most popular SQL implementations, including Microsoft SQL Server, Oracle, DB2, and MySQL.

REPLACE

The REPLACE function searches a character string and replaces characters found in a search string with characters listed in a replacement string. Here is the general syntax:

```
REPLACE(character_string, search_string, replacement_string)
```

- *character_string* is the string to be searched and is most often a table column name, but it can be any expression that yields a character string.
- *search_string* is the string of one or more characters to be found in *character_string*.
- *replacement_string* is the string that replaces any occurrences of *search_string* that are found in *character_string*.

Here is an example that replaces all hyphens (dashes) found in a person's phone number with periods (only the first two rows in the result set are shown):

```
SELECT PERSON_PHONE,
       REPLACE(PERSON_PHONE,'-','.') AS DISPLAY_PHONE
   FROM PERSON;
```

```
PERSON_PHONE    DISPLAY_PHONE
---------------  ---------------
230-229-8976    230.229.8976
401-617-7297    401.617.7297
```

LTRIM

The LTRIM function removes any leading (left-hand) spaces in a character string. Note that only leading spaces are removed—embedded and trailing spaces are left in the string. There is no data with leading and/or trailing spaces in the video store database, so here is a general example:

```
LTRIM ('  String with spaces  ')
Returns this string: 'String with spaces  '
```

RTRIM

The RTRIM function works like LTRIM, but it removes trailing spaces. If you need to remove both leading and trailing spaces, you can nest LTRIM and RTRIM like this:

```
RTRIM(LTRIM ('  String with spaces  '))
Returns this string: 'String with spaces'
```

NOTE: *Oracle provides a convenient function named TRIM that trims both leading and trailing spaces. For other implementations, you can always nest the LTRIM and RTRIM functions and achieve the same result.*

Null Value Function (NVL, ISNULL, IFNULL)

Oracle, Microsoft SQL Server, and MySQL all provide a function that replaces null values with a selected value. Unfortunately, they each give the function a different name: NVL in Oracle, ISNULL in SQL Server, and IFNULL in MySQL. Apparently, DB2 has no equivalent function. The following examples select the LATE_OR_LOSS_FEE from the MOVIE_RENTAL table with null values replaced by 0. Transaction 9 was selected because it has two movies on it, one of which has a null value for LATE_OR_LOSS_FEE (a good example that shows that null values are transformed while non-null values are left just the way they are).

Oracle:

```
SELECT NVL(LATE_OR_LOSS_FEE, 0) AS LATE_OR_LOSS_FEE
  FROM MOVIE_RENTAL
 WHERE TRANSACTION_ID=9;


LATE_OR_LOSS_FEE
----------------
               0
           29.98


2 rows selected.
```

Microsoft SQL Server:

```
SELECT ISNULL(LATE_OR_LOSS_FEE, 0) AS LATE_OR_LOSS_FEE
  FROM MOVIE_RENTAL
WHERE TRANSACTION_ID=9;


LATE_OR_LOSS_FEE
----------------
           29.98
             .00


(2 rows affected)
```

MySQL:

```
SELECT IFNULL(LATE_OR_LOSS_FEE, 0) AS LATE_OR_LOSS_FEE
  FROM MOVIE_RENTAL
WHERE TRANSACTION_ID=9;


+------------------+
| LATE_OR_LOSS_FEE |
+------------------+
|            29.98 |
|             0.00 |
+------------------+
2 rows in set (0.16 sec)
```

Notice how differently the MySQL command line client formats its output. While SQL clients from different vendors typically format results differently, the good news is that the data is the same.

ASCII

The ASCII function returns the ASCII character set value (a number between 0 and 255) for a character string containing a single character. For example, the ASCII code for a space is 32, so ASCII(' ') would return a value of 32.

CHAR (CHR)

The CHAR function (named CHR in Oracle and DB2) returns the character associated with an ASCII value (a number between 0 and 255). For example, the function ASCII(44) returns a comma since the ASCII value for a comma is 44. This function is particularly useful for concatenating characters that either cannot be displayed or would be awkward to handle in SQL. Some of the ASCII characters typically used with this function are listed in the following table. You can use the ASCII function or an ASCII character set table (easily found on the Internet) if you need to know other values.

ASCII Value	Character
9	Tab
10	Line feed
13	Carriage return
39	Single quote

Some examples follow. Keep in mind that the concatenation operators are not the same for all DBMS implementations ('+' for Microsoft SQL Server, '||' for most others).

- Find any movie titles that have a Tab character in them:

Microsoft SQL Server:

```
SELECT MOVIE_ID FROM MOVIE
  WHERE MOVIE_TITLE LIKE '%'+CHAR(9)+'%';


MOVIE_ID
(0 rows affected)
```

Oracle and DB2:

```
SELECT MOVIE_ID FROM MOVIE
  WHERE MOVIE_TITLE LIKE '%' || CHR(9) || '%';


no rows selected
```

> **NOTE:** *You may modify the Tab query to find movies with single quotes in their titles by changing the 9 to 39. You should find Movie ID 3 (Something's Gotta Give).*

Mathematical Functions

As you might guess from the name, mathematical functions return the result of a mathematical operation and usually require a numeric expression as an input parameter, which can be a literal value, a numeric table column value, or any expression (including the output of another function) that yields a numeric value.

SIGN

The SIGN function takes in a numeric expression and returns one of the following values based on the sign of the input number:

Return Value	Meaning
−1	Input number is negative
0	Input number is zero
1	Input number is positive
null	Input number is null

Here is an example:

```
SELECT LATE_OR_LOSS_FEE,
       SIGN(LATE_OR_LOSS_FEE) AS FEE_SIGN
  FROM MOVIE_RENTAL
 WHERE LATE_OR_LOSS_FEE IS NOT NULL;

LATE_OR_LOSS_FEE    FEE_SIGN
----------------    ----------
           29.99           1
               4           1
               4           1
           29.98           1
```

SQRT

The SQRT function takes in a single numeric expression and returns its square root. The general syntax is

```
SQRT (numeric_expression)
```

The result is a bit meaningless, but let's take the square root of the non-null Late or Loss Fees we just looked at:

```
SELECT LATE_OR_LOSS_FEE,
       SQRT(LATE_OR_LOSS_FEE) AS FEE_SQRT
  FROM MOVIE_RENTAL
 WHERE LATE_OR_LOSS_FEE IS NOT NULL;
```

```
LATE_OR_LOSS_FEE      FEE_SQRT
----------------    ----------
           29.99    5.47631263
               4             2
               4             2
           29.98    5.47539953
```

CEILING (CEIL)

The CEILING function returns the smallest integer that is greater than or equal to the value of the numeric expression provided as an input parameter. In other words, it rounds up to the next nearest whole number. There are some interesting naming compatibility issues across SQL implementations: Microsoft SQL Server uses the name CEILING, Oracle uses the name CEIL, and both DB2 and MySQL allow either name (CEIL or CEILING) to be used.

As an example, let's apply CEILING to the Late or Loss Fees (if you are using Oracle, change CEILING to CEIL):

```
SELECT LATE_OR_LOSS_FEE,
       CEILING(LATE_OR_LOSS_FEE) AS FEE_CEILING
  FROM MOVIE_RENTAL
 WHERE LATE_OR_LOSS_FEE IS NOT NULL;
```

```
LATE_OR_LOSS_FEE    FEE_CEILING
----------------    -----------
            4.00              4
            4.00              4
           29.99             30
           29.98             30
```

FLOOR

The FLOOR function is the logical opposite of the CEILING function—it returns the integer that is less than or equal to the value of the numeric expression provided as an input parameter. In other words, it rounds *down* to the next nearest whole number.

Here is an example showing FLOOR applied to Late or Loss Fees:

```
SELECT LATE_OR_LOSS_FEE,
       FLOOR(LATE_OR_LOSS_FEE) AS FEE_FLOOR
  FROM MOVIE_RENTAL
 WHERE LATE_OR_LOSS_FEE IS NOT NULL;

LATE_OR_LOSS_FEE   FEE_FLOOR
----------------   ---------
            4.00           4
            4.00           4
           29.99          29
           29.98          29
```

Date and Time Functions

There is very little consistency in date and time functions across different DBMS vendors. Largely, this is because most of them developed date and time data types ahead of the development of standards. Because of this diversity, date and time functions are presented in summary form for Microsoft SQL Server, Oracle, DB2, and MySQL. As always, the vendor documentation should be consulted for detailed explanations of the use of these functions. Terms shown in italics are defined in the notes at the bottom of each table. The term "datetime" is used throughout this section to mean a character string that contains both a date and time in a format that is acceptable to the particular DBMS.

Microsoft SQL Server Date and Time Functions

Microsoft SQL Server offers the date and time functions shown in the following table:

Function	Purpose	Input Parameters
DATEADD	Returns a new datetime calculated by adding an interval to the *datepart* of the supplied date	*datepart*, interval quantity, datetime
DATEDIFF	Returns the number of datetime boundaries crossed between two dates	*datepart*, start datetime, end datetime
DATENAME	Returns a text name representing the selected *datepart* of the input datetime	*datepart*, datetime

Function	Purpose	Input Parameters
DATEPART	Returns an integer representing the selected *datepart* of the supplied datetime	*datepart*, datetime
DAY	Returns an integer representing the day contained in the supplied datetime	datetime
GETDATE	Returns the current system datetime	None
GETUTCDATE	Returns the current UTC (Universal Coordinated Time) datetime	None
MONTH	Returns an integer representing the month contained in the supplied datetime	datetime
YEAR	Returns an integer (four digits) representing the year contained in the supplied datetime	datetime

Note: Datepart *is a parameter that specifies a part of a date, such as year, month, day, hour, minute, second, and millisecond. Refer to Microsoft SQL Server documentation for values and options.*

Oracle Date and Time Functions

Oracle has more than 24 date and time functions. Remember that while Oracle calls the data type DATE, all dates contain a time component—it's just set to zeros (representing midnight) when it's not used. The functions you are most likely to use are listed in the following table:

Function	Purpose	Input Parameters
ADD_MONTHS	Adds the supplied number of months to the supplied date	date, number of months (positive or negative value)
CURRENT_DATE	Returns the current date in the time zone set for the database session	None
EXTRACT	Extracts the specified datetime field from the supplied date	*datetime field keyword*, date
LAST_DAY	Returns the supplied date with the day shifted to the last day of the month	date

Function	Purpose	Input Parameters
MONTHS_BETWEEN	Returns the number of months (including fractional parts) between the two supplied dates; result is negative if second date is before the first date	first date, second date
SYSDATE	Returns the current system date and time	None
TO_CHAR	When used with a date, converts the date to a character string in a format specified by the *format string*	date, *format_string*
TO_DATE	Converts the supplied character string into an Oracle internally formatted date, using the *format string* as a template for interpreting the character string's contents	date, *format_string*
TRUNC	Truncates a date to the time unit specified in the datetime field keyword. If the keyword is omitted, the date is truncated to the current day	date, *datetime field keyword*

NOTE:

- Datetime field keyword *is a keyword that specifies one of the fields contained within an Oracle date, such as YEAR, MONTH, DAY, HOUR, MINUTE, and SECOND.*

- Format string *is a character string of symbols that specify the format that is to be used for the date when converted to or from a character string. There are over 40 different symbols that may be used in the format string (see Oracle documentation for an exhaustive list). For example, the format string 'MM/DD/YYYY HH:MI' would refer to a date character string that would look like '12/01/2004 11:58', while the format string 'DD-MON-RR' (the Oracle default format) would refer to a string that would look like '01-Dec-04'.*

- *TO_CHAR can also be used to convert numeric values to character strings.*

- *TRUNC can also be used to truncate numeric values, which chops off any numbers to the right of the decimal point.*

MySQL Date and Time Functions

MySQL has well over 30 date and time functions. Of those, the ones you are most likely to use are listed in the following table:

Function	Purpose	Input Parameters
ADDDATE	Adds two date, interval, or datetime expressions, yielding a new date	expression 1, expression 2
ADDTIME	Adds two time expressions, yielding a new time	expression 1, expression 2
CURDATE	Returns the current date in YYYY-MM-DD format	None
DATE	Returns the date part of a date or datetime expression	datetime expression
DATEDIFF	Returns the number of days between two dates	start date, end date
DATE_FORMAT	Formats a date according to a format string	date, *format string*
DAYNAME	Returns the text name for the day of the week contained in a date	date
DAYOFMONTH	Returns the day of the month, in the range 1 to 31	date
DAYOFWEEK	Returns a weekday index number for the day contained in a date (1 for Sunday, 2 for Monday, and so forth)	date
DAYOFYEAR	Returns the day of the year for the day contained in a date with a valid range of 1 to 366	date
LAST_DAY	Changes the day in a date to the last day of the month	date
MONTH	Returns the month contained in a date with a valid range of 1 to 12	date
MONTHNAME	Returns the text name of the month contained in a date	date
NOW	Returns the current date and time	None
STR_TO_DATE	Converts a character string to a datetime format data item; the *format string* indicates the format of the date information in the input character string	character string, *format string*
TIME	Extracts the time part of a datetime or time expression	datetime

Function	Purpose	Input Parameters
TIMEDIFF	Returns the time difference between two datetime or time expression parameters	expression 1, expression 2
TIME_FORMAT	Formats a time according to the format string	time, *format string*
UTC_DATE	Returns the current UTC (Universal Coordinated Time) date	None
UTC_TIME	Returns the current UTC (Universal Coordinated Time) time	None
WEEKOFYEAR	Returns the week of the year for a date, in the range 1 to 54	date

Note: Format string *is a string of characters that indicates formatting options for parts of the date. Consult MySQL documentation for details.*

DB2 Date and Time Functions

DB2 UDB contains over 20 date and time functions. Of those, the ones you are most likely to use are listed in the table that follows:

Function	Purpose	Input Parameters
DATE	Converts an expression into a date	expression
DAY	Returns the day part of a datetime expression	datetime expression
DAYNAME	Returns the text name of the day of the week for a date or datetime expression	datetime expression
DAYOFWEEK	Returns the day of the week (1 for Sunday, 2 for Monday, and so forth) for a datetime expression	datetime expression
DAYS	Returns an integer representation of a date	datetime expression
MINUTE	Returns the minute part of a datetime expression	datetime expression
MONTH	Returns the month part of a datetime expression	datetime expression
MONTHNAME	Returns the text name of the month for a date or datetime expression	datetime expression
QUARTER	Returns an integer in the range 1 to 4 representing the calendar quarter in which a date falls	datetime expression
SECOND	Returns the seconds part of a date or datetime expression	datetime expression

Function	Purpose	Input Parameters
TIME	Returns the time part of a date or datetime expression	datetime expression
WEEK	Returns the week of the year as an integer in the range 1 to 54	datetime expression
YEAR	Returns the year part of a date or datetime expression	datetime expression

Taking Advantage of Views

From Chapter 1, you should recall that a *view* is a stored database query that provides a database user with a customized subset of the data from one or more tables in the database. Note that Microsoft Access uses the term *query* instead of view. The inherent beauty of views is that, once created, they can be queried just like tables. In fact, the user never needs to know they are using a view instead of a real table. There can be some restrictions when data manipulation (inserts, updates, and deletes) is attempted using views (check your DBMS documentation), but queries work just the same against views as they do against tables. Furthermore, views provide a number of very useful benefits:

- Hiding columns a user does not need or should not see
- Hiding rows a user does not need or should not see
- Hiding complex operations such as joins
- Improving query performance (in some RDBMSs, such as Microsoft SQL Server)

The examples in this section show views that provide the aforementioned benefits. From Chapter 4, the general syntax for creating a view is

```
CREATE [OR REPLACE] VIEW view_name AS sql_query;
```

Here are some practical examples using the video store sample database:

- Obvious privacy rules require that the store manager keep employee tax IDs (social security numbers) and rates of pay in strict confidence. However, there are a number of web-based applications that require some employee information, such as the name of the employee and their supervisor's name (if any). What is required in such cases is a view that can be safely used by those web applications without the possibility of a developer who's using the data accidentally revealing confidential information. The query in the view must join with the PERSON table to find the name of the employee

and again (using an outer join) for the name of the employee's supervisor. Furthermore, column names should be as user friendly to a U.S.-based web development team as possible. Here is the SQL statement to create the view:

```
CREATE VIEW EMPLOYEE_LIST AS
  SELECT A.PERSON_ID AS ID,
         B.PERSON_GIVEN_NAME AS FIRST_NAME,
         B.PERSON_MIDDLE_NAME AS MIDDLE_NAME,
         B.PERSON_FAMILY_NAME AS LAST_NAME,
         C.PERSON_GIVEN_NAME AS MANAGER_FIRST_NAME,
         C.PERSON_FAMILY_NAME AS MANAGER_LAST_NAME
    FROM EMPLOYEE A JOIN PERSON B
           ON A.PERSON_ID = B.PERSON_ID
         LEFT OUTER JOIN PERSON C
           ON A.SUPERVISOR_PERSON_ID = C.PERSON_ID

View created.
```

Once the view is created, you can write queries against it just like you can with tables. Here is a simple query against the view just created:

```
SELECT LAST_NAME, MANAGER_LAST_NAME
  FROM EMPLOYEE_LIST
 ORDER BY LAST_NAME;

LAST_NAME                        MANAGER_LAST_NAME
------------------------         ------------------------
Alexander
Bernstein                        Alexander
Chung                            Alexander
```

- For a movie catalog listing, you want to list the MPAA Rating Description and the Movie Genre Description. It seems obvious that this three-table join will be needed quite often, so you help the video store staff by creating a view with the joins already done for them. Here is the SQL statement to create the view:

```
CREATE VIEW MOVIE_LISTING AS
SELECT A.MOVIE_ID, B.MOVIE_GENRE_DESCRIPTION AS GENRE,
       C.MPAA_RATING_CODE AS RATING,
       C.MPAA_RATING_DESCRIPTION AS RATING_DESC,
       A.MOVIE_TITLE, A.RETAIL_PRICE_VHS,
       A.RETAIL_PRICE_DVD, A.YEAR_PRODUCED
  FROM MOVIE A JOIN MOVIE_GENRE B ON
       A.MOVIE_GENRE_CODE = B.MOVIE_GENRE_CODE
            JOIN MPAA_RATING C ON
       A.MPAA_RATING_CODE = C.MPAA_RATING_CODE
```

Here is a simple query that uses the view instead of the base tables:

```
SELECT GENRE, RATING, MOVIE_TITLE
  FROM MOVIE_LISTING
 ORDER BY GENRE, RATING, MOVIE_TITLE;


GENRE                  RATING MOVIE_TITLE
--------------------   ------ ------------------------------
Action and Adventure   PG-13  Master and Commander: The Far
Action and Adventure   PG-13  Pirates of the Caribbean: The
Action and Adventure   PG-13  The Day After Tomorrow
Action and Adventure   PG-13  The Italian Job
Action and Adventure   R      Kill Bill: Vol. 1
Action and Adventure   R      Man on Fire
Action and Adventure   R      The Last Samurai
Comedy                 PG-13  50 First Dates
Comedy                 PG-13  Matchstick Men
Comedy                 PG-13  Something's Gotta Give
Comedy                 PG-13  The School of Rock
Drama                  PG-13  Big Fish
Drama                  R      Cold Mountain
Drama                  R      Lost in Translation
Drama                  R      Monster
Drama                  R      Mystic River
Drama                  R      Road to Perdition
Foreign                R      Das Boot
Romance                PG-13  13 Going on 30
Romance                PG-13  Two Weeks Notice

20 rows selected.
```

- The video store is very interested in placing a computer-based kiosk in the children's section to allow youngsters to search for movies online. However, the store manager wants to be sure only G, PG, and PG-13 rated movies show up on the children's kiosk. It would be simple enough to enforce this rule in the application program that will control the kiosk. However, if a database view is used and the kiosk application is forced to use only the view, there can be no accidental slip-ups in the application program's logic, and it will be easy to adjust the view later if the MPAA changes its rating system again (as they have done several times in the past). Rather than repeat the join logic in the MOVIE_LISTING view again in this view, you can simply use the MOVIE_LISTING view to create the

new view. Yes, you can create a view based on *another view*! It provides unparalleled flexibility. Here is the example:

```
CREATE VIEW CHILDRENS_MOVIE_LISTING AS
SELECT * FROM MOVIE_LISTING
  WHERE RATING IN ('G','PG','PG-13')
```

Using the same select you used against MOVIE_LISTING, here is the new result:

```
SELECT GENRE, RATING, MOVIE_TITLE
  FROM CHILDRENS_MOVIE_LISTING
 ORDER BY GENRE, RATING, MOVIE_TITLE;


GENRE                  RATING MOVIE_TITLE
--------------------   ------ -------------------------------
Action and Adventure   PG-13  Master and Commander: The Far
Action and Adventure   PG-13  Pirates of the Caribbean: The
Action and Adventure   PG-13  The Day After Tomorrow
Action and Adventure   PG-13  The Italian Job
Comedy                 PG-13  50 First Dates
Comedy                 PG-13  Matchstick Men
Comedy                 PG-13  Something's Gotta Give
Comedy                 PG-13  The School of Rock
Drama                  PG-13  Big Fish
Romance                PG-13  13 Going on 30
Romance                PG-13  Two Weeks Notice

11 rows selected.
```

Notice how the WHERE clause in the CHILDRENS_MOVIE_LISTING view blocks the unwanted rows from the query results. However, a word of caution on creating views based on other views: the CHILDRENS_MOVIE_LISTING view is dependent on the MOVIE_LISTING view and may become invalid or otherwise malfunction any time the MOVIE_LISTING view is changed. Without a bit of planning and control, a house of cards can result that will fall down every time changes are made. Nevertheless, views are a powerful tool that simply cannot be ignored.

Using SQL to Generate SQL

Most RDBMS products come with a set of catalog views that allow query access to the metadata that describes the database objects contained in the database. Experienced database administrators know how to use the data in the catalog to their advantage and actually use SQL statements to generate other SQL statements.

Generating SQL in Oracle

In Oracle, the USER_TABLES view contains information about each table that belongs to the current database user. You can use the command "DESCRIBE USER_TABLES" to see the definition of the view, or refer to the Oracle Server Reference manual for descriptions of this and other catalog views.

Here is an SQL statement that creates a DROP TABLE command for every table found in USER_TABLES. The WHERE clause was added to eliminate some Oracle internal tables that might otherwise appear in the result set. There are also techniques available for sending the query results to a file that can then be used as a script, but they are beyond the scope of this text (see the Oracle SQL*Plus SPOOL command for details).

```
SELECT 'DROP TABLE ' || TABLE_NAME ||
       ' CASCADE CONTRAINTS;' AS SQL
  FROM USER_TABLES
 WHERE TABLE_NAME NOT LIKE 'BIN$%';


SQL
-------------------------------------------------------------
DROP TABLE MOVIE_RENTAL CASCADE CONSTRAINTS;
DROP TABLE CUSTOMER_TRANSACTION CASCADE CONSTRAINTS;
DROP TABLE CUSTOMER_ACCOUNT_PERSON CASCADE CONSTRAINTS;
DROP TABLE EMPLOYEE CASCADE CONSTRAINTS;
DROP TABLE MOVIE_LANGUAGE CASCADE CONSTRAINTS;
DROP TABLE MOVIE_COPY CASCADE CONSTRAINTS;
DROP TABLE MOVIE CASCADE CONSTRAINTS;
DROP TABLE PERSON CASCADE CONSTRAINTS;
DROP TABLE MPAA_RATING CASCADE CONSTRAINTS;
DROP TABLE MOVIE_GENRE CASCADE CONSTRAINTS;
DROP TABLE LANGUAGE CASCADE CONSTRAINTS;
DROP TABLE CUSTOMER_ACCOUNT CASCADE CONSTRAINTS;
```

Generating SQL in Microsoft SQL Server

Microsoft uses the term "system tables" for the SQL Server tables that contain metadata. You can find descriptions of them in Books Online under the topic "system tables." Here is the SQL Server equivalent of the previous example (dropping all tables) using the SQL Server SYSOBJECTS table. The WHERE clause filters out all objects except those with the "user table" object type.

```
SELECT 'DROP TABLE ' + NAME + ';'
  FROM SYSOBJECTS
 WHERE XTYPE='U'

DROP TABLE PERSON;
DROP TABLE MOVIE;
DROP TABLE MOVIE_COPY;
DROP TABLE MOVIE_LANGUAGE;
DROP TABLE EMPLOYEE;
DROP TABLE CUSTOMER_ACCOUNT_PERSON;
DROP TABLE CUSTOMER_TRANSACTION;
DROP TABLE MOVIE_RENTAL;
DROP TABLE CUSTOMER_ACCOUNT;
DROP TABLE LANGUAGE;
DROP TABLE MOVIE_GENRE;
DROP TABLE MPAA_RATING;
```

NOTE: *These generated DROP statements won't run without some additional work because of the referential constraints. SQL Server doesn't support the "CASCADE CONSTRAINTS" clause with the DROP command, so the referential constraints would have to be dropped before the tables could be, or the DROP statements would have to be placed in the proper order before being run.*

The CASE Expression

The CASE expression is a recent addition to the SQL standard but an important one. For the first time, parts of SQL statements can be executed conditionally. For example, a column in the query results may be formatted based on the values contained in another column. However, your SQL implementation may not support it just yet because it is so new.

The CASE expression allows two general forms.

Simple CASE Expression

Here is the general syntax of the simple form of the CASE expression:

```
CASE input_expression
  WHEN comparison_expression THEN result_expression
 [WHEN comparison_expression THEN result_expression ...]
 [ELSE result_expression]
END
```

NOTE:

- *Each WHEN condition is evaluated as* input_expression = comparision_expression, *and if the result is a logical TRUE, the* result_expression *is returned and no other WHEN conditions are evaluated.*

- *If none of the WHEN conditions evaluates to TRUE, and there is an ELSE condition, the* result_expression *associated with the ELSE condition is returned.*

- *If none of the WHEN conditions evaluates to TRUE, and there is no ELSE condition, a null value is returned.*

As an example, you can use the CASE expression to translate the MPAA Rating Code to a simple message that can be displayed at the checkout counter in the video store to remind sales clerks to check customer ages for movies rated above PG-13. Note the placement of the AS keyword just after the END keyword to assign a column name to the generated column in the result set. Here is the example:

```
SELECT MOVIE_ID, MPAA_RATING_CODE AS RATING,
   CASE MPAA_RATING_CODE
      WHEN 'G' THEN 'All ages'
      WHEN 'PG' THEN 'Parental guidance'
      WHEN 'PG-13' THEN 'Ages 13 and up'
      ELSE 'MUST be at least 17'
      END AS RATING_DESC
   FROM MOVIE
 ORDER BY MOVIE_ID;

  MOVIE_ID RATING RATING_DESC
---------- ------ -------------------
         1 R      MUST be at least 17
         2 R      MUST be at least 17
         3 PG-13  Ages 13 and up
         4 PG-13  Ages 13 and up
         5 R      MUST be at least 17
         6 PG-13  Ages 13 and up
         7 PG-13  Ages 13 and up
         8 R      MUST be at least 17
         9 PG-13  Ages 13 and up
        10 R      MUST be at least 17
        11 PG-13  Ages 13 and up
        12 PG-13  Ages 13 and up
        13 PG-13  Ages 13 and up
        14 R      MUST be at least 17
```

```
15 R       MUST be at least 17
16 PG-13   Ages 13 and up
17 PG-13   Ages 13 and up
18 R       MUST be at least 17
19 PG-13   Ages 13 and up
20 R       MUST be at least 17
```

Searched CASE Expression

The so-called searched CASE expression allows for more flexible comparison conditions because each one is written as a complete condition, including the comparison operator. Here is the general syntax:

```
CASE
  WHEN condition THEN result_expression
  [WHEN condition THEN result_expression ...]
  [ELSE result_expression]
END
```

NOTE:

- *Each* condition *can be any SQL expression that evaluates to TRUE or FALSE.*

- *Each WHEN is evaluated in sequence, and if one of them evaluates to TRUE, the associated* result_condition *is returned and no other WHEN conditions are evaluated.*

- *If none of the WHEN conditions evaluates to TRUE, and there is an ELSE condition, the* result_expression *associated with the ELSE condition is returned.*

- *If none of the WHEN conditions evaluates to TRUE, and there is no ELSE condition, a null value is returned.*

As an example, here is a query that classifies VHS movies by price range:

```
SELECT MOVIE_ID, RETAIL_PRICE_VHS,
  CASE
    WHEN RETAIL_PRICE_VHS IS NULL THEN 'Not Available'
    WHEN RETAIL_PRICE_VHS < 10 THEN 'Bargain'
    WHEN RETAIL_PRICE_VHS < 20 THEN 'Budget'
    WHEN RETAIL_PRICE_VHS < 40 THEN 'Average'
    ELSE 'Premium'
```

```
 END AS PRICE_CATEGORY
FROM MOVIE
ORDER BY MOVIE_ID;
```

```
MOVIE_ID RETAIL_PRICE_VHS PRICE_CATEGORY
---------- ---------------- --------------
        1            58.97 Premium
        2            15.95 Budget
        3            14.95 Budget
        4            11.95 Budget
        5            24.99 Average
        6            24.99 Average
        7            14.95 Budget
        8            50.99 Premium
        9            12.98 Budget
       10            49.99 Premium
       11             6.93 Bargain
       12             9.95 Bargain
       13             6.93 Bargain
       14            24.99 Average
       15             9.99 Bargain
       16            11.69 Budget
       17            14.94 Budget
       18            24.99 Average
       19            12.98 Budget
       20            17.99 Budget
```

Quiz

Choose the correct responses to each of the multiple-choice questions. Note that there may be more than one correct response to each question.

1. SQL functions
    a. Return a set of values
    b. Return a single value
    c. Can be used in the WHERE clause of an SQL statement
    d. Can be used as a table name alias in an SQL statement
    e. Can be used in the column list of an SQL statement

2. The REPLACE function
   a. Replaces a table name with a view name
   b. Replaces a column name with a column alias
   c. Replaces a character string in a column with another character string
   d. Replaces all values in a column with a new set of values
   e. Replaces all rows in a view with rows containing data from another table

3. The null value function
   a. Is called NVL in Oracle databases
   b. Is called ISNULL in IBM DB2 databases
   c. Is called ISNULL in Microsoft SQL Server databases
   d. Is called ISNULL in MySQL databases
   e. Is called IFNULL in the SQL standard

4. The LTRIM function
   a. Removes trailing spaces from character strings
   b. Removes leading spaces from character strings
   c. Can be nested with other functions
   d. Replaces null values with other values in character strings
   e. Removes both leading and trailing spaces from character strings

5. The CHAR function
   a. Is named CHR in some SQL implementations
   b. Is identical to the ASCII function in some SQL implementations
   c. Returns the ASCII character set value for a character
   d. Returns the character for an ASCII character set value
   e. Converts a numeric value to a character string

6. The SIGN function
   a. Returns −1 if the supplied parameter has a negative value
   b. Returns 0 if the supplied parameter has a value of zero
   c. Returns +1 if the supplied parameter has a value greater than or equal to zero
   d. Returns 0 if the supplied parameter is null
   e. Returns a null value if the supplied parameter is not a number

7. The CEILING function

   a. Rounds a number down to the next whole number

   b. Rounds a number up to the next whole number

   c. Always returns an integer

   d. Returns either an integer or a null value

   e. Is named CEIL in some SQL implementations

8. The FLOOR function

   a. Rounds a number down to the next whole number

   b. Rounds a number up to the next whole number

   c. Always returns an integer

   d. Returns either an integer or a null value

   e. Is named FLR in some SQL implementations

9. Date and time functions

   a. Are very similar across different vendor implementations

   b. Vary markedly across different vendor implementations

   c. Include functions that format date and time data items for display

   d. Include functions that convert character strings to dates and times

   e. Include functions that convert date and time data items to character strings

10. CASE expressions

   a. Allow for conditional execution of clauses within an SQL statement

   b. Come in two forms named static and dynamic

   c. Come in two forms named searched and nonsearched

   d. Come in two forms named simple and searched

   e. Come in two forms named standard and searched

Write SQL statements to solve each of the following problems.

11. List the MPAA_RATING_CODE values from the MPAA_RATING table, with hyphens (dashes) translated to spaces.

12. Using the CHAR function (called CHR in Oracle), list the MOVIE_ID and MOVIE_TITLE for all movies that have a single quote (ASCII character 39) in their names.

13. Find the ASCII character set value for an exclamation point (!).

14. Find the average price of a DVD movie (column DVD_RETAIL_PRICE in the MOVIE table), with the calculated average rounded up to the nearest whole dollar.

15. Find the average price of a VHS movie (column VHS_RETAIL_PRICE in the MOVIE table), with the calculated average rounded down to the nearest whole dollar.

16. For an Oracle database, generate the SQL commands to drop all the referential constraints owned by the current user. The Oracle catalog view is called USER_CONSTRAINTS, and referential constraints have a CONSTRAINT_TYPE of 'R'. The table name on which the constraint is based is in the TABLE_NAME column of the catalog view. Remember that you have to use the ALTER TABLE command to drop table constraints.

17. For a Microsoft SQL Server database, list all the foreign key constraints. Use the SYSOBJECTS system table, where NAME is the name of the constraint, and XTYPE has the value 'F' for foreign key constraints.

18. Write an SQL statement that lists each Customer Account (CUSTOMER_ACCOUNT_ID) with a character string based on the value of CHILD_RENTAL_ALLOWED_INDIC where the string shows 'Child Rental OK' if the value is 'Y' and 'NO CHILD RENTAL' if the value is 'N'. Hint: A simple CASE expression should work the best here.

19. Write an SQL statement that lists each Movie (MOVIE_ID) along with the decade based on the value of YEAR_PRODUCED (80s, 90s, 00s, Unknown). A search CASE expression should be helpful here.

20. Write an SQL statement that lists each movie rental (MOVIE_RENTAL table) with the LATE_OR_LOSS_FEE categorized as follows: None (data value null or 0), Minor (data value < 10), Major (data value >=10).

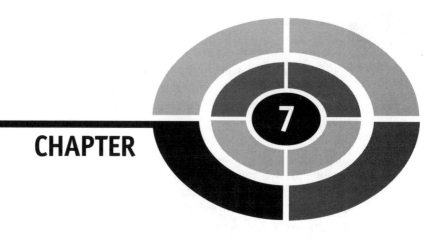

Maintaining Data Using DML

Thus far we have looked at Data Definition Language (DDL), which is used to create and modify the database objects that hold and organize the data in the database, and Data Query Language (DQL), which is used to select data from the database. This chapter covers Data Manipulation Language (DML), which is the part of SQL that is used to maintain the data that is stored in the database's relational tables.

DML is comprised of three SQL commands:

- **INSERT**   Adds new rows to a database table
- **UPDATE**   Updates existing database table rows
- **DELETE**   Deletes rows from a database table

Keep in mind that each individual DML statement can affect data in only one table. It is possible to reference a view in a DML statement, including one that contains data from more than one table (that is, a view that contains a table join), but in that case, the DML statement may only reference the columns from *one* of the tables in the view. Said another way, when a DML statement references a view, the view columns referenced in the DML statement must all map to columns of *one* physical table in the database.

The DBMS you are using most likely offers some form of transaction support, wherein a series of SQL DML statements can be considered an "all or nothing" group of statements that must either all be successful or all fail. This feature is very useful when SQL statements are used in business transactions and is covered in detail in Chapter 9. If you try out any of the statements in this chapter (as I strongly recommend), you can ignore transaction support, *unless* you are using Oracle. With the Oracle database, transaction support is automatically activated when you connect to the database. This means that none of the modifications you make will be permanently made in the database until you either disconnect (exit) from the database normally or issue a commit command. That won't be an issue under normal circumstances, but if your computer system or your Oracle session crashes (that is, you exit the database *abnormally*), any changes you have made since you connected to the database will be automatically rolled back. Moreover, if you have multiple connections to the database at the same time, the changes made by one connection (session) won't be seen by any other concurrent connection until a commit has been performed. If you are using Oracle and want to change the default behavior, see Chapter 9 for details on how to do so.

Even if transaction support is not specifically enabled, the DBMS will handle each individual DML statement as a transaction. This means that if the DBMS finds an error with a modification to any row identified by the DML statement, it will "roll back" the statement so that the net effect is a complete failure of the DML statement for all rows in the table. In other words, the DBMS will never leave the data in an inconsistent state. For example, if I tried to delete all rows in the MOVIE table, and the DBMS encountered an error deleting the third row in the table (having already deleted the first two rows in the table), the *entire* statement would fail and the rollback operation would automatically (some say "automagically") put the first two rows back.

The SQL statements in this chapter assume that your DBMS is using the format YYYY-MM-DD for date values in SQL statements. If your DBMS uses a different format, you will have to alter the examples in this chapter to run them successfully on your DBMS. For Oracle databases, the following statement will change Oracle's default date format to the one that is used in this chapter but only for the current session (the default format will be assumed every time you re-connect to the database):

```
ALTER SESSION SET NLS_DATE_FORMAT='YYYY-MM-DD';
```

Another important consideration is the constraints defined on the table referenced by the DML statement. The DBMS will not perform any modification to the data in the database if it violates one of the constraints. When forming DML statements, you need to consider the following in regard to the constraints on the table being modified:

- **Primary key constraints** When you insert a new row into a table, the primary key of the new row must be unique among all rows in the table. When you modify a primary key value (which is rarely done), the new value must be unique among all rows in the table.

- **Unique constraints** As with primary key columns, columns with a unique constraint defined on them must always have values that are unique among all rows in the table.

- **Referential constraints** You cannot insert or update a foreign key value unless the corresponding parent row containing the key value in its primary key column(s) already exists. Conversely, you cannot delete a parent row if there are any child rows that still reference it unless the constraint includes an ON DELETE CASCADE option. In general, table inserts have to be in hierarchical sequence (parents before children) and deletes done in the reverse sequence (children before parents).

- **NOT NULL constraints** For an INSERT, you must provide values for any columns that have NOT NULL constraints. For an UPDATE, you cannot change columns to null values if they have a NOT NULL constraint. If the DML statement references a view, you cannot use it for INSERTS if any of the table's required columns (those with NOT NULL constraints) are missing from the view definition.

- **CHECK constraints** An INSERT or UPDATE statement cannot apply a value to a table column that violates any CHECK constraint on that column.

The INSERT Statement

The INSERT statement in SQL is used to add new rows of data to tables. It comes in two basic forms: one where column values are provided in the statement itself, and the other where values are selected from a table or view using a subselect. Let's have a look at those two forms.

Single Row Inserts Using the VALUES Clause

The INSERT statement that uses a VALUES clause can create only one row each time it is run because the values for that one row of data are provided in the statement itself. Here is the general syntax for the statement:

```
INSERT INTO table_or_view_name
  [(column_list)]
  VALUES (value_list);
```

Note the following:

- The column list is optional but if included must be enclosed in a pair of parentheses.

- If the column list is omitted, a value must be provided for every column in the table in the same order as the columns are defined in the table. It is *always* a good idea to provide the column list, because leaving it out makes the INSERT statement dependent on the table's definition, which means that if the column order is changed, or a new column is added to the table (even an optional one), the INSERT statement will most likely fail the next time it is run.

- If the column list is provided, the value list must provide a value for each column in the column list and in the same order. In other words, the column list and value list must have a one-to-one correspondence. Any column that is omitted from the column list will be set to a null value, provided nulls are allowed for that column.

- The keyword NULL may be used in the value list to specify a null value for any column.

- In Microsoft SQL Server and Sybase Adaptive Server, you cannot insert values into a column with the IDENTITY property set. The IDENTITY property is a commonly used method for assigning sequential values to a primary key, such as the MOVIE_ID column in the MOVIE table. If the IDENTITY property is set, you can simply not reference the column in the SQL INSERT statement and the DBMS will assign the next unique value to the primary key. Alternatively, you can turn off the restriction by running this statement:

```
SET identity_insert table_name ON
```

Here is an example containing two INSERT statements, one that creates a new row in the MOVIE table with the optional column list that skips the RETAIL_PRICE_VHS column, and another that creates a MOVIE_COPY table row for the same movie but without the optional column list:

```
INSERT INTO MOVIE
  (MOVIE_ID, MOVIE_GENRE_CODE, MPAA_RATING_CODE,
   MOVIE_TITLE, RETAIL_PRICE_DVD, YEAR_PRODUCED)
 VALUES (21, 'Drama', 'PG-13', 'Ray', 29.95, '2004');


INSERT INTO MOVIE_COPY
 VALUES (21, 1, '2005-04-01', null, 'V');
```

For Microsoft SQL Server and Sybase Adaptive Server with the IDENTITY property set for the MOVIE table, you can use this variation of the MOVIE table INSERT statement:

```
INSERT INTO MOVIE
  (MOVIE_GENRE_CODE, MPAA_RATING_CODE,
   MOVIE_TITLE, RETAIL_PRICE_DVD, YEAR_PRODUCED)
 VALUES ('Drama', 'PG-13', 'Ray', 29.95, '2004');
```

Bulk Inserts Using a Nested SELECT

As you likely noticed, it takes a lot of typing to insert a single row of data with an INSERT statement that uses a VALUES clause. An alternative that can be used to create multiple rows in a table with a single statement is the form that uses a nested SELECT statement. This form is also useful for finding the next value for sequentially assigned primary key values, such as the MOVIE_ID column in the MOVIE table. It is also quite useful if a temporary table is created for testing and you want to populate the table with all the data from another table. The general syntax is

```
INSERT INTO table_or_view_name
  [(column_list)]
  SELECT select_statement;
```

Note the following:

- The column list is optional, but if included must be enclosed in a pair of parentheses.

- If the column list is omitted, the nested SELECT must provide a value for every column in the table, in the same order as the columns are defined in the table. It is *always* a good idea to provide the column list, because leaving it out makes the INSERT statement dependent on the table's definition, which means that if the column order is changed, or a new column is added to the table (even an optional one), the INSERT statement will most likely fail the next time it is run.

- If the column list is provided, the nested SELECT must provide a value for each column in the column list and in the same order. In other words, the column list and the columns in the result set of the SELECT must have a one-to-one correspondence. Any column that is omitted from the column list will be set to a null value, provided nulls are allowed for that column.

- The keyword NULL may be used in the SELECT to specify a null value for any column.

As an example, let us assume that all movies are now available in French. The MOVIE_LANGUAGE table has French language rows for only some movies, and you want to add the missing ones. This is a deliberately complicated example intended to show just how sophisticated the nested SELECT statement can be. Here is the INSERT statement that will handle the task:

```
INSERT INTO MOVIE_LANGUAGE
    (MOVIE_ID, LANGUAGE_CODE)
  SELECT MOVIE_ID, 'fr'
    FROM MOVIE
  WHERE MOVIE_ID NOT IN
      (SELECT MOVIE_ID
         FROM MOVIE_LANGUAGE
        WHERE LANGUAGE_CODE = 'fr');
```

The following example inserts a new row in the MOVIE table, using the SELECT to find the maximum value for the MOVIE_ID column and incrementing it by 1 to form the primary key value for the new row:

```
INSERT INTO MOVIE
  (MOVIE_ID, MOVIE_GENRE_CODE, MPAA_RATING_CODE,
   MOVIE_TITLE, RETAIL_PRICE_DVD, YEAR_PRODUCED)
 SELECT MAX(MOVIE_ID)+1, 'Drama', 'PG-13',
        'The Terminal', 24.95, '2004'
   FROM MOVIE;
```

The UPDATE Statement

The UPDATE statement in SQL is used to update the data values for table (or view) columns listed in the statement. Here is the general syntax for an UPDATE statement:

```
UPDATE table_or_view_name
   SET column_name = expression
      [,column_name = expression ...]
 [WHERE Clause];
```

Note the following:

- The SET clause contains a list of one or more columns along with an expression that specifies the new value for each column. Essentially, it is a comma-separated list of name and value pairs with an equal operator between each name and value.

- The *expression* can be a constant, another column name, or any other expression that SQL can resolve to a single value to be assigned to the column.

- The WHERE clause contains an expression that limits the rows that are to be updated. If the WHERE clause is omitted, the SQL engine will attempt to update every row in the table or view.

Here are some examples:

- The movie added earlier in this chapter (MOVIE_ID = 21) was input with incorrect prices. The VHS price should be 29.95 and the DVD price 34.95. The following statement updates the prices to the correct amounts. Note that it updates two columns in a single row in the MOVIE table.

```
UPDATE MOVIE
   SET RETAIL_PRICE_VHS = 29.95,
       RETAIL_PRICE_DVD = 34.95
 WHERE MOVIE_ID = 21;
```

- The video store has decided to give all the clerical employees (EMPLOYEE_ JOB_CATEGORY = 'C') an 8 percent raise. This will update one column for several rows (all those with a matching job category). You can use a calculation to increase each rate by 8 percent by multiplying the existing

rate by 1.08 and rounding to two decimal places using the ROUND function. Here is the statement:

```
UPDATE EMPLOYEE
   SET EMPLOYEE_HOURLY_RATE =
       ROUND(EMPLOYEE_HOURLY_RATE * 1.08, 2)
 WHERE EMPLOYEE_JOB_CATEGORY = 'C';
```

The DELETE Statement

The DELETE statement removes one or more rows from a table. The statement may also reference a view but only a view based on a single table (that is, views that contain joins may not be referenced by DELETE statements). The DELETE statement never references any columns because it removes entire rows of data, including all data values (all columns) for each affected row. If you wish to remove single data values in existing rows, use an UPDATE statement to set those column values to null values (assuming nulls are permitted in those columns). The general syntax of the DELETE statement is

```
DELETE FROM table_or_view_name
[WHERE Clause];
```

Note the following:

- The WHERE clause is optional. However, it is almost always included because a DELETE without a WHERE clause attempts to delete *all* the rows in the table, which is usually not the desired result.

- When included, the WHERE clause specifies the rows to be deleted. Any row for which the WHERE clause evaluates to TRUE is deleted.

- Keep in mind that you cannot delete rows when the DELETE would violate a referential constraint. In general, children have to be deleted before parents.

Here are a few examples:

- Delete the movie you added earlier in this chapter (MOVIE_ID = 21). Note that you must delete any corresponding MOVIE_COPY and MOVIE_ LANGUAGE rows first because they would be children of the MOVIE table row. You might try deleting the MOVIE table row first just to see what error message your DBMS displays when a referential constraint is violated.

```
DELETE FROM MOVIE_COPY
 WHERE MOVIE_ID = 21;
```

```
DELETE FROM MOVIE_LANGUAGE
 WHERE MOVIE_ID = 21;

DELETE FROM MOVIE
 WHERE MOVIE_ID = 21;
```

- Delete all rows in the MOVIE_LANGUAGE table for the Spanish language (LANGUAGE_CODE = 'es'). Note that in many SQL implementations the data is case sensitive, and in those cases the language code value must be provided in lowercase to match the data.

```
DELETE FROM MOVIE_LANGUAGE
 WHERE LANGUAGE_CODE = 'es';
```

Quiz

Choose the correct responses to each of the multiple-choice questions. Note that there may be more than one correct response to each question.

1. DML includes the following SQL commands:
   a. INSERT
   b. REMOVE
   c. UPDATE
   d. SELECT
   e. DROP

2. A DML statement may reference
   a. Columns from multiple tables
   b. Columns from a single table
   c. A view that contains columns from only one table
   d. View columns that come from multiple tables
   e. View columns that come from a single table

3. When forming DML statements, the following types of constraints must be considered:
   a. Referential constraints
   b. Security constraints
   c. NOT NULL constraints

  d. Unique constraints

  e. Primary key constraints

4. An INSERT statement with a VALUES clause

  a. Must have a column list

  b. Must have a values list

  c. Can insert multiple rows with one statement execution

  d. May use the keyword NULL to assign null values to columns

  e. May include a WHERE clause

5. An INSERT statement with a nested SELECT is useful for

  a. Finding the next value for a sequentially assigned primary key

  b. Moving rows from one table to another

  c. Populating a test table with data from another table

  d. Eliminating duplicate rows in a table

  e. Inserting multiple rows with a single statement

6. An INSERT statement with a nested SELECT

  a. Must have two column lists, one with the INSERT clause and one in the nested SELECT

  b. Must have an embedded SELECT that returns only one row of data

  c. May use the keyword NULL to assign null values to columns

  d. May include a WHERE clause

  e. Must have a column list in the nested SELECT that corresponds with either the INSERT column list or the columns in the table being inserted

7. An UPDATE statement without a WHERE clause

  a. Updates all rows in the table to null values

  b. Attempts to update every row in the table

  c. Fails with an error condition

  d. Deletes all rows in the table

  e. Results in a Cartesian product

8. A DELETE statement without a WHERE clause

  a. Updates all rows in the table to null values

  b. Fails with an error condition

   c. Attempts to delete every row in the table

   d. Results in a Cartesian product

   e. Must include a column list

9. An UPDATE statement

   a. Must include a SET clause

   b. Must provide a new value for at least one column

   c. Must include a WHERE clause

   d. May set a column to the value of another column

   e. May set a column to a list of values derived by an expression

10. A DELETE statement

   a. May include an optional column list

   b. May include an optional WHERE clause

   c. May use the FORCE keyword to force deletion of rows

   d. Cannot violate any referential constraints on the table

   e. May have a nested SELECT as part of the WHERE clause

11. The SET clause in an UPDATE statement may assign a value to a column that is

   a. A constant

   b. Another column name

   c. A list of values

   d. Any expression that yields a single value

   e. The NULL keyword

12. The SELECT statement that may be nested in a bulk INSERT statement may include

   a. A WHERE clause

   b. A GROUP BY clause

   c. One or more aggregate functions

   d. A join of multiple tables

   e. A UNION clause

Write SQL statements to solve each of the following problems.

13. Using an INSERT with a VALUES clause but no column list, insert a new row into the MOVIE_GENRE table with a MOVIE_GENRE_CODE of 'TRAIN' and a MOVIE_GENRE_DESCRIPTION of 'Training'.

14. Using an INSERT with a VALUES clause and a column list, insert a new row in the MOVIE table with the following data values:

MOVIE_ID:	99
MOVIE_GENRE_CODE:	TRAIN
MPAA_RATING_CODE:	NR
MOVIE_TITLE:	Employee Training Video

15. Using an INSERT with a nested SELECT, insert a row into MOVIE_LANGUAGE for the Japanese language (LANGUAGE_CODE = 'ja') for every movie in the MOVIE table. (There are currently no rows for Japanese in the MOVIE_LANGUAGE table.)

16. Create a table called RENTAL_TOTAL using the CREATE statement below. Using an INSERT with a nested SELECT, insert a row into RENTAL_TOTAL for each movie in MOVIE_RENTAL that contains the total number of rentals and the total rental fee amount for that movie.

```
CREATE TABLE RENTAL_TOTAL
   (MOVIE_ID            INTEGER      NOT NULL,
    NUMBER_OF_RENTALS   INTEGER      NOT NULL,
    TOTAL_RENTAL_FEES   NUMERIC(7,2) NOT NULL);
```

17. Delete all rows in the RENTAL_TOTAL table.

18. Delete the Japanese Language rows that you created in question 15.

19. Copy 1 of Movie 1 (MOVIE_ID=1, COPY_NUMBER=1) was sold on January 15, 2005. Update the correct row in the MOVIE_COPY table to set DATE_SOLD accordingly.

20. Update the MOVIE table to increase all non-null VHS prices (RETAIL_PRICE_VHS) by 10 percent.

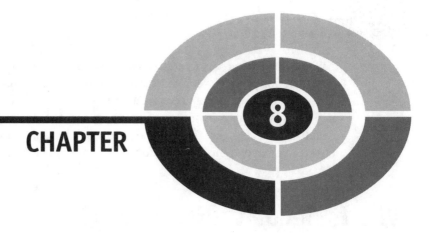

Applying
Security Controls
Using DCL

Security has become an essential consideration in modern computer systems. Nothing can be more embarrassing to an organization than a media story regarding sensitive data or trade secrets that were electronically stolen from their computer systems. Recent federal security legislation places significant restrictions on the use of personal information. In California, a new law requires that notification be sent to any California resident who *might* have had their data compromised. The new laws significantly add to the expense and embarrassment related to the cleanup effort, and it is very likely that stricter laws will be passed at the state and federal levels in the near future.

This chapter introduces some general security concepts that must be taken into consideration with any computer system. However, the focus will be on how SQL is used to implement data access security controls. A good database administrator will participate in all aspects of securing the computer system and network on which the database is deployed, but security measures implemented outside the DBMS are beyond this book's scope.

Why Is Security Necessary?

Murphy's Law states that anything that can go wrong will go wrong. Seasoned information technology security professionals will tell you that Murphy was an optimist. Reports of security breaches in computer systems are far too common. There are many threats, ranging from malicious programs such as viruses and spyware to hackers and thieves intent on stealing identities and anything of value they can get using a stolen identity or credit card. In fact, identity theft and credit card fraud are now the number one white collar crime in the United States (they're combined into a single category because one so often leads to the other). The ill effects of security breaches range from public embarrassment to losses that can amount to millions of dollars. In one of the more bizarre cases, thieves stole the identity of an elderly couple and sold their house while they were still living in it—the couple found out when they were served an eviction notice. It took them months to straighten out the mess and restore their credit standing.

A computer system is only as secure as its weakest component. Therefore, one must take a holistic approach to security and make every component as resistant to intrusion as possible. This includes securing the computer network, the servers on which applications and databases run, the operating systems on the servers, data files that contain the database data (including any backups), the DBMS, access to the data in the DBMS, and the client systems that connect to the servers and databases. Servers placed on the Internet with default configurations and passwords have been compromised within *minutes*. Default database passwords and common security vulnerabilities are widely known. In early 2003, the Slammer worm infected tens of thousands of Microsoft SQL Server databases that had been set up with a default "sa" (system administrator) account that had no password. Oddly, the worst damage done by this worm was the loss of service when infected computers sent out hundreds of thousands of packets on the network in search of other computers on the network to infect, so it could have been a lot worse. If you think this cannot happen to you, think again. Here are some reasons security must be designed into your computer systems:

- Databases connected to the Internet or any other network are vulnerable to hackers and other criminals who are determined to damage or steal the data. These include the following:

  - Spies from competitors who are after your secrets.

  - Hackers interested in a sense of notoriety from penetrating your systems.

  - Individuals interested in whatever they can obtain that has economic value.

  - Disgruntled employees. (It seems odd that we never hear of gruntled employees—gruntle means "to make happy"—but only of disgruntled ones.)

  - Zealots interested in making a political statement at the expense of your organization.

  - The emotionally unbalanced and just plain evil people.

- Fraud attempts. Any bank auditor will tell you that 80 percent of fraud is committed by or with the assistance of employees. So, don't assume your system is immune just because the database is not accessible from the Internet.

- Honest mistakes by authorized users can cause security exposures, loss of data, and processing errors.

- Security controls keep people honest in the same way that locks on homes and offices do.

It must be understood that security precautions can never completely prevent the most determined adversary from breaching a system. The only way to completely guarantee that a system cannot ever be penetrated is to power it down and leave it that way. However, the right precautions can *slow down* even the most determined and talented adversary long enough to allow for detection and intervention. Above all, the use of *layers* of security at all system levels offers the best protection for valuable data resources.

Database Security Architectures

For database administrators who support databases from multiple vendors, one of the challenges is that, with the exception of Microsoft SQL Server and Sybase Adaptive Server, no two databases have the same architecture for database security. Of course, this is a side effect of the overall database architectures being different.

The only reason that Microsoft SQL Server and Sybase Adaptive Server have such similar architectures is that the former was derived from the latter. Because Microsoft SQL Server and Oracle are among the most popular databases today, let's have a quick look at how each implements database security.

Database Security in Microsoft SQL Server and Sybase Adaptive Server

With Microsoft SQL Server and Sybase Adaptive Server, once the DBMS software is installed on the server, a database server is created. This is a confusing term, of course, because we call the hardware a "server." In this case, the *server* or *SQL Server* is a copy of the DBMS software running in memory as a set of processes (also called *services* in Windows environments) with related control information that is stored in a special database on the SQL Server. I will use the term *SQL Server* to mean the DBMS software and the term *database server* to mean the hardware platform on which the database is running. In this architecture, each SQL Server manages many databases, with each database representing a logical grouping of data as determined by the database designer. Figure 8-1 shows a simplified view of the security architecture for Microsoft SQL Server and Sybase Adaptive Server.

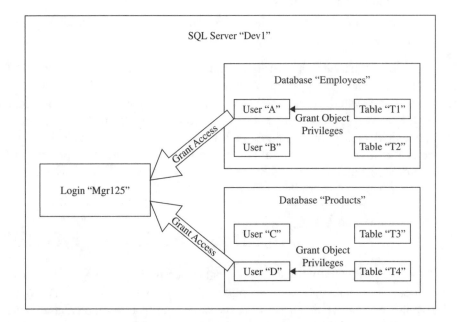

Figure 8-1   Database security in Microsoft SQL Server and Sybase Adaptive Server

Security in Microsoft SQL Server and Sybase Adaptive Server may be administered using either GUI tools (such as Enterprise Manager) or the vendor-provided stored procedures invoked using SQL statements. Here's a list of the components of the security architecture:

- **Login**   This is a user account on the SQL Server, also called a *user login*. It is created using a GUI tool such as Enterprise Manager or the sp_addlogin stored procedure supplied with the DBMS. The SQL Server login is not the same as any operating system account the user may have on the database server. However, on database servers running Microsoft Windows, the login can use Windows authentication, meaning the Windows operating system stores the credentials (login name and password) and authenticates users when they connect to the SQL Server. An obvious advantage to Windows authentication is that user access to the various SQL Servers in the enterprise can be centrally managed through the Windows account, rather than locally managed on each SQL Server. Note that once a login is defined in the SQL Server, the database user may connect to the SQL Server, but a login alone does *not* give them access to any database information. There is, however, a master login called "sa" (system administrator) that, similar to "root" in Unix and "Administrator" in Microsoft Windows, has full privileges to everything in the SQL Server environment. Figure 8-1 shows only one user login, called Mgr125.

- **Database**   A database is a logical collection of database objects (tables, views, indexes, and so on) as defined by the database designer. Figure 8-1 shows two databases: Employees and Products. It is important to understand that a login is allowed to connect to a database only after it has been granted that privilege by an administrator. (See the "User" topic that follows.) In addition to databases holding system data, some special databases are created when the SQL Server is created (not shown in Figure 8-1) and are used by the DBMS to manage the SQL Server. Among these are the following databases:

  - **master**   The master database contains system-level information, initialization settings, configuration settings, login accounts, the list of databases configured in the SQL Server, and the location of primary database data files.

  - **tempdb**   The tempdb database contains temporary tables and temporary stored procedures.

  - **model**   The model database contains a template for all other databases created on the system.

  - **msdb**   In Microsoft SQL Server databases only, the msdb database contains information used for scheduling jobs and alerts.

- **User**   Each database has a set of users assigned to it. Each database user maps to a login, so each user is a pseudo-account that is an alias to an SQL Server login account. User accounts do not necessarily have to have the same user name as their corresponding login accounts. When an administrator grants access to a database for a particular login account, using either a GUI tool such as Enterprise Manager or the sp_adduser stored procedure supplied with the DBMS, the user account corresponding to the login account is created by the DBMS. In Figure 8-1, the Mgr125 login corresponds to User A in the Employees database and to User D in the Products database. These privileges permit the login to connect to the database(s) but do not give the user any privileges against objects in those databases. I discuss how this happens later in this chapter.

- **Privileges**   Each user account in a database may be granted any number of privileges (also called *permissions*). *System privileges* are general privileges applied at the database level. Microsoft SQL Server divides these into *server privileges,* which include such permissions as starting up, shutting down, and backing up the SQL Server, and *statement privileges*, which include such permissions as creating a database and creating a table. *Object privileges* allow specific actions on a specific object, such as allowing select and update on Table T1. Figure 8-1 contains arrows that show the granting of object privileges on Table T1 to User A in the Employees database and on Table T4 to User D in the Products database. These privileges work in much the same way across all relational databases, thanks to SQL standards, and are therefore covered in the "Database Privileges" section a little later in this chapter.

Database Security in Oracle

Oracle's security architecture, shown in Figure 8-2, is markedly different compared to that of Microsoft SQL Server and Sybase Adaptive Server. The differences between the two are highlighted as each component is introduced:

- **Instance**   This is a copy of the Oracle DBMS software running in memory. Each instance manages only *one* database.

- **Database**   This is the collection of files managed by a single Oracle instance. Taken together, the Oracle instance and database comprise what Microsoft SQL Server and Sybase Adaptive Server call the *SQL Server*. Figure 8-2 depicts the Dev1 database.

- **User**   Each database account is called a *user*. As with Microsoft SQL Server and Sybase Adaptive Server, the user account may be authenticated

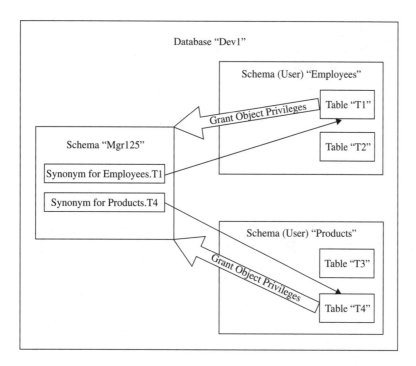

Figure 8-2 Database security in Oracle

externally (that is, by the operating system) or internally (by the DBMS). Each user is automatically allocated a schema (defined next), and this user is the *owner* of that schema, meaning it automatically has full privileges over any object in the schema. The following predefined users are created automatically when the database is created (not shown in Figure 8-2):

- The SYS user is the owner of the Oracle instance and its schema contains objects that Oracle uses to manage the instance. This user is equivalent to the "sa" user in Microsoft SQL Server and Sybase Adaptive Server.

- The SYSTEM user is the owner of the Oracle database and its schema contains objects that Oracle uses to manage the database. This user and its corresponding schema are similar to the "dbo" (database owner) user in the master database in Microsoft SQL Server and Sybase Adaptive Server.

- Many Oracle database options create their own user accounts when those options are installed.

- **Schema** This is the collection of database objects that belong to a specific Oracle user. The Oracle schema is equivalent to what Microsoft SQL Server

and Sybase Adaptive Server call a *database*. Figure 8-2 shows the Employees, Products, and Mgr125 schemas, which are owned by the Employees, Products, and Mgr125 users, respectively. Schema and user names are *always* identical in Oracle. "Mgr125" is a workaround to a special challenge you face with Oracle's security architecture, as discussed in the "Schema Owner Accounts" section later in this chapter.

- **Privileges** As with Microsoft SQL Server and Sybase Adaptive Server, privileges are divided into system and object privileges. These are covered in the "Database Privileges" section later in this chapter.

Implementing Database Access Security

The purpose of database access security is to protect the data from unauthorized usage. In order to accomplish this, the database administrator must determine which users are permitted to perform which actions against which objects in the database. The permissions given to users are called database *privileges*. The next topic takes a look at privileges, followed by a topic that covers the SQL statements used for security administration.

Database Privileges

Privileges provide the authorization for database users to perform various actions in the database. Remember that a database user can be a person or a process that connects to the database. In general, when a database user is given permission to connect to a database, they cannot do anything without being given some additional privileges. That is, a user who can connect to the database generally cannot access any data or perform any administrative function on the database until they are granted privileges to do so. In SQL, privileges are given to a database user with the GRANT statement, and taken away with the REVOKE statement, both of which are covered later in this chapter. Privileges are divided into two categories, as described in the topics that follow: "System Privileges" and "Object Privileges."

System Privileges

System privileges are general permissions to perform functions in managing the server and the database(s). Hundreds of permissions are supported by each database vendor, with most of those being system privileges. Some of the most commonly used ones are listed in the sections that follow. Complete details may be found in vendor-supplied documentation.

Here are some commonly used Microsoft SQL Server system privileges:

- **SHUTDOWN**   Provides the ability to issue the server shutdown command.
- **CREATE DATABASE**   Provides the ability to create new databases on the SQL Server.
- **BACKUP DATABASE**   Provides the ability to run backups of the databases on the SQL Server.

Here are some commonly used Oracle system privileges:

- **CREATE SESSION**   Provides the ability to connect to the database.
- **CREATE TABLE**   Provides the ability to create tables in your own schema. Similar privileges exist for other object types, such as indexes, synonyms, procedures, and so on.
- **CREATE ANY TABLE**   Provides the ability to create tables in *any* user's schema. Similar privileges are available for other object types, such as indexes, synonyms, procedures, and so on.
- **CREATE USER**   Provides the ability to create new users in the database.

Oracle permits the WITH ADMIN OPTION clause to be included when granting system permissions. When this option is included, the user(s) not only acquires the privilege but also the ability to grant the permission to other users. I do *not* recommend this practice because it opens up too many potential security exposures, especially because revocation of permissions granted in this way do not cascade.

Object Privileges

Object privileges provide authorization to perform specific actions upon specific database objects. For example, a database user may be given SELECT and UP-DATE privileges against a particular table but not INSERT or DELETE. The GRANT statement that gives database privileges to a database user may include a WITH GRANT OPTION clause that allows the recipient to then grant the privilege to others. If the privilege is subsequently revoked, a cascading revoke takes place if this user has, in turn, granted the permission to anyone else. I do *not* recommend use of the WITH GRANT OPTION clause because it is far too easy to lose control over who has which privileges.

SQL Statements Used for Security Administration

This topic describes the SQL statements used to administer data access security. Keep in mind that there is a lot of variation in the way that security is implemented in different SQL implementations, so as always, you should consult the documentation supplied by your database vendor.

The CREATE USER Statement

Many database vendors provide a GUI (graphical user interface) for security administration. However, the SQL standard contains a CREATE USER statement that can be used to define users in the database. The general syntax of the CREATE USER statement is

```
CREATE USER username
   [IDENTIFIED BY password]
   [options];
```

NOTE:

- *The IDENTIFIED BY CLAUSE is used for users that are authenticated by the DBMS. For users authenticated externally (that is, by the operating system), the syntax will vary.*

- *The options (if any apply) are DBMS specific and may include such things as defaults for various database connection properties.*

- *Microsoft SQL Server and Sybase Adaptive Server do not support the CREATE USER statement. Instead, they use stored procedures supplied by the database vendor: sp_addlogin is used to add logins to the SQL Server, which gives users the ability to connect to the SQL Server, and sp_adduser is used to add users to a database, which associates a login with a user account to permit access to the particular database.*

The GRANT Statement

The GRANT statement is used to bestow one or more privileges to a database user. The general syntax of the GRANT statement is

```
GRANT privilege [,privilege ...]
   [ON object]
   TO grantee [,grantee ...]
   [WITH GRANT OPTION | WITH ADMIN OPTION];
```

NOTE:

- *The privilege list can be either one or more system privileges, or one or more object privileges. System and object privileges cannot be mixed in the same GRANT statement.*

- *The ON object clause applies only to object privileges. It specifies the object on which object privileges listed in the privilege list are being granted.*

- *The grantee list specifies one or more database users or roles that are to receive the privilege(s). Roles are discussed later in this chapter.*

- *The WITH GRANT OPTION or WITH ADMIN OPTION clause allows the grantee to then grant the privilege to others. The syntax and usage will vary some across different SQL implementations. As already mentioned, I don't recommend using these because they essentially give away control of database privileges.*

One example follows. You will find more examples in the "Simplifying Administration Using Roles" section toward the end of this chapter.

- Grant the SELECT privilege on the MPAA_RATING table to PUBLIC. In most SQL implementations, PUBLIC is a keyword that is used to assign a privilege to all users of the database. In general, this is not a great idea, but the MPAA_RATING is just a code reference table, so allowing everyone to select from it is not much of a security exposure.

```
GRANT SELECT ON MPAA_RATING TO PUBLIC;
```

The REVOKE Statement

The general syntax of the REVOKE statement is shown here, along with some examples:

```
REVOKE privilege [,privilege ...]
  [ON object]
   FROM grantee [,grantee ...];
```

NOTE:

- *The privilege list can be either one or more system privileges, or one or more object privileges. System and object privileges cannot be mixed in the same REVOKE statement.*

- *The ON object clause applies only to object privileges. It specifies the object for which object privileges listed in the privilege list are being revoked.*

- *The grantee list specifies one or more database users or roles that are to lose the privilege(s). Roles are discussed later in this chapter.*

Here is an example—it reverses the GRANT from the previous topic:

```
REVOKE SELECT ON MPAA_RATING FROM PUBLIC;
```

Schema Owner Accounts

With all databases, you want to avoid giving database users more privileges than they need to do their job. This not only prevents errors made by humans from becoming data disasters (including those errors contained in the application programs and database queries they write), but it also keeps people honest.

In Microsoft SQL Server and Sybase Adaptive Server, you want to avoid having database users connect as the "sa" user. You want to create database logins that have the minimal privileges required. Sadly, this is often not done, and applications connect as "sa" or to a database with a user account that has the DBO (database owner) or DBA (database administrator) role. Roles are a collection of privileges and are discussed in an upcoming section. Whether done out of lack of understanding or out of laziness, this practice represents a *huge* security exposure that should be forbidden as a matter of policy.

In Figure 8-2, note that the Mgr125 user owns no tables but does have some privileges granted to it by the Employees and Products users. This is to work around a fundamental challenge with Oracle's security architecture. If you allowed a database user to connect to the database using a user such as Employees or Products, the user would automatically have full privileges to every object in the schema, including insert, delete, and update against any table, and also the ability to create and alter tables without restriction. This is fundamentally the same issue as allowing use of the "sa" user or the DBO and DBA roles in Microsoft SQL Server and Sybase Adaptive Server. The Mgr125 user mimics the behavior of the login with the same name shown in Figure 8-1. With the right system privileges, you can prevent the Mgr125 user in Oracle from being able to create any tables of its own.

You may have noticed the synonyms for user Mgr125 in Figure 8-2. A *synonym* is merely an alias or nickname for a database object. The synonyms are for the convenience of the user so that names do not have to be qualified with their schema name. To select from the T1 tables in the Employees schema directly, user Mgr125 would have to refer to the table name as "Employees.T1" in the SQL statement. This is not only inconvenient, but also can cause no end to problems if you ever decide to change the name of the Employees user. By creating a synonym called "T1" in the Mgr125 schema that points to Employees.T1, the user may now refer to the table as just "T1". Incidentally, you may recall that all user and object names in Oracle are case insensitive, so the use of mixed case here is only for illustration. The syntax for creating this synonym is as follows:

```
CREATE SYNONYM T1 FOR EMPLOYEES.T1;
```

Simplifying Administration Using Roles

A *role* is a named collection of privileges that can, in turn, be granted to one or more users. Most RDBMS systems have predefined roles that come with the system, and database users with the CREATE ROLE privilege may create their own. Roles have the following advantages:

- **Roles may exist before user accounts do.**   For example, you can create a role that contains all the privileges required to work on a particular development project. When a new hire joins the project team, one GRANT statement gives their new user account all the permissions they need.

- **Roles relieve the administrator of a lot of tedium.**   Many privileges may be granted with a single command when a role is used.

- **Roles survive when user accounts are dropped.**   In cases where the DBA must drop and re-create a user account, it can be a lot of work to reinstate all the privileges, which is simplified if all the privileges are assembled into one role.

The only potential disadvantage of roles, especially predefined ones, is that they can be granted without sufficient attention to all the privileges contained in them, thereby giving a user more privileges than the minimum they need. For example, the CONNECT role in Oracle includes CREATE SESSION and ALTER SESSION, as you would expect, but it also includes CREATE CLUSTER, CREATE DATA-BASE LINK, CREATE SEQUENCE, CREATE SYNONYM, CREATE TABLE, and CREATE VIEW. This is probably a more powerful collection than you would want a business user of the database to have, so it might be better to grant CREATE SESSION instead.

For administrators, a common role is DBA, which conveys a lot of powerful privileges (over 125 separate privileges in Oracle). Obviously, such a high-powered privilege must be granted judiciously.

Administering Roles in Microsoft SQL Server and Sybase Adaptive Server

Many SQL implementations use the SQL standard CREATE ROLE statement to establish roles, and the GRANT statement to assign the privileges contained in a role to a user. However, Microsoft SQL Server and Sybase Adaptive Server have a proprietary solution that requires the use of vendor-supplied stored procedures to invoke role-based security.

Roles are created using the sp_addrole stored procedure. The stored procedure sp_droprole may subsequently be used to drop the role. The general syntax for the stored procedure is

```
sp_addrole 'rolename' [,'ownername']
```

- The *rolename* parameter assigns a name to the role, which must be unique among all user and role names in the current database.

- The optional *ownername* parameter specifies the owner of the role, with a default of "dbo" (the database owner user account).

Here are two statements that add roles for the manager of the video store and the clerks who work in the store:

```
sp_addrole 'manager'
sp_addrole 'clerk'
```

Privileges are granted to the role using a standard GRANT statement. In the following examples, note how the same privileges can be granted to multiple roles when that fits the needs of the business, but at the same time, different privileges can be granted when required.

```
GRANT SELECT ON MPAA_RATING
    TO manager, clerk;
GRANT SELECT ON MOVIE
    TO clerk;
GRANT SELECT, INSERT, UPDATE, DELETE ON MOVIE
    TO manager;
```

Roles are assigned to database users using the vendor supplied sp_addrolemember stored procedure. The stored procedure sp_droprolemember can be used to remove a user from a role. The general syntax for sp_addrolemember is

```
sp_addrolemember 'rolename','username'
```

- The *rolename* parameter specifies that role to which the user is to be assigned.
- The *username* parameter specifies the database user account that is to be assigned the privileges contained in the role.

Administering Roles in Oracle

The SQL standard specifies the CREATE ROLE statement to be used for the creation of roles. The DROP ROLE statement can be used to subsequently drop the role if necessary. You must have the CREATE ROLE privilege to run the statement, which usually means that you must be a high-powered user in Oracle, such as SYSTEM. The general syntax of the CREATE ROLE statement is

```
CREATE ROLE rolename [options];
```

- The *rolename* provides the name of the new role.
- The *options* provide optional security specifications for the new role.

Here are two statements that add roles for the manager of the video store and the clerks who work in the store:

```
CREATE ROLE manager;
CREATE ROLE clerk;
```

As with Microsoft SQL Server and Sybase Adaptive Server, privileges are granted to the role using a standard GRANT statement. In the following examples, note how the same privileges can be granted to multiple roles when that fits the needs of the business, but at the same time, different privileges can be granted when required.

```
GRANT SELECT ON MPAA_RATING
    TO manager, clerk;
GRANT SELECT ON MOVIE
    TO clerk;
GRANT SELECT, INSERT, UPDATE, DELETE ON MOVIE
    TO manager;
```

Roles are assigned to database users using the standard GRANT statement. The syntax follows the same general syntax for the GRANT statement as described earlier in this chapter.

Using Views to Implement Column and Row Level Security

One of the common security issues to be addressed is how to allow database users access to some rows and columns in a table while preventing access to other rows and columns. Views are an excellent way to accomplish this. Here are some of the benefits of using views to accomplish security objectives:

- **Columns that a database user does not require may be omitted from the view.** Assuming the user has been granted access to the view rather than the underlying table, this method totally prevents them from seeing the information in the columns that were omitted from the view.

- **A WHERE clause may be included in the view to limit returned rows.** Joins may be included to match to other tables as a way of limiting rows. For example, the view could limit Product table rows to only those products for a Division ID that matches the division in which the employee works.

- **Joins to "lookup" tables can be used to replace code values in a table with their corresponding descriptions.** A lookup table typically contains a list of code values (for example, department codes, transaction codes, status codes) and their descriptions, and it's used to "look up" the descriptions for the codes. Although this is a minor point, employees trying to hack database records during fraud attempts have a much more difficult time if they cannot see the codes used to categorize the transactions. Furthermore, employees trying to do their best usually have a better time reading and understanding code descriptions than the corresponding code values.

There are other ways to accomplish these objectives, however. Many modern RDBMSs, including Oracle and Microsoft SQL Server, have provisions for column-level security wherein a DBA may grant access by table column. For row-level restrictions, a feature called Virtual Private Database, available in Oracle starting with version 9*i*, can be used to accomplish the objective. Finally, some prefer to use stored procedures for all database access and thus use custom programming to control all database access.

Quiz

Choose the correct responses to each of the multiple-choice questions. Note that there may be more than one correct response to each question.

1. Recent security legislation

   a. Requires the use of roles in administering database security

   b. Restricts the use of personal data

   c. Requires database administrators to secure the computer network

   d. Requires posting stolen identities on the Internet

   e. Requires notification to individuals who might have had their data compromised

2. Security is necessary because

   a. Honest people make mistakes

   b. Application security controls alone are inadequate

   c. 80 percent of fraud is committed by outside hackers

   d. Databases connected to the Internet are vulnerable

   e. Security controls keep people honest

3. Intruders who attempt to penetrate systems connected to the Internet include

   a. Bank auditors

   b. Spies from competitors

   c. Web bloggers

   d. Hackers

   e. Disgruntled employees

4. Components that must be secured include

   a. Client workstations

   b. Servers

   c. Databases

   d. Operating systems

   e. Networks

5. In Microsoft SQL Server, a login (user login)

   a. Can connect to any number of databases

   b. Automatically has database access privileges

   c. Can use Windows authentication

   d. Can be authenticated by Microsoft SQL Server

   e. Owns a database schema

6. In Microsoft SQL Server, a database

   a. Is owned by a login

   b. May have one or more users assigned to it

   c. May contain system data (for example, master) or user (application) data

   d. May be granted privileges

   e. Is a logical collection of database objects

7. In Oracle, a user account

   a. Can connect (log in) to any number of databases

   b. Automatically has database privileges

   c. Can use operating system authentication

   d. Can be authenticated by the Oracle DBMS

   e. Owns a database schema

8. In Oracle, a database

   a. Is owned by a user

   b. May have one or more user accounts defined in it

   c. May contain system data (for example, system schema) and user (application) data

   d. Is the same as a schema

   e. Is managed by an Oracle instance

9. System privileges

   a. Are granted in a similar way in Oracle, Sybase, and Microsoft SQL Server

   b. Are specific to a database object

   c. Allow the grantee to perform certain administrative functions on the server, such as shutting it down

   d. Are rescinded using the SQL REMOVE statement

   e. Vary across databases from different vendors

10. Object privileges

    a. Are granted in a similar way in Oracle, Sybase, and Microsoft SQL Server

    b. Are specific to a database object

    c. Allow the grantee to perform certain administrative functions on the server, such as shutting it down

    d. Are rescinded using the SQL REMOVE statement

    e. Are granted using the SQL GRANT statement

11. Using the WITH GRANT OPTION when granting object privileges

    a. Allows the grantee to grant the privilege to others

    b. Gives the grantee DBA privileges on the entire database

    c. Can lead to security issues

    d. Will cascade if the privilege is subsequently revoked

    e. Is a highly recommended practice because it is so convenient to use

12. Roles

    a. May be assigned to only one user

    b. May be shared by many users

    c. May exist before users do

    d. May contain any number of object privileges

    e. May contain only one object privilege

13. Potential downsides of using roles for security include:

    a. They are more difficult to administer than individual privileges

    b. They are dropped when the user is dropped

    c. They are dropped when the privileges are dropped

    d. They can be granted without consideration for all the privileges they contain

    e. Additional training time is required for administrators who must use them

14. Views may assist with security policy implementation by

    a. Restricting the table columns to which a user has access

    b. Restricting the databases to which a user has access

    c. Restricting table rows to which a user has access

    d. Storing database audit results

    e. Monitoring for database intruders

15. Roles are created in Microsoft SQL Server and Sybase Adaptive Server using

    a. The sp_create_role stored procedure

    b. The sp_add_role stored procedure

    c. The sp_addrole stored procedure

    d. The CREATE ROLE statement

    e. The GRANT statement

16. Roles are created in Oracle using

    a. The sp_create_role stored procedure

    b. The sp_add_role stored procedure

    c. The sp_addrole stored procedure

    d. The CREATE ROLE statement

    e. The GRANT statement

17. Role privileges are granted to database users in Microsoft SQL Server and Sybase Adaptive Server using

    a. The sp_create_role_member stored procedure

    b. The sp_add_role_member stored procedure

    c. The sp_addrolemember stored procedure

    d. The CREATE ROLE MEMBER statement

    e. The GRANT statement

18. Role privileges are granted to database users in Oracle using

    a. The sp_create_role_member stored procedure

    b. The sp_add_role_member stored procedure

    c. The sp_addrolemember stored procedure

    d. The CREATE ROLE MEMBER statement

    e. The GRANT statement

19. Write the SQL statement to give users manager_1 and manager_2 privileges to SELECT, INSERT and DELETE rows in the EMPLOYEE table. If you want to test the statement, you will first have to create the manager_1 and manager_2 users.

20. Write the SQL statement to rescind INSERT, UPDATE, and DELETE privileges for the clerk_127 user from the MOVIE table. If you want to test the statement, you will first have to create the clerk_127 user.

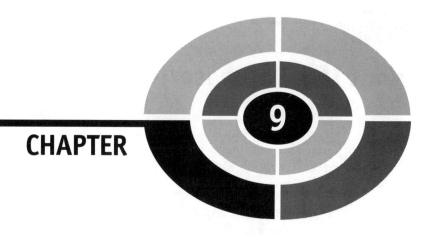

Preserving Database Integrity Using Transactions

In the next chapter, we'll look at how SQL can be incorporated into application programs, such as those written in Java, the Microsoft .NET Framework, C, and other programming languages/environments. However, before we do that, you need to understand the concept of database transactions because you will need them in order to properly implement business processes that update the database.

What Is a Database Transaction?

A *transaction* is a discrete series of actions that must be either completely processed or not processed at all. Some call a transaction a *unit of work* as a way of further emphasizing its all-or-nothing nature. Transactions have properties that can be easily remembered using the acronym ACID (Atomicity, Consistency, Isolation, Durability):

- **Atomicity**   A transaction must remain whole. That is, it must completely succeed or completely fail. When it succeeds, all changes that were made by the transaction must be preserved by the system. Should a transaction fail, all changes that were made by it must be completely undone. In database systems, we use the term *rollback* for the process that backs out any changes made by a failed transaction, and we use the term *commit* for the process that makes transaction changes permanent.

- **Consistency**   A transaction should transform the database from one consistent state to another. For example, a transaction that creates an invoice for an order transforms the order from a *shipped* order to an *invoiced* order, including all the appropriate database changes.

- **Isolation**   Each transaction should carry out its work independent of any other transaction that might occur at the same time.

- **Durability**   Changes made by completed transactions should remain permanent, even after a subsequent shutdown or failure of the database or other critical system component. In object terminology, the term *persistence* is used for permanently stored data. The concept of "permanent" here can be confusing, because nothing seems to ever stand still for long in an OLTP (online transaction processing) database. Just keep in mind that *permanent* means the change will not disappear when the database is shut down or fails—it does *not* mean that the data is in a permanent state that can never be changed again.

Transaction Support in Relational DBMSs

Aside from personal computer database systems, most relational DBMSs provide transaction support. This includes provisions in SQL for identifying the beginning and end of each transaction, along with a facility for logging all changes made by transactions so that a rollback may be performed when necessary. As you might guess, standards lagged behind the need for transaction support, so support for transactions varies a bit across RDBMS vendors.

Most RDBMSs record all transactions and the modifications made by them in a *transaction log*. The before and after image of each database modification made by a transaction is recorded in the transaction log. This facilitates any necessary roll-back because the before images can be used to reverse the database changes made by the transaction. A transaction commit is not complete until the commit record has been written to the transaction log. Because database changes are not always written to disk immediately, the transaction log is sometimes the only means of recovery when there is a system failure.

Let's look at transaction support in some of today's most popular RDBMS products.

Transaction Support in Microsoft SQL Server

Microsoft SQL Server supports transactions in three modes: autocommit, explicit, and implicit. All three modes are available when you're connected directly to the database using a client tool designed for this purpose. However, if you plan to use an ODBC or JDBC driver, you should consult the driver's documentation for information on the transaction support it provides. The three modes are

- **Autocommit mode**   In autocommit mode, each SQL statement is automatically committed as it completes. Essentially, this makes every SQL statement a discrete transaction. Every connection to Microsoft SQL Server uses autocommit until either an explicit transaction is started or the implicit transaction mode is set. In other words, autocommit is the default transaction mode for each SQL Server connection.

- **Explicit mode**   In explicit mode, each transaction is started with a BEGIN TRANSACTION statement and ended with either a COMMIT TRANSACTION statement (for successful completion) or a ROLLBACK TRANSACTION statement (for unsuccessful completion). This mode is used most often in application programs, stored procedures, triggers, and scripts. The general syntax of the three SQL statements follows:

```
BEGIN TRAN[SACTION]  [tran_name | @tran_name_variable]
 [WITH MARK ['description']]

COMMIT [TRAN[SACTION]  [tran_name | @tran_name_variable]]

ROLLBACK [TRAN[SACTION]  [tran_name | @tran_name_variable |
        savepoint_name | @savepoint_name_variable]]
```

- **Implicit mode**   Implicit transaction mode is toggled on or off with the command SET IMPLICIT_TRANSACTIONS {ON | OFF}. When implicit mode is on, a new transaction is started whenever any of a list of specific SQL statements is executed, including DELETE, INSERT, SELECT, and UPDATE, among others. Once a transaction is implicitly started, it continues until the transaction is either committed or rolled back. If the database user disconnects before submitting a transaction-ending statement, the transaction is automatically rolled back.

Transaction Support in Sybase Adaptive Server

Transaction support in Sybase Adaptive Server is very much like that in Microsoft SQL Server, but there are differences. Sybase Adaptive Server supports transactions in two modes: autocommit and explicit. Both modes are available when you're connected directly to the database using a client tool designed for this purpose. However, if you plan to use an ODBC or JDBC driver, you should consult the driver's documentation for information on the transaction support it provides. Here's a description of the two modes:

- **Autocommit mode**   In autocommit mode, each SQL statement is automatically committed as it completes. Essentially, this makes every SQL statement a discrete transaction. Every connection to Sybase Adaptive Server uses autocommit until an explicit transaction is started. In other words, autocommit is the default transaction mode for each connection.

- **Explicit mode**   In explicit mode, each transaction is started with a BEGIN TRANSACTION statement and ended with either a COMMIT TRANSACTION statement (for successful completion) or a ROLLBACK TRANSACTION statement (for unsuccessful completion). There is also a *savepoint*, which provides a consistent point in the processing of a transaction that can be used in a rollback. The explicit mode is used most often in application programs, stored procedures, triggers, and scripts. The general syntax of the SQL statements that support transactions is

```
BEGIN TRAN[SACTION] transaction_name

SAVE TRAN[SACTION] savepoint_name

COMMIT TRAN | TRANSACTION | WORK [transaction_name]

ROLLBACK [TRAN | TRANSACTION | WORK]
         [transaction_name | savepoint_name]
```

Transaction Support in Oracle

Oracle supports only two transaction modes: autocommit and implicit. As with Microsoft SQL Server and Sybase Adaptive Server, support varies when ODBC and JDBC drivers are used, so the driver vendor's documentation should be consulted in those cases. The two transaction modes in Oracle are

- **Autocommit mode**   As with other DBMSs, in autocommit mode each SQL statement is automatically committed as it completes. However, in Oracle, autocommit is *not* the default mode. Autocommit mode is toggled on and off using the SET AUTOCOMMIT command, as shown here, and it is off by default:

```
SET AUTOCOMMIT ON

SET AUTOCOMMIT OFF
```

- **Implicit mode**   A transaction is implicitly started when the database user connects to the database (that is, when a new database session begins). This is the default transaction mode in Oracle. When a transaction ends with a commit or rollback, a new transaction is automatically started. Unlike Microsoft SQL Server and Sybase Adaptive Server, nested transactions (transactions within transactions) are not permitted. A transaction ends with a commit when any of the following occurs: 1) the database user issues the SQL COMMIT statement; 2) the database session ends normally (that is, the user issues an EXIT command); 3) the database user issues an SQL DDL statement (that is, a CREATE, DROP, or ALTER statement). A transaction ends with a rollback when either of the following occurs: 1) the database user issues the SQL ROLLBACK statement; 2) the database sessions ends abnormally (that is, client connection is canceled or the database crashes or is shut down using one of the shutdown options that aborts client connections instead of waiting for them to complete).

Transaction Support in MySQL

Transaction support was added to MySQL beginning with version 3.23.0. However, in order to provide upward compatibility from older releases, transaction support was added using new storage engines. Tables created using the default storage engine (ISAM, which is called MyISAM in newer versions of MySQL) do not have transaction support. In order to enable transaction support, either the InnoDB or

BDB (Berkeley DB) storage engine must be specified when the table is created. For example:

```
CREATE TABLE LANGUAGE
 (LANGUAGE_CODE          CHAR(2)      NOT NULL,
  LANGUAGE_NAME          VARCHAR(40)  NOT NULL,
 PRIMARY KEY (LANGUAGE_CODE))
 ENGINE = INNODB;
```

There are many implications to using a different storage engine, so you should consult the documentation for the version of MySQL you are running before making a decision.

For tables that are created using either the InnoDB or BDB storage engines, transaction support is available in two modes:

- **Autocommit mode**   Autocommit mode is toggled on and off using a SET statement where a value of 0 turns off autocommit and a value of 1 turns it on:

```
SET AUTOCOMMIT=0;
```

```
SET AUTOCOMMIT=1;
```

- **Implicit mode**   Implicit mode takes effect whenever autocommit mode is turned off. The following SQL statements may be used in implicit transaction mode:

```
START TRANSACTION [WITH CONSISTENT SNAPSHOT];
```

```
SAVEPOINT savepoint_identifier;
```

```
ROLLBACK [TO savepoint_identifier];
```

```
COMMIT;
```

Transaction Support in DB2 UDB

All transactions in DB2 UDB (Universal Database) are implicit. The behavior is quite similar to transaction support in Oracle. The SQL statements used for transaction support are

```
COMMIT [WORK];
```

```
SAVEPOINT savepoint_name [options];
```

```
RELEASE [TO] SAVEPOINT savepoint_name;

ROLLBACK [WORK] [TO SAVEPOINT [savepoint_name]];
```

Locking and Transaction Deadlock

Although the simultaneous sharing of data among many database users has significant benefits, there also is a serious drawback that can cause updates to be lost.
Fortunately, the database vendors have worked out solutions to the problem. This
section presents the concurrent update problem and various solutions.

The Concurrent Update Problem

Figure 9-1 illustrates the concurrent update problem that occurs when multiple
database sessions are allowed to concurrently update the same data. Recall that
a session is created every time a database user connects to the database, which
includes the same user connecting to the database multiple times. The concurrent
update problem happens most often between two different database users who are
unaware that they are making conflicting updates to the same data. However, one
database user with multiple connections can trip themselves up if they apply
updates using more than one of their database sessions.

The scenario presented uses a fictitious company that sells products and creates an
invoice for each order shipped. Figure 9-1 illustrates User A, a clerk in the shipping
department who is preparing an invoice for a customer, which requires updating the
customer's data to add to the customer's balance due. At the same time, User B,
a clerk in the accounts receivable department, is processing a payment from the very

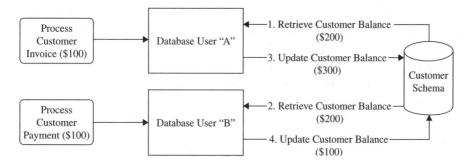

Figure 9-1   The concurrent update problem

same customer, which requires updating the customer's balance due to subtract the amount they paid. Here is the exact sequence of events, as illustrated in Figure 9-1:

1. User A queries the database and retrieves the customer's balance due, which is $200.

2. A few seconds later, User B queries the database and retrieves the same customer's balance, which is still $200.

3. In a few more seconds, User A applies her update, adding the $100 invoice to the balance due, which makes the new balance $300 in the database.

4. Finally, User B applies his update, subtracting the $100 payment from the balance due he retrieved from the database ($200), resulting in a new balance due of $100. He is unaware of the update made by User A and thus sets the balance due (incorrectly) to $100.

The balance due for this customer should be $200, but the update made by User A has been overwritten by the update made by User B. The company is out $100 that either will be lost revenue or will take significant staff time to uncover and correct. As you can see, allowing concurrent updates to the database without some sort of control can cause updates to be lost. Most database vendors implement a locking strategy to prevent concurrent updates to the exact same data.

Locking Mechanisms

A *lock* is a control placed in the database to reserve data so that only one database user may update it. When data is locked, no other database session can update the data until the lock is released, which is usually done with a COMMIT or ROLL-BACK SQL statement. Any other session that attempts to update locked data will be placed in a *lock wait* state, and the session will stall until the lock is released. Some database products, such as IBM's DB2, will time out a session that waits too long and return an error instead of completing the requested update. Others, such as Oracle, may leave a session in a lock wait state for an indefinite period of time.

By now it should be no surprise that there is significant variation in how locks are handled by different vendors' database products. A general overview is presented here with the recommendation that you consult your database vendor's documentation for details on how locks are supported. Locks may be placed at various levels (often called *lock granularity*), and some database products, including Sybase Adaptive Server, Microsoft SQL Server, and DB2, support multiple levels with automatic *lock escalation,* which raises locks to higher levels as a database session places more and more locks on the same database objects. Locking and unlocking small amounts of data requires significant overhead, so escalating locks to higher levels can substantially improve performance. Typical lock levels are as follows:

- **Database**   The entire database is locked so that only one database session may apply updates. This is obviously an extreme situation that should not happen very often, but it can be useful when significant maintenance is being performed, such as upgrading to a new version of the database software. Oracle supports this level indirectly when the database is opened in exclusive mode, which restricts the database to only one user session.

- **File**   An entire database file is locked. Recall that a file can contain part of a table, an entire table, or parts of many tables. This level is less favored in modern databases because the data locked can be so diverse.

- **Table**   An entire table is locked. This level is useful when you're performing a table-wide change such as reloading all the data in the table, updating every row, or altering the table to add or remove columns. Oracle calls this level a *DDL lock,* and it is used when DDL statements (CREATE, DROP, and ALTER) are submitted against a table or other database object.

- **Block or page**   A block or page within a database file is locked. A *block* is the smallest unit of data that the operating system can read from or write to a file. On most personal computers, the block size is called the *sector size.* Some operating systems use pages instead of blocks. A *page* is a virtual block of fixed size, typically 2K or 4K, which is used to simplify processing when there are multiple storage devices that support different block sizes. The operating system can read and write pages and let hardware drivers translate the pages to appropriate blocks. As with file locking, block (page) locking is less favored in modern database systems because of the diversity of the data that may happen to be written to the same block in the file.

- **Row**   A row in a table is locked. This is the most common locking level, with virtually all modern database systems supporting it.

- **Column**   Some columns within a row in the table are locked. This method sounds terrific in theory, but it's not very practical because of the resources required to place and release locks at this level of granularity. Very sparse support for it exists in modern commercial database systems.

Locks are always placed when data is updated or deleted. Most RDBMSs also support the use of a FOR UPDATE OF clause on a SELECT statement to allow locks to be placed when the database user declares their *intent* to update something. Some locks may be considered *read-exclusive,* which prevents other sessions from even reading the locked data. Many RDBMSs have session parameters that can be

set to help control locking behavior. One of the locking behaviors to consider is whether all rows fetched using a cursor are locked until the next COMMIT or ROLLBACK, or whether previously read rows are released when the next row is fetched. Consult your database vendor documentation for more details.

The main problem with locking mechanisms is that locks cause *contention*, meaning that the placement of locks to prevent loss of data from concurrent updates has the side effect of causing concurrent sessions to compete for the right to apply updates. At the least, lock contention slows user processes as sessions wait for locks. At the worst, competing lock requests can stall sessions indefinitely, as you will see in the next section.

Deadlocks

A *deadlock* is a situation where two or more database sessions have locked some data and then each requests a lock on data that another session has locked. Figure 9-2 illustrates this situation.

This example again uses two users from our fictitious company, cleverly named A and B. User A is a customer representative in the customer service department and is attempting to correct a payment that was credited to the wrong customer account. He needs to subtract (debit) the payment from Customer 1 and add (credit) it to Customer 2. User B is a database specialist in the IT department, and she has written an SQL statement to update some of the customer phone numbers with one area code to a new area code in response to a recent area code split by the phone company. The statement has a WHERE clause that limits the update to only those customers having a phone number with certain prefixes in area code 510 and updates those phone numbers to the new area code. User B submits her SQL UPDATE statement while User A is working on his payment credit problem. Customers 1 and 2 both have

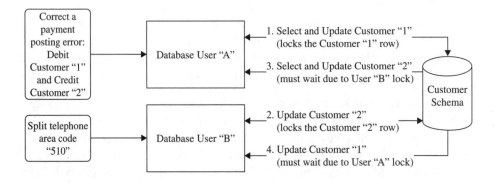

Figure 9-2 The deadlock

phone numbers that need to be updated. The sequence of events (all happening within seconds of each other), as illustrated in Figure 9-2, takes place as follows:

1. User A selects the data from Customer 1 and applies an update to debit the balance due. No commit is issued yet because this is only part of the transaction that must take place. The row for Customer 1 now has a lock on it due to the update.

2. The statement submitted by User B updates the phone number for Customer 2. The entire SQL statement must run as a single transaction, so there is no commit at this point, and thus User B holds a lock on the row for Customer 2.

3. User A selects the balance for Customer 2 and then submits an update to credit the balance due (same amount as debited from Customer 1). The request must wait because User B holds a lock on the row to be updated.

4. The statement submitted by User B now attempts to update the phone number for Customer 1. The update must wait because User A holds a lock on the row to be updated.

These two database sessions are now in deadlock. User A cannot continue due to a lock held by User B, and vice versa. In theory, these two database sessions will be stalled forever. Fortunately, modern DBMSs contain provisions to handle this situation. One method is to prevent deadlocks. Few DBMSs have this capability due to the considerable overhead this approach requires and the virtual impossibility of predicting what an interactive database user will do next. However, the theory is to inspect each lock request for the potential to cause contention and not permit the lock to take place if a deadlock is possible. The more common approach is deadlock detection, which then aborts one of the requests that caused the deadlock. This can be done either by timing lock waits and giving up after a preset time interval or by periodically inspecting all locks to find two sessions that have each other locked out. In either case, one of the requests must be terminated and the transaction's changes rolled back in order to allow the other request to proceed.

Quiz

Choose the correct responses to each of the multiple-choice questions. Note that there may be more than one correct response to each question.

1. A transaction
   a. May be partially processed
   b. May not be partially processed

   c. Changes the database from one consistent state to another

   d. Is sometimes called a *unit of work*

   e. Has properties described by the ACID acronym

2. The *A* in the ACID acronym stands for

   a. Automatically

   b. Auxiliary

   c. Atomicity

   d. Augmented

   e. Availability

3. The *C* in the ACID acronym stands for

   a. Correlated

   b. Consistency

   c. Committed

   d. Calculated

   e. Consolidated

4. The *I* in the ACID acronym stands for

   a. Integration

   b. Immediacy

   c. Iconic

   d. Isolation

   e. Information

5. The *D* in the ACID acronym stands for

   a. Durability

   b. Dedication

   c. Duality

   d. Database

   e. Distribution

6. The process that backs out changes made by a failed transaction is called

   a. Transaction logging

   b. Commit

   c. Rollback

      d. Recovery

      e. Savepoint creation

7. The process that makes transaction changes permanent is called

      a. Transaction logging

      b. Commit

      c. Rollback

      d. Savepoint creation

      e. Saving the transaction

8. Support for transactions in relational databases includes

      a. Identifying the beginning of each transaction

      b. Identifying the end of each transaction

      c. Distributed database management

      d. Periodic database backups

      e. The transaction log

9. Microsoft SQL Server supports the following transaction modes:

      a. Autocommit

      b. Automatic

      c. Durable

      d. Explicit

      e. Implicit

10. Oracle supports the following transaction modes:

      a. Autocommit

      b. Automatic

      c. Durable

      d. Explicit

      e. Implicit

11. In implicit transaction mode in Microsoft SQL Server, a new transaction is started by

      a. Connecting to the database

      b. A COMMIT statement

      c. A ROLLBACK statement

    d. An INSERT statement

    e. A SELECT statement

12. In implicit transaction mode in Oracle, a new transaction is started by

    a. Connecting to the database

    b. A Commit statement

    c. A Rollback statement

    d. An INSERT statement

    e. A SELECT statement

13. The SQL statements used to manage transactions in Microsoft SQL Server and Sybase Adaptive Server include

    a. BEGIN TRANSACTION

    b. END TRANSACTION

    c. COMMIT

    d. ROLLBACK

    e. SET AUTOCOMMIT

14. SQL statements used to manage transactions in Oracle are

    a. BEGIN TRANSACTION

    b. END TRANSACTION

    c. COMMIT

    d. ROLLBACK

    e. SET AUTOCOMMIT

15. In MySQL, transaction support

    a. Only applies to the ISAM and MyISAM storage engines

    b. Only applies to the InnoDB and BDB storage engines

    c. Includes autocommit, implicit, and explicit modes

    d. Includes autocommit and implicit modes

    e. Includes autocommit and explicit modes

16. SQL statements used to manage transactions in DB2 UDB are

    a. BEGIN TRANSACTION

    b. END TRANSACTION

    c. COMMIT

    d. ROLLBACK

    e. SAVEPOINT

17. The amount of data held by a lock (lock granularity) can be a

    a. Database

    b. Table

    c. Row

    d. Column

    e. Block or page

18. The concurrent update problem

    a. Is a consequence of simultaneous data sharing

    b. Cannot occur when AUTOCOMMIT is set to ON

    c. Is the reason that transaction locking must be supported

    d. Occurs when two database users submit conflicting SELECT statements

    e. Occurs when two database users make conflicting updates to the same data

19. A lock

    a. Is a control placed on data to reserve it so that the user may update it

    b. Is usually released when a COMMIT or ROLLBACK takes place

    c. Has a timeout set in DB2 and some other RDBMS products

    d. May cause contention when other users attempt to update locked data

    e. May have levels and an escalation protocol in some RDBMS products

20. A deadlock

    a. Is a lock that has timed out and is therefore no longer needed

    b. Occurs when two database users each request a lock on data that is locked by the other

    c. Can theoretically put two or more users in an endless lock wait state

    d. May be resolved by deadlock detection on some RDBMSs

    e. May be resolved by lock timeouts on some RDBMSs

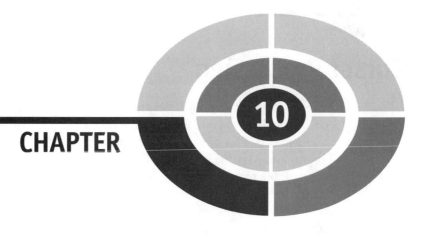

Integrating SQL into Applications

In this chapter, we'll have a look at how SQL is used in applications. An *application* is a set of computer programs designed to solve a particular business problem, such as an order-entry system, a payroll-processing system, or an accounting system. Applications can be built using a general-purpose procedural programming language such as Java, C, or C++, or a programming environment such as the Microsoft .NET Framework. A *procedural* programming language specifies an explicit sequence of steps to follow in order to complete a transaction. In applications that use relational databases, the application developers use various techniques for communicating with the database, which of course includes sending SQL statements to the database for processing and dealing with the results. This chapter explores some of those techniques.

Cursor Processing

Procedural programming languages are designed to handle one record at a time (one object instance or collection at a time in the case of object-oriented languages such as Java). This presents a dilemma when SQL is used in conjunction with the programming language because SQL queries typically produce result sets that contain multiple records (rows) of data. There is a mismatch that must be addressed.

To overcome the mismatch, most relational databases support the concept of a *cursor*, which is merely a pointer to a single row in the result set. In Oracle, cursor support is included in a procedural language SQL extension called PL/SQL (Procedural Language/SQL) and similarly is included in Transact-SQL in Sybase Adaptive Server and Microsoft SQL Server. These procedural SQL extensions are discussed later in this chapter. The use of a cursor parallels the use of a traditional flat file in that the cursor must be defined and opened before it may be used, it may be read from by fetching rows in a programming loop, and it should be closed when the program no longer needs it.

The DECLARE CURSOR Statement

A cursor must be declared before it can be referenced by any other SQL statements. Here is the general syntax of the DECLARE CURSOR statement that defines a cursor:

```
DECLARE cursor_name CURSOR FOR
select_statement
[FOR UPDATE [OF column_name [, column_name...]]]
```

NOTE:

- *The exact syntax will vary from one DBMS to another. For example, the SQL standard specifies the keyword FOR, but the Oracle syntax uses the keyword IS, and the Microsoft SQL Server syntax makes the keyword optional. Also, Oracle requires the keyword CURSOR to appear before the cursor name instead of after it. As usual, consult your DBMS documentation for details.*

- *The DECLARE CURSOR statement only defines the cursor—no data is selected until the cursor is subsequently opened and used. This is very much like defining a file in a traditional programming language—nothing really happens until the file is opened and used.*

- *The cursor_name must be unique within the program and will be used to reference the declared cursor in subsequent statements.*

- *The SQL statement included in the cursor declaration can contain most SELECT statement clauses. However, the INTO clause may not be included here because it is used in the FETCH statement as shown later in this section.*

- *The FOR UPDATE clause is optional, but some SQL implementations require it if subsequent SQL statements update and/or delete data selected by the cursor. As usual, consult your RDBMS documentation for specifics.*

Here is an example of a DECLARE CURSOR statement written in Oracle syntax. It selects movie rentals that are currently overdue.

```
DECLARE CURSOR overdue_rentals IS
SELECT MOVIE_ID, COPY_NUMBER, TRANSACTION_ID, DUE_DATE
  FROM MOVIE_RENTAL
 WHERE DUE_DATE < CURRENT_DATE
   FOR UPDATE OF DUE_DATE;
```

You can tell that this is an Oracle example because of the syntax and the use of CURRENT_DATE, which is an Oracle function that returns the current date and time. For other SQL implementations, substitute the expression that yields the current date and time in the RDBMS and adjust other syntax as required. For example, for Microsoft SQL Server, the statement would be

```
DECLARE overdue_rentals CURSOR FOR
SELECT MOVIE_ID, COPY_NUMBER, TRANSACTION_ID, DUE_DATE
  FROM MOVIE_RENTAL
 WHERE DUE_DATE < getdate()
   FOR UPDATE OF DUE_DATE;
```

The OPEN CURSOR Statement

The cursor must be opened before it can be used. In this example, the RDBMS may not have to retrieve any rows when you open the cursor, but for efficiency it might decide to retrieve some number of rows and place them in a buffer for you. A *buffer* is merely an area of computer memory used to temporarily hold data. It is far more efficient to use a buffer to hold some number of prefetched rows than it is going to

the database files for every single row because computers can access memory so much faster than files in the file system. In some cases, however, the RDBMS *must* fetch all the rows matching a query and sort them before the first row may be returned to the application program. You may have guessed that these are queries containing an ORDER BY to sequence the returned rows for us. If there is no index on the column(s) used for sequencing, then the RDBMS must find and sort all of them before it knows which one is the correct one to return as the *first* row (the one that sorts the lowest in the requested sequence). Although a lot goes on when a cursor is opened, the statement itself is quite simple. Here is the OPEN CURSOR statement for our example:

```
OPEN overdue_rentals;
```

The FETCH Statement

Each time your program requires a new row from the result set, simply issue a FETCH command against the cursor. This is very much like reading the next record from a file in an older flat file system. Remember that the cursor is merely a pointer into the result set. Every time a fetch is issued, the cursor is advanced one row, and the row currently pointed to is returned to the calling program (that is, the program that issued the FETCH). If there are no more rows in the result set (that is, if the cursor has been advanced past the last row in the result set), a code is returned to the calling program to indicate this. Another detail handled by the fetch is mapping the columns returned to programming language variables (called *host language variables,* or just *host variables*). This is done with the INTO clause, and naturally the syntax of the variable names will vary from one programming language to another. The general form of the FETCH statement is

```
FETCH cursor_name
 [INTO variable_list];
```

Notice that the FETCH statement refers only to the cursor name and the host variables. The cursor declaration ties the cursor to the table(s) and column(s) being referenced. In most SQL implementations, host variables must be declared before they can be referenced in a FETCH statement. The syntax and rules for declaring host variables vary across SQL implementations, so you should consult your vendor's documentation for details. Here is an example that will run in most SQL implementations (the INTO clause has been intentionally left out). However, Oracle requires the INTO clause along with some other statements that start and end a PL/SQL statement block, so this example won't work in Oracle without some modifications:

```
FETCH overdue_rentals;
```

Cursor UPDATE and DELETE Statements

SQL provides a convenient way to update data selected with a cursor or to delete rows from tables referenced by a cursor fetch. Keep in mind that no SQL statement can update or delete data in more than one table, so a cursor that contains a join has some update and delete restrictions. And as noted earlier, many SQL implementations require the FOR UPDATE clause for cursors that are to be used for updates and/or deletes. A special form of UPDATE and DELETE statement is used when a cursor is involved. It contains the WHERE CURRENT OF clause that names the cursor. The row that is updated or deleted is the last one fetched by the named cursor. If no row was successfully fetched from the cursor, any statement containing WHERE CURRENT OF will fail.

Here is the general syntax of the cursor UPDATE statement, followed by Oracle and Microsoft SQL Server examples:

```
UPDATE table_name
  SET column_and_value_list
 WHERE CURRENT OF cursor_name;

UPDATE MOVIE_RENTAL
   SET DUE_DATE = CURRENT_DATE
 WHERE CURRENT OF overdue_rentals;

UPDATE MOVIE_RENTAL
   SET DUE_DATE = getdate()
 WHERE CURRENT OF overdue_rentals;
```

Here is the general syntax of the cursor DELETE statement, followed by an example:

```
DELETE FROM table_name
 WHERE CURRENT OF cursor_name;

DELETE FROM MOVIE_RENTAL
 WHERE CURRENT OF overdue_rentals;
```

The CLOSE Statement

As previously stated, you should always close the cursor when the program no longer needs it because this frees up any resources the cursor has used, including memory for buffers. The CLOSE statement is as simple as the OPEN statement:

```
CLOSE overdue_rentals;
```

In Transact-SQL (Microsoft SQL Server and Sybase), memory used by a cursor is not completely freed up when the cursor is closed, so it is also good programming practice to deallocate the cursor as shown in this example:

```
DEALLOCATE overdue_rentals;
```

Embedding SQL in Application Programs

Now that you have seen how applications handle database query result sets using cursors, you need to understand how the application connects to and interacts with the database. Most connections between an application and database use a standard API. An *API* (*application programming interface*) is a set of calling conventions by which an application program accesses services. Such services can be provided by the operating system or by other software products such as the DBMS. The API provides a level of abstraction that allows the application to be portable across various operating systems and vendors.

ODBC Connections

ODBC (Open Database Connectivity) is a standard API for connecting application programs to DBMSs. ODBC is based on a Call Level Interface (CLI, a convention that defines the way calls to services are made), which was first defined by the SQL Access Group and released in September 1992. Although Microsoft was the first company to release a commercial product based on ODBC, it is not a Microsoft standard, and in fact there are now versions available for Unix, Macintosh, and other platforms.

ODBC is independent of any particular language, operating system, or database system. An application written to the ODBC API can be ported to another database or operating system merely by changing the ODBC driver. It is the ODBC driver that binds the API to the particular database and platform, and a definition known as the *ODBC data source* contains the information necessary for a particular application to connect with a database service. On Windows systems, the most popular ODBC drivers are shipped with the operating system, as is a utility program to define ODBC data sources (found on the Control Panel or Administrative Tools Panel, depending on the version of Windows).

Most commercial software products and most commercial databases support ODBC, which makes it far easier for software vendors to market and support products across a wide variety of database systems. One notable exception is applications written in Java. They use a different API known as JDBC, which is covered in the next section.

A common dilemma is that relational database vendors do not handle advanced functions in the same way. This problem can be circumvented using an escape clause that tells the ODBC driver to pass the proprietary SQL statements through the ODBC API untouched. The downside of this approach, of course, is that applications written this way are not portable to a different vendor's database (and sometimes not even to a different version of the same vendor's database).

Connecting Databases to Java Applications

Java started as a proprietary programming language (originally named Oak) that was developed by Sun Microsystems. It rapidly became the de facto standard programming language for web computing, at least in non-Microsoft environments. Java is a type-safe, object-oriented programming language that can be used to build client components (applets) as well as server components (servlets). It has a machine-independent architecture, making it highly portable across hardware and operating system platforms.

You may also run across the terms *JavaScript* and *JScript*. These are scripting languages with a Java-like syntax that are intended to perform simple functions on client systems, such as editing dates. They are not full-fledged implementations of Java and are not designed to handle database interactions.

JDBC (Java Database Connectivity)

JDBC (Java Database Connectivity) is an API, modeled after ODBC, for connecting Java applications to a wide variety of relational DBMS products. Some JDBC drivers translate the JDBC API to corresponding ODBC calls and thus connect to the database via an ODBC data source. Other drivers translate directly to the proprietary client API of the particular relational database, such as the Oracle Call Interface (OCI). As with ODBC, an escape clause is available for passing proprietary SQL statements through the interface. The JDBC API offers the following features:

- **Embedded SQL for Java**   The Java programmer codes SQL statements as string variables, the strings are passed to Java methods, and an embedded SQL processor translates the Java SQL to JDBC calls.

- **Direct mapping of RDBMS tables to Java classes**   The results of SQL calls are automatically mapped to variables in Java classes. The Java programmer may then operate on the returned data as native Java objects.

Java examples are a bit too involved for this book, but you can find lots of them on the websites of vendors who support JDBC. For instance, the Oracle Technology Network site contains many JDBC examples: http://www.oracle.com/technology.

JSQL (Java SQL, SQLJ)

JSQL (also called Java SQL and SQLJ) is a method of embedding SQL statements in Java without having to do special coding to put the statements into Java strings. It is an extension of the ISO/ANSI standard for SQL embedded in other host languages, such as C. A special program called a *precompiler* is run on the source program that automatically translates the SQL statements written by the Java programmer into pure Java. This method can save a considerable amount of development effort.

Middleware Solutions

Middleware can be thought of as software that mediates the differences between an application program and the services available on a network or between two disparate application programs. In the case of Java database connections, middleware products can make the RDBMS look as if it is an object-oriented database running on a remote server. The Java programmer then accesses the database using standard Java methods, and the middleware product takes care of the translation between objects and relational database components. There are a number of application development environments that can be purchased that provide a middleware solution between the Java class structure and relational databases. Most of these provide a GUI tool for mapping relational data to Java classes, and using the mapping specification, they automatically generate the SQL statements required to retrieve the data from the database and populate the classes, as well as the SQL statements to apply any data updates to the relational database.

The .NET Framework

.NET is the Microsoft web services strategy for applications that are integrated across the Microsoft platform. The .NET Framework is a development and execution environment that allows different programming languages and libraries to work together to create applications. The .NET Framework consists of:

- **The Common Language Runtime (CLR)** A language-neutral development and execution environment. Support is provided for standard languages such as C and C++ as well as Microsoft proprietary languages such as Visual Basic .NET, C#, and J#.

- **The Framework Class Libraries (FCL)**   A consistent, object-oriented library of prepackage functions.

- **Infrastructure**   Support for standard networking protocols and specifications, programming libraries of various languages, and different platforms.

Applications built using the .NET Framework can use classes and libraries within the framework to send SQL to a relational database (typically Microsoft SQL Server) and to process the results of the execution of the SQL statements by the DBMS. I included the .NET Framework here as an example of a vendor-proprietary development environment that includes provisions for embedding SQL in the application. There are many such environments available from a variety of vendors.

Computationally Complete SQL

As originally developed, SQL was solely a data language because it lacked several types of statements that are essential in general programming languages, including statements for looping, branching, and error handling. SQL that includes all the statements required for the creation of complete programs is called *computationally complete*. When database developers and DBAs needed to perform complex operations on the database, they had to resort to a general-purpose programming language such as C. For business applications, the use of a general-purpose language was (and still is) an appropriate solution. However, forcing DBAs to write triggers and stored procedures in a general-purpose programming language, which was the only option available in some early RDBMS products such as DB2, was not such a great idea, especially since DBAs often were not well-versed in the supported programming language.

Triggers and *stored procedures* are program modules that are stored in the database. The difference between the two is that a trigger executes (fires) automatically based on an event in the database, such as inserting a row into a particular table, while a stored procedure executes when it is invoked using a special SQL statement such as CALL or EXECUTE. Stored procedures are useful for hiding complex SQL statements from application programs, developers, and end users of the database.

In fact, some believe that all database access should be via stored procedures in order to insulate the database users from any database design changes. Triggers are useful for automating events such as logging data changes and replicating (copying) data to another database, along with anything else that must be run automatically based on an event. However, it is a good idea to keep business logic in the application programs themselves instead of in the database to minimize requirements to change the database as the business changes.

RDBMS vendors were quick to provide proprietary language extensions to SQL that permitted complete programs to be written. The next two sections of this chapter present high-level overviews of two such languages: Transact-SQL as offered with Microsoft SQL Server and Sybase Adaptive Server (the two are similar but not exactly identical implementations) and PL/SQL as offered with the Oracle RDBMS. Keep in mind that entire books can (and have) been written on Transact-SQL and PL/SQL, while only a brief overview is offered here.

Transact-SQL (Microsoft SQL Server and Sybase Adaptive Server)

Microsoft SQL Server and Sybase Adaptive Server share a common SQL language because they have the same roots. In 1987, Microsoft recognized that it lacked an SQL implementation that would run on its new Windows Server operating system. A partnership with Sybase was formed, and the result was an adaptation of Sybase's database technology that ran on both Windows and Unix. When the partnership ended in 1993, both companies retained rights to the technology they developed, which became Microsoft SQL Server and Sybase DataServer (later renamed to Adaptive Server). Over time, these two product lines have diverged, but to this day, if you know Transact-SQL for one of them, you can easily adapt your knowledge and skills to the other.

Transact-SQL includes all the SQL statements and functions you have seen thus far, including SELECT, INSERT, UPDATE, and DELETE, plus all the statements required to make it a computationally complete language. In addition, Sybase and Microsoft have provided a considerable number of stored procedures, written in Transact-SQL, to assist in the management and use of the database. They are easy to spot because their names all begin with "sp_".

The following table provides an overview of the Transact-SQL language elements:

Language Element	Description
BACKUP	Backs up the database, transaction log, or one or more files or filegroups
BEGIN	Starts a statement block
BREAK	Exits a WHILE loop
CASE	Evaluates a lists of conditions and returns one of multiple possible result expressions
CONTINUE	Restarts a WHILE loop
Cursor Control statements	Includes the DECLARE CURSOR, OPEN, FETCH, CLOSE, and DEALLOCATE statements as described in this chapter
DCL statements	Includes the standard SQL GRANT and REVOKE statements as described in Chapter 8
DDL statements	Includes the CREATE, ALTER, and DROP statements as described in Chapter 3, with extensions for the creation and management of triggers and stored procedures written in Transact-SQL
DECLARE	Defines Transact-SQL variables
DML statements	Includes the standard SQL INSERT, UPDATE, and DELETE statements as described in Chapter 7
END	Ends a statement block
EXEC	Executes a stored procedure
Functions	Includes SQL functions as described in Chapters 4 and 6
GOTO	Transfers control unconditionally (branches) to a statement label
IF...ELSE	Evaluates one or more conditions, providing statements to execute when a condition evaluates to TRUE
PRINT	Returns a message to the client
RESTORE	Restores a database, transaction log, or one or more files or filegroups from a backup
RETURN	Ends the current procedure, returning control to the calling module

Language Element	Description
SELECT [INTO]	Includes standard SQL SELECT, as described in Chapters 4 through 6, with an optional INTO clause added to allow storage of selected data in declared Transact-SQL language variables
SHUTDOWN	Immediately stops the RDBMS engine
Transaction statements	Includes BEGIN TRANSACTION, END TRANSACTION, COMMIT, and ROLLBACK statements as described in Chapter 9
TRUNCATE TABLE	Clears a table of all data, but without firing any triggers defined on the table
USE	Names the database that all subsequent Transact-SQL will use
WAITFOR	Delays statement execution
WHILE	Repeats statements while a specific condition is TRUE

Oracle PL/SQL

PL/SQL (Programming Language/SQL), originally known as the "procedural option," was first released in 1991 as part of Oracle version 6. It was modeled after Ada, a programming language that at the time was the standard programming language for the United States government. This may seem like an odd choice, but Oracle Corporation has always had close ties with the federal government. In fact, it is now well known that the CIA was Oracle's very first customer.

Unlike Transact-SQL, Oracle SQL is not considered a part of PL/SQL, but rather a separate language that can be invoked from within PL/SQL as needed. Like Microsoft SQL Server and Sybase Adaptive Server, Oracle provides a host of stored procedures with the database, mostly written in PL/SQL, and usually with names that begin with "DBMS_". The combination of SQL, PL/SQL, and the SQL*Plus client (which has its own set of commands) can be confusing at times because it is difficult to remember to which language a particular statement belongs. However, other than finding which product manual describes the command when you need help with syntax, you don't have to worry much because SQL*Plus, Oracle SQL, and PL/SQL all interoperate seamlessly.

Here is a table that provides an overview of PL/SQL language elements:

Language Element	Description
BEGIN	Starts a block of statements.
CALL	Calls a PL/SQL procedure as a subprogram.
CURSOR FOR LOOP	Defines a loop tied to a cursor that is repeated for each row returned by the cursor.
Cursor statements	Includes the DECLARE CURSOR, OPEN, FETCH, and CLOSE statements as described in Chapter 10. There are also special variables (attributes) associated with cursors to allow for operations such as testing whether a FETCH found a row of data or not.
DECLARE	Defines PL/SQL variables. PL/SQL supports all the Oracle SQL data types, plus it adds a bunch of its own, including arrays, memory tables, record structures, and user-defined types.
END	Ends a block of statements.
END LOOP	Marks the end of a LOOP or FOR LOOP.
EXCEPTION	Starts a special section of the PL/SQL program that handles exceptions (errors) trapped during statement execution. A WHEN statement is included for each condition to be handled.
EXECUTE	Invokes (executes) a PL/SQL stored procedure.
EXIT [WHEN]	Exits from a loop.
FOR LOOP	Defines a loop that iterates a numeric variable. An optional range can be included to control the number of loop executions.
GOTO	Transfers control (branches) unconditionally to a statement label.
IF...THEN...ELSE	Evaluates one or more conditions, providing statements to execute when a condition evaluates to TRUE.
LOOP	Defines a simple loop that will execute continuously until stopped with an EXIT statement.
NULL	Is a statement that does absolutely nothing (which reminds me of a few coworkers I once had). It is often used as a placeholder in a block of conditional statements.
RAISE	Raises an error condition. If a WHEN statement is defined for the condition, it takes over to handle the condition; otherwise, the PL/SQL program fails.

Language Element	Description
RETURN	Exits from a PL/SQL block or procedure, returning control to the block or procedure that invoked it.
Transaction statements	Includes the COMMIT, ROLLBACK, and SAVEPOINT statements as described in Chapter 9.
WHEN	Used in an EXCEPTION section, defines an exception condition and the actions to be taken when the exception is raised. Note that exceptions can be raised when errors occur or when the RAISE statement is executed.
WHILE	Repeats statements while a specific condition is TRUE.

Quiz

Choose the correct responses to each of the multiple-choice questions. Note that there may be more than one correct response to each question.

1. A cursor is
   a. The collection of rows returned by a database query
   b. A pointer into a result set
   c. The same as a result set
   d. A buffer that holds rows retrieved from the database
   e. A method to analyze the performance of SQL statements

2. A result set is
   a. The collection of rows returned by a database query
   b. A pointer into a cursor
   c. The same as a cursor
   d. A buffer that holds rows retrieved from the database
   e. A method to analyze the performance of SQL statements

3. Before rows may be fetched from a cursor, the cursor must first be
   a. Declared
   b. Committed
   c. Opened
   d. Closed
   e. Deallocated

4. Cursors are

   a. Intended to overcome the mismatch between the way object-oriented languages and relational databases handle query results

   b. Intended to overcome the mismatch between the way procedural languages and relational databases handle query results

   c. Included in the Oracle PL/SQL language

   d. Included in the Sybase Transact-SQL language

   e. Included in the Microsoft Transact-SQL language

5. The cursor name is included in

   a. The DECLARE CURSOR statement

   b. The SELECT statement

   c. The OPEN statement

   d. The FETCH statement

   e. The CLOSE statement

6. The cursor name must be unique within

   a. A table

   b. A row

   c. A result set

   d. A database

   e. A program

7. A cursor OPEN statement

   a. Always causes the query to be run and the result set to be filled with data

   b. May cause the query to be run and some rows placed in the result set

   c. Must include an INTO clause

   d. Must include the cursor name

   e. Must include the table name(s)

8. ODBC is

   a. A standard API for connecting to DBMSs

   b. Independent of any particular language, operating system, or DBMS

   c. A Microsoft standard

   d. Used by Java programs

   e. Flexible in handling proprietary SQL

9. JDBC is

    a. A standard API for connecting to DBMSs

    b. Independent of any particular language, operating system, or DBMS

    c. A Microsoft standard

    d. Used by Java programs

    e. Flexible in handling proprietary SQL

10. JSQL is

    a. A Sun Microsystems standard

    b. A method of embedding SQL statements in Java

    c. An extension of an ISO/ANSI standard

    d. A middleware solution

    e. Independent of any particular language, operating system, or DBMS

11. Middleware solutions for Java connections

    a. Use standard Java methods for access to an RDBMS

    b. Make the RDBMS look like an object-oriented database

    c. Provide a method for embedding SQL statements in Java

    d. Are independent of any particular language, operating system, or DBMS

    e. Usually run on a remote server

12. The Microsoft .NET Framework includes

    a. The Transact-SQL language

    b. The Common Language Runtime (CLR)

    c. The Common Gateway Interface (CGI)

    d. The Framework Class Libraries (FCL)

    e. Infrastructure to support various network specifications, programming languages, and platforms

13. Computationally complete SQL includes statements for

    a. Report writing

    b. Error handling

    c. Looping

    d. Branching

    e. Cursor processing

14. A trigger is

    a. Executed only when called

    b. Executed automatically based on an event in the database

    c. Written in a nonprocedural language

    d. Written in a procedural language

    e. Stored in the database

15. A stored procedure is

    a. Executed only when called

    b. Executed automatically based on an event in the database

    c. Written in a nonprocedural language

    d. Written in a procedural language

    e. Stored in the database

16. Transact-SQL

    a. Appears in Oracle and Microsoft SQL Server

    b. First appeared in 1987

    c. Includes standard SQL with procedural extensions

    d. Was developed jointly by Oracle and Sybase

    e. Is the language used for many stored procedures provided by Microsoft and Sybase

17. Language elements included in Transact-SQL are

    a. BEGIN and END to start and end statement blocks

    b. WHILE for statement repetition

    c. SQL DDL, DQL, DML, and DCL statements

    d. DECLARE for definition of variables

    e. GOTO and EXIT to branch out of loops

18. PL/SQL

    a. Was originally known as Ada

    b. Was first released in 1991

    c. Was developed by the CIA

    d. Does not include standard SQL statements

    e. First appeared with Oracle version 6

19. Language elements included in PL/SQL are

    a. DECLARE for the definition of variables

    b. WAITFOR to delay execution of statements

    c. EXCEPTION for the handling of exceptions

    d. FOR LOOP and WHILE for forming loops

    e. The SELECT statement

20. Language elements included in both PL/SQL and Transact-SQL are

    a. BACKUP and RESTORE to back up and restore database elements

    b. IF...ELSE for conditional execution of statements

    c. NULL as a placeholder that does nothing

    d. DECLARE for the definition of variables

    e. RETURN to exit from a block of statements

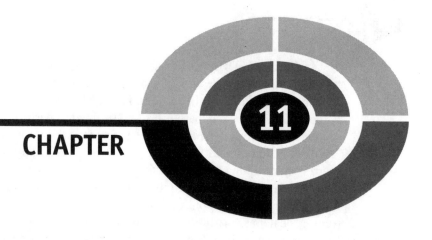

CHAPTER 11

SQL Performance
and Tuning
Considerations

This final chapter covers performance and tuning considerations for making the SQL statements you write run faster and more efficiently. First, we'll have a look at general things that can be done at the DBMS level, followed by guidelines for writing efficient SQL. The many differences across RDBMSs (even different versions from the same vendor) make universal solutions to performance issues difficult to develop. What works well in one DBMS often has a lesser, or even negative, effect on another. While I have made every attempt to include guidelines in this chapter that are universally applicable, I have also included some of the most important vendor-specific guidelines. In all cases, be sure to check your RDBMS documentation for current information.

Any seasoned DBA (Database Administrator) will tell you that database performance tuning is a neverending task. It seems there is always something that can be tweaked to make it run better. The key to success is managing your time and the expectations of the database users and setting the performance requirements for an application before it is even written. Simple statements such as "every database update must complete within four seconds" are usually the best. With that done, performance tuning becomes a simple matter of looking for things that do not conform to the performance requirement and tuning them until they do. The law of diminishing returns applies to database tuning, and you can put lots of effort into tuning a database process for little or no gain. The beauty of having a standard performance requirement is that you can stop when the process meets the requirement and then move on to the next problem.

General RDBMS Tuning Considerations

Most RDBMS performance problems are the result of poorly written SQL statements, but there are things that the DBA can do to make the entire database system run more efficiently. So, before we move on to tuning SQL queries, the sections that follow offer some general considerations for tuning the RDBMS.

Minimize Disk Reads and Writes

This may seem obvious, but the slowest operation on most computer systems is I/O (input/output), such as reading data from and writing data to the storage system (the hard disks). Moving data around in memory and performing various calculations and transformations on the data are both much faster than an I/O operation. So why wouldn't you just put the entire database in memory and keep it there? Actually, that may happen someday. However, for now, memory is too expensive to be a complete replacement for disks, and most memory is *volatile*, meaning that the data held in it is lost when the computer system is shut down. There is nonvolatile memory, but it costs considerably more. Therefore, the best thing the DBA can do is to make efficient use of the available memory to minimize I/O operations and the time spent waiting for them to complete. Here are some ways to do that:

- **Allocate correctly sized buffers.** You may recall that a buffer is an area of memory used to hold data that has been recently read from or is destined to be written to the storage system. With properly sized buffers, recently read data will stay in memory for a reasonable time, improving the probability that a new query will find the data it needs already sitting in a buffer. On the output side, if there is room in the correct buffer, the RDBMS can write the data to the buffer and copy the buffer from memory to the storage system for permanent storage at a later time. This is called *asynchronous I/O*, which is fundamental to an efficient RDBMS.

- **Spread out disk I/O.**   If you have multiple physical disk drives, spread the database files out to allow for parallel I/O. (Multiple partitions on a personal computer hard drive don't count because those partitions are all on the same physical drive.) In general, a disk drive can access only one spot on the drive at a time, so multiple I/O operations on a single drive must be handled serially. By spreading files out, multiple I/O operations can happen at the same time (one per drive at any instant).

Tune the Computer System and Environment

It should be obvious that the computer system on which the DBMS runs should be as fast and efficient as possible. Here are some general considerations:

- **Select fast and reliable hardware.**   The faster the hardware on your computer system, particularly disk drives and processors, the faster your database queries will run.

- **Tune the operating system.**   While there is a lot of variation across vendors and operating system versions, there are usually some things that can be done to improve performance. For example, in Microsoft Windows the size of the swap file can have a significant effect on operating system performance. Consult a tuning manual or white paper on your operating system for specifics.

Design the Tables Efficiently

Relational table design can have a huge effect on performance. Most popular RDBMSs have manuals or white papers that cover best practices for designing efficient tables. Here are some general guidelines that apply to all SQL implementations:

- **CHAR vs. VARCHAR**   For character columns that are five characters or less, the CHAR data type is most appropriate, even if the data length varies. The VARCHAR data type is better for variable length columns that are usually

longer than five characters in size. For columns that always contain data of the same length, CHAR is an obvious choice. The reason for using CHAR for short columns is that VARCHAR columns include 1 to 3 bytes to hold the length of the column data, and there is additional processing overhead for calculating the length when the column data changes.

- **Numeric column data types** Use the smallest data type in which the data will fit. A lot of space is wasted if, for example, the BIGINT data type is used when the data would always fit in INT or SMALLINT.

- **Identical data types for primary and foreign key columns** Joins work much more efficiently if the data types of the columns used in the join predicate (usually the primary key in one table and a foreign key in the other table) have identical data types. When the data types are different, the DBMS has to convert one of them so that the data values can be compared correctly, and such conversion amounts to unnecessary overhead.

- **Beware of triggers** Triggers placed on database tables are sometimes convenient and/or necessary ways to solve specific problems such as enforcing complicated constraints. However, the work that the trigger does is part of the unit of work of the SQL statement that modifies the table (the statement that caused the trigger to fire), and therefore, it slows down that SQL statement.

Tuning SQL Queries

About 80 percent of database query performance problems can be solved by adjusting the SQL statement. However, you must understand how the particular DBMS being used processes SQL statements in order to know what to tweak. For example, placing SQL statements inside stored procedures can yield remarkable performance improvement in Microsoft SQL Server and Sybase, but the same is not true in Oracle.

A query *execution plan* is a description of how an RDBMS will process a particular query, including index usage, join logic, and estimated resource cost. It is important to learn how to use the "explain plan" utility in your DBMS, if one is available, because it will show you exactly how the DBMS will process the SQL statement you are attempting to tune. Examples of obtaining execution plans for Oracle and Microsoft SQL Server databases appear later in this chapter.

The next section covers some general query design and tuning tips for SQL, followed by sections that offer recommendations for several of the most popular RDBMS products currently on the market.

General RDBMS Considerations

This section covers design and tuning considerations that apply to most SQL implementations. As always, consult the documentation for the DBMS you are using for applicability information.

Know Your Optimizer

The *query optimizer* is the software component in the RDBMS that analyzes an SQL statement to determine the best way to execute it. Most modern optimizers are *cost-based*, which means that they estimate the cost of all possible ways to execute a statement and then chose the one with the lowest cost. An important component of cost-based optimizers is statistics gathered from the database, such as the number of rows in each table and the number of unique values each indexed column has. However, some optimizers are *rule-based*, which means that they apply a set of rules to the SQL statement instead of cost estimates when deciding how to best execute it. A few optimizers such as Oracle's allow a choice of either cost-based or rule-based. Here are some considerations regarding query optimizers:

- **Order of table names** Does the order of the table names in the FROM or JOIN clause have any influence on the order in which tables are accessed when performing the joins? This is more likely the case with a rule-based optimizer. Ideally, the DBMS should access the most selective table (the one that will eliminate the most number of rows from the result set) first. For rule-based optimizers, you may find some surprising differences. For example, Oracle version 7 processed the table name list from right to left, but this was changed to left to right order starting with version 8.

- **Order of search predicates** Does the order of the predicates in the WHERE clause have any influence on the order in which the predicates are evaluated? Ideally, the most restrictive predicate (the one that eliminates the most number of rows) should be evaluated first.

- **Lack of statistics** If a cost-based optimizer is being used, what does it do when statistics have not been collected for one or more tables? Some optimizers, such as Oracle's, revert back to rule-based, while others assume default values for the required statistics or simply refuse to use any indexes and do full table scans of all the tables. A *full table scan* is where the DBMS reads every row in the table to find the desired ones, which of course can be a performance disaster for tables with very large numbers of rows.

- **Query rewrites**   Are queries rewritten into more efficient forms by the optimizer? For example, many optimizers automatically rewrite subselects into equivalent joins in order to simplify subsequent processing. In some cases, you may find that certain DBMS options must be enabled in order to allow the optimizer to rewrite queries.

- **View definition merges**   For queries that use views, at what point does the DBMS merge the view definition (the query that defines the view) into the SQL statement submitted by the database user? This has obvious implications for the optimizer —the sooner it can evaluate the entire SQL statement, the smarter its decision should be.

- **Other criteria**   What other criteria influence the optimizer? For example, some optimizers will favor unique indexes over nonunique ones, and some will favor the use of an index to sequence rows over sorting the result set.

Efficient Query Design

Many application developers simply write SQL statements off the top of their heads without giving much thought to designing them for efficient processing. This is an easy trap to fall into because SQL is a nonprocedural language that gives the false impression that the form of the statement does not matter provided it produces the correct result set. Statements that are not designed can introduce enormous performance issues. For example, I recently reviewed an SQL statement that retrieved about six million rows of data each time it was executed. The application that issued the SQL only required the first row found. When this statement was run, the entire database seized until the processing was complete. It felt like the lights dimmed in the building from all the resources this one query consumed. It took the developer who fixed the problem only about an hour to turn the query into a very efficient one, but a little bit of thought by the original developer would have avoided the crisis entirely. Here are some considerations regarding query design:

- **Know your data.**   When writing the SQL statement, you should have some idea of how many rows are in each table, how selective your WHERE predicates are, and how many rows you expect in the result set. The larger the number of rows involved, the more time you should spend thinking about the best way to write the SQL statement.

- **Minimize returned rows.**   The fewer the rows in the result set, the more efficiently the query will run.

- **Avoid scans of large tables.**   For tables over 1000 rows or so, scanning all the rows in the table instead of using an index can be expensive in terms of resources required. And, of course, the larger the table, the more expensive a table scan becomes. Full table scans occur in the following situations:

- The query does not contain a WHERE clause to limit rows.

- None of the columns referenced in the WHERE clause matches the leading column of an index on the table.

- Index and table statistics have not been updated. Most RDBMS query optimizers use statistics to evaluate available indexes, and without statistics, a table scan may be seen as more efficient than using an index.

- At least one column in the WHERE clause does match the first column of an available index, but the comparison used obviates the use of an index. These cases include the following:

    - Use of the NOT operator (for example, WHERE NOT CITY = 'New York'). In general, indexes can be used to find what *is* in a table, but cannot be used to find what is *not* in a table.

    - Use of the NOT EQUAL operator (for example, WHERE CITY <> 'New York').

    - Use of a wildcard in the first position of a comparison string (for example, WHERE CITY LIKE '%York%').

    - Use of an SQL function in the comparison (for example, WHERE UPPER(CITY) = 'NEW YORK').

- **Avoid unnecessary columns.**   The wider the data in each row in the result set, the more disk space and memory that is required for intermediate operations such as sorts and to hold the result set.

- **Avoid unnecessary tables.**   The fewer the tables, the more efficient the query.

- **Avoid sorts of large result sets.**   Sorts are expensive, especially when the rows being sorted will not fit in memory. When the result set is expected to be very large, sorts should be avoided. Most optimizers will use an index if it can eliminate the need for a sort, but creating an index solely to avoid a sort of a large number of rows is probably not wise because of the overhead required to maintain the index.

- **Match data types in predicates.**   Whether a predicate compares two column values as is done with joins, or a column value and a literal as is done when filtering rows, it is important for the data types to match. When

the data types do not match, the DBMS must convert one of them before performing the comparison, and while the work to do this is relatively small, it mounts quickly when it has to be done for each row in a large table.

- **Use IN instead of OR when possible.** The IN operator can be rewritten as a JOIN, but the OR operator often requires multiple queries to be run with the results combined by the DBMS. The former is far more efficient.

- **Use GROUP BY instead of DISTINCT.** In most DBMSs, a GROUP BY is a more efficient way to eliminate duplicate rows compared with the DISTINCT keyword. The reason for this is that a GROUP BY invokes the sort required to find the duplicates earlier in the processing of the query, while a DISTINCT applies the sort as the very last step (applied to the final result set). The sooner the duplicate rows are eliminated, the more efficiently the remainder of the processing on that result set can be performed.

- **Use hints if you must.** *Hints* are special syntax that can be placed in the SQL statement to direct the optimizer to take certain actions, such as forcing the use of a particular index or a particular method to join tables. While this can be a very attractive option, it should only be used as a last resort because hints are not portable across database vendors, and they sometimes stop working when the DBMS software is upgraded to a newer version. The Oracle, MySQL, and Microsoft SQL Server optimizers all respond to hints, but the syntax accepted by each is different.

- **Temporary tables may help.** Temporary tables can help in some situations, such as assembling large result sets and then adding an index or two to support multiple subsequent queries against the temporary table. However, remember that you're doubling up the reads and writes when you do this because all the data selected from the original (base) tables must be written to the temporary table(s) and then read back from there. In short, there are no free lunches.

- **Views may help.** Views can help because they hide complex operations such as nested aggregate functions. And with DBMSs that don't have an SQL statement cache, views may process more efficiently than ordinary queries because the SQL statement that defines the view has already been parsed and optimized, which means this work does not have to be done every time the view is accessed. But above all, remember that views are also SQL queries, so they are subject to all the tuning considerations you apply to any SQL statement.

Use Indexes Wisely

Indexes can greatly improve data access times. However, always keep in mind that indexes take up storage space and they have to be maintained. Here are some considerations related to the use of indexes to improve query performance:

- **Avoid indexes on frequently updated columns.**   Creating an index on a column that is frequently updated doubles up the amount of writes required when the column is updated. Always remember that when column data is updated, the DBMS must also update any indexes that include that column.

- **Create only selective indexes.**   *Index selectivity* is a ratio of the number of distinct values a column has divided by the number of rows in a table. For example, if a table has 1000 rows and a column has 800 distinct values, the selectivity of the index is 0.8, which is considered good. However, a column such as gender that only has two distinct values (M and F) has very poor selectivity (.002 in this case). Unique indexes always have a selectivity ratio of 1.0, which is the best possible. A good rule of thumb is to avoid indexes with a selectivity of less than 0.33 unless they are indexes especially designed for low selectivity such as bit-map indexes.

- **Foreign key indexes improve joins.**   With most optimizers, an index on a foreign key column greatly improves join performance, and it can enable additional join methods for the optimizer to use.

- **Index columns frequently used in predicates.**   For large tables, every query should contain a WHERE predicate that references an indexed column. Therefore, it is best to find the columns that are most frequently referenced by predicates and to index them.

- **Don't overindex.**   As a rule of thumb, don't create more than three or four indexes for any table. As already stated, indexes take up storage and must be maintained. Too many indexes on a table can cripple the performance of an INSERT or UPDATE issued against that table.

- **Avoid overlapping indexes.**   Nearly every RDBMS can use an index even when the WHERE predicate references only the first column of the index. Therefore, overlapping indexes (those that have the same leading column) are redundant and unnecessary.

- **Consider unique indexes.**   With some RDBMSs, such as DB2, unique indexes are so superior that DBAs often add otherwise unnecessary columns to an index just to make it unique.

- **Drop indexes for bulk loads.**   For mass loads of data into a table, consider dropping some of the indexes and re-creating them after the load is complete. This can save a substantial amount of time in some DBMSs.

MySQL Considerations

Here are a few tuning considerations that are particular to the MySQL DBMS:

- **Storage engine** MySQL has a unique feature that provides multiple storage engines, one of which may be selected for each new table. These storage engines include MyISAM (a replacement for the original ISAM), HEAP, MERGE, InnoDB, and BDB (Berkeley DB). The differences are too involved to explain here, but there are several chapters of the MySQL Reference Manual devoted to them. Suffice it to say that the choice of storage engine has a profound effect on the optimizer and the performance of SQL statements issued against the table.

- **Hash indexes** MySQL supports hash indexes where the data values are sent through a hashing algorithm before being added to the index. While this technique scatters sequentially assigned values so new rows of data end up more uniformly spread out in the index, hash indexes have the disadvantage of not being useful as a replacement for sorts because the index entries are not in key sequence.

Oracle Considerations

This section covers some tuning considerations that are specific to Oracle databases.

Oracle Index Considerations

Oracle provides some additional indexing options that are worth consideration:

- **Function-based indexes** Normally a predicate such as WHERE UPPER(MOVIE_TITLE) LIKE 'BIG%' precludes the use of an index. However, Oracle allows an index to be created on a function, such as UPPER(MOVIE_TITLE), which then is usable for queries that reference the function. There are several prerequisites for the use of this option, so you may need some help from your Oracle DBA before you can use it. The syntax for a function-based index simply uses the function specification instead of the column name in the ON clause of the CREATE INDEX statement:

```
CREATE INDEX IX_MOVIE_TITLE_UPPER
  ON MOVIE (UPPER(MOVIE_TITLE));
```

- **Bit-map indexes** Oracle bit-map indexes are designed to handle columns where the cardinality is low (that is, where there are relatively few data values among many rows). A *bit-map index* contains records that have one bit for every row in the indexed table and one index record for every possible data value in the indexed column. A bit is "on" (a binary 1) if the corresponding row in the table contains the value that the index record represents, and "off" (a binary 0) if not. For example, if the MOVIE table contained 5000 rows and you built a bit-map index on the MPAA_RATING_CODE column, the index would contain records that were 5000 bits (roughly 625 bytes) in size, and there would be 6 such records (one for each value of MPAA_RATING_CODE). The first index record would represent the first MPAA_RATING_CODE value ("G") and bits in that record would be "on" when the corresponding row in the MOVIE table had a rating of "G". The DBMS can use matrix algebra to quickly find desired data rows, particularly when the search predicates reference multiple columns that have bit-map indexes. A bit-map index is created using the normal CREATE INDEX syntax with the keyword BITMAP used instead of the keyword UNIQUE:

```
CREATE BITMAP INDEX IX_MOVIE_MPAA_RATING
   ON MOVIE (MPAA_RATING_CODE);
```

- **Index organized tables**   It's a good practice to create an index on the primary key of every table. However, for tables with only a few columns, such as reference tables and small intersection tables, this always seems wasteful because most or all of the data in the table is repeated in the index. Oracle provides a nice solution that allows the entire table to be stored in the index. Essentially, an index organized table (IOT) is a primary key index and a table rolled into a single structure. While you can create additional indexes on an IOT, in those cases you might be better off using a conventional table. Here is an example that creates a reference table for media formats as an IOT:

```
CREATE TABLE MEDIA_FORMAT (
   MEDIA_FORMAT_CODE    CHAR(1),
   MEDIA_FORMAT_DESC    VARCHAR(50),
   CONSTRAINT PK_MEDIA_FORMAT
      PRIMARY KEY (MEDIA_FORMAT_CODE))
   ORGANIZATION INDEX;
```

Using EXPLAIN PLAN

In Oracle, the SQL EXPLAIN PLAN statement analyzes an SQL statement and posts analysis results to a special plan table. The plan table must be created exactly as specified by Oracle, so it is best to use the script they provide for this purpose, which can be found under the Oracle Home directory as /RDBMS/ADMIN/

catplan.sql. After running the EXPLAIN PLAN statement, you must then retrieve the results from the plan table using a SELECT statement. Fortunately, Oracle's Enterprise Manager has a GUI version available that makes query tuning a lot easier.

Here is an example of an EXPLAIN PLAN statement:

```
EXPLAIN PLAN
  SET STATEMENT_ID = 'STMT_1'
 FOR
  SELECT MOVIE_ID,
         MOVIE_GENRE.MOVIE_GENRE_DESCRIPTION AS GENRE,
         MOVIE.MPAA_RATING_CODE AS RATING,
         MPAA_RATING.MPAA_RATING_DESCRIPTION AS RATING_DESC
    FROM MOVIE
         JOIN MOVIE_GENRE ON MOVIE.MOVIE_GENRE_CODE =
                             MOVIE_GENRE.MOVIE_GENRE_CODE
         JOIN MPAA_RATING ON MOVIE.MPAA_RATING_CODE =
                             MPAA_RATING.MPAA_RATING_CODE
  WHERE MOVIE_ID < 6
  ORDER BY MOVIE_ID;

Explained.
```

NOTE:

- *STATEMENT_ID is any character string that the statement author wishes to use to identify the explain results. This feature allows multiple explains to be run with the STATEMENT_ID as the identifier that keeps the information about each execution plan separate in the plan table.*

- *The statement to be explained follows the FOR keyword and can be any valid SQL statement.*

- *When the EXPLAIN PLAN statement is run, the SQL statement is not actually executed. Instead of a result set containing rows of data, only the message "Explained." is returned to the user. This indicates that the explain plan information has been successfully written to the plan table.*

Following is the statement commonly used to retrieve and display the execution plan. It is a complex SQL statement, but the only thing that has to be changed when it is run is the STATEMENT_ID. The CONNECT BY clause is an Oracle proprietary SQL extension that joins a recursive relationship in a table through all iterations (from child to parent to grandparent, and so forth). This SQL was included here to illustrate one method of viewing explain plan results. As mentioned before, there is also a GUI tool in Oracle's Enterprise Manager.

```
SELECT rtrim(substr(LPAD(' ',2*(LEVEL-1))||operation,1,30))||' '
                ||rtrim(options)||' '||rtrim(object_name)|| ' '
                ||'(cost= '||cost||', cardinality='||cardinality||')'
                "Query Plan"
    FROM plan_table
  START WITH id = 0
          AND upper(statement_id) = upper('STMT_1')
CONNECT BY PRIOR id = parent_id
          AND upper(statement_id) = upper('STMT_1');

Query Plan
------------------------------------------------
SELECT STATEMENT    (cost= 10, cardinality=5)
  SORT ORDER BY  (cost= 10, cardinality=5)
    HASH JOIN    (cost= 9, cardinality=5)
      MERGE JOIN    (cost= 5, cardinality=5)
        TABLE ACCESS BY INDEX ROWID MPAA_RATING
                      (cost= 2, cardinality=6)
          INDEX FULL SCAN SYS_C005440
                      (cost= 1, cardinality=6)
        SORT JOIN  (cost= 3, cardinality=5)
          TABLE ACCESS BY INDEX ROWID MOVIE
                      (cost= 2, cardinality=5)
            INDEX RANGE SCAN SYS_C005449
                      (cost= 1, cardinality=5)
      TABLE ACCESS FULL MOVIE_GENRE
                      (cost= 3, cardinality=16)

10 rows selected.
```

Here are some key points regarding the query plan that appears in the result set:

- The indentation shows the order of execution, with the innermost steps being performed first.

- The cost values show a relative cost. The numbers have no meaning beyond their relative differences. For example, a cost of 10 represents a step that uses twice the resources of a step that has a cost of 5.

- The cardinality values show the estimated number of rows that are processed by the step.

- "TABLE ACCESS FULL" indicates a full table scan where all rows in the table are read sequentially.

- "INDEX RANGE SCAN" indicates the scan of a portion of the rows in an index.

- "TABLE ACCESS BY INDEX" indicates access to a table using the index shown.

- The sorts and joins should be self evident by the step names.

Microsoft SQL Server Considerations

This section covers some tuning considerations that are specific to Microsoft SQL Server databases.

SQL Server Query Performance Considerations

Here are some considerations for running queries in Microsoft SQL Server databases:

- **Access via stored procedures.** Placing frequently used SQL queries in stored procedures can yield significant performance gains. In fact, in older versions of Microsoft SQL Server, it was essential to do so in order to achieve reasonable performance because there was no SQL cache to hold recently used SQL statements. In SQL Server 2005, the SQL cache allows the DBMS to recognize a statement similar to one that has already been run and to bypass statement preparation and optimization steps when the statement is reused from the cache. Nonetheless, any statement that is accessed through a stored procedure is precompiled and optimized, so it will always perform well (even if it is not found in the cache at the time it is run). This is one reason why seasoned developers strive to do most or all of their SQL Server database access using stored procedures.

- **Avoid nulls in unique indexes.** Unlike most other SQL implementations, unique indexes in SQL Server do not handle null column values well. You can define a unique index that includes a column that is allowed to be null, but the second index entry that contains a null is considered a duplicate of the first, and therefore results in a duplicate key error. Most other SQL implementations avoid this issue by not indexing null values.

- **Consider clustered indexes.** A *clustered index* causes the table rows to be physically ordered by the indexed column(s). This can help considerably in search and join operations, but it's at the expense of table maintenance, particularly when new rows force existing rows to be moved to maintain their sequence.

Displaying Execution Plans Using SQL Query Analyzer

Microsoft provides a facility for explaining query execution plans just as Oracle and DB2 do. In Microsoft SQL Server 2000, the SQL Query Analyzer tool has a button labeled "Display Estimated Execution Plan" that graphically displays how the SQL statement will be executed. This feature is also accessible from the Query menu item as the option Show Execution Plan. These items may have different names in other versions of Microsoft SQL Server. In SQL Server 2005, there does not appear to be a tool called SQL Query Analyzer, and it is not clear what the tool will be called when the product is formally released.

In the Query Analyzer tool, the default mode is Object Browser. To display an execution plan, click the Display Estimated Execution Plan icon or press CTRL-L. The execution plan is displayed graphically as shown in Figure 11-1. Each step is shown as an icon and the number near the icon shows the percentage of the total query cost that applies to that step. You can place your cursor pointer over any icon to see a pop-up window showing more detailed information for that step.

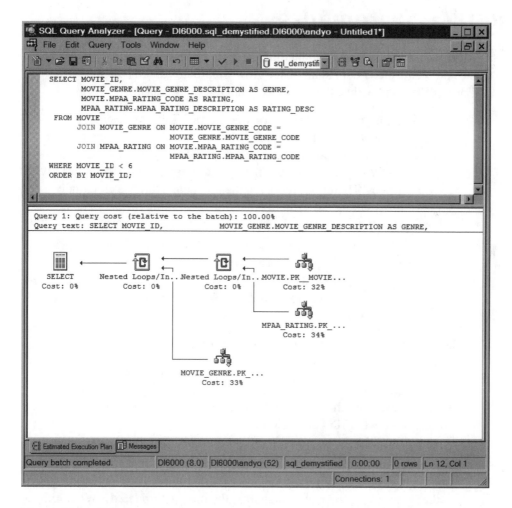

Figure 11-1   SQL Query Analyzer output

DB2 UDB Considerations

Like Oracle and Microsoft SQL Server, DB2 also provides a utility to display query execution plans. IBM provides a script called EXPLAIN.DDL that creates the tables needed to hold the output of the explain facility. Once the explain tables are created, the explain facility can be used to create execution plans for queries, and the plans can then be displayed using either Visual Explain in the Control Center or by querying the explain tables using SQL.

Tuning DML Statements

DML (Data Manipulation Language) statements generally produce fewer performance problems than query statements. However, there can be issues.

For INSERT statements, there are two main considerations:

- **Ensuring adequate free space for new rows**   Tablespaces that are short on space present problems as the DBMS searches for free space to hold rows being inserted. Moreover, inserts do not usually put rows into the table in primary key sequence because there usually isn't free space in exactly the right places. Therefore, reorganizing the table, which is essentially a process of unloading the rows to a flat file, re-creating the table, and then reloading the table can improve both insert and query performance.

- **Index maintenance**   Every time a row is inserted into a table, a corresponding entry must be inserted into every index built on the table (although null values are usually not indexed). The more indexes, the more overhead every insert will require. Index free space can usually be tuned just as table free space can.

UPDATE statements have the following considerations:

- **Index maintenance**   If columns that are indexed are updated, the corresponding index entries must also be updated. In general, updating primary key values has particularly bad performance implications, so much so that some RDBMSs prohibit them.

- **Row expansion**   When columns are updated in such a way that the row grows significantly in size, the row may no longer fit in its original location, and there may not be free space around the row for it to expand in place (other rows might be right up against the one just updated). When this occurs, the row must either be moved to another location in the data file where it will fit or be split with the expanded part of the row placed in a new location, connected to the original location by a pointer. Both of these situations are not only expensive when they occur but are also detrimental to the performance of subsequent queries that touch those rows. Table reorganizations can resolve the issue, but it's better to prevent the problem by designing the application so that rows tend not to grow in size after they are inserted.

DELETE statements are the least likely to present performance issues. However, a table that participates as a parent in a relationship that is defined with the ON DELETE CASCADE option can perform poorly if there are many child rows to delete. Moreover, index maintenance also comes into play here because index entries must be removed for any deleted rows.

Quiz

Choose the correct responses to each of the multiple-choice questions. Note that there may be more than one correct response to each question.

1. Performance requirements
   a. Should be set after the SQL statements are tuned
   b. Provide a way to identify statements that need tuning
   c. Are best when they contain complex criteria
   d. Provide a way to know when to stop tweaking a query
   e. Are developed just to make the auditors happy

2. Disk reads and writes can be minimized by
   a. Allocating buffers of sufficient size
   b. Placing all the database files on one disk drive
   c. Putting the entire database in memory
   d. Adding indexes for all the important table columns
   e. Spreading files across all available disk drives

3. The computer system can be tuned by
   a. Collecting database statistics
   b. Applying available security patches
   c. Selecting fast and reliable hardware

    d. Following the DBMS tuning recommendations

    e. Consulting a tuning guide for the operating system

4. Efficient table design includes

    a. Using VARCHAR for all variable-length character columns

    b. Using the smallest possible numeric data type that holds the data values

    c. Using triggers whenever possible

    d. Using identical data types for primary keys and their matching foreign keys

    e. Using identical data types for all primary key columns

5. A query execution plan

    a. Describes how the DBMS will execute a query

    b. Is stored in the SQL cache

    c. Is created using the explain plan feature of the RDBMS

    d. Requires a plan table to hold the explain results

    e. Requires the use of a stored procedure

6. The query optimizer

    a. Creates a query execution plan in the plan table

    b. Determines the best way to execute an SQL statement

    c. May use statistics gathered from the database

    d. May use rules applied to the way the statement was written

    e. Can be cost-based or rule-based

7. In order to design proper queries, the developer should

    a. Know the characteristics of the data in the database

    b. Match data types in predicates

    c. Use hints as much as possible

    d. Avoid unnecessary tables and columns

    e. Maximize the number of rows in each result set

8. Table scans can be avoided by

    a. Including a WHERE clause that references an indexed column

    b. Using GROUP BY instead of DISTINCT

    c. Making sure that statistics are up to date

d. Making at least one predicate references the leading column of an index

    e. Avoiding unnecessary columns

9. An index cannot be used when

    a. The WHERE clause references the second column of an index

    b. A LIKE clause references a comparison string that contains a wildcard (except in the first position of the string)

    c. The NOT operator is used in a predicate

    d. An SQL function is included in a column comparison (except when they match a function-based index)

    e. The NOT EQUAL operator is used in a predicate

10. Considerations for using indexes include

    a. Placing indexes on all frequently updated columns

    b. Placing indexes on foreign key columns

    c. Avoiding overlapping indexes

    d. Creating indexes on columns that have only a few possible values

    e. Avoiding unique indexes

11. Tuning considerations for MySQL include

    a. Function-based indexes

    b. Hash indexes

    c. Clustering indexes

    d. Storage engine options

    e. Bit-map indexes

12. Tuning considerations for Oracle include

    a. Function-based indexes

    b. Hash indexes

    c. Clustering indexes

    d. Storage engine options

    e. Bit-map indexes

13. Tuning considerations for Microsoft SQL Server include

    a. Function-based indexes

    b. Hash indexes

   c. Clustering indexes

   d. Storage engine options

   e. Bit-map indexes

14. An explain plan in Oracle

   a. Requires the use of a plan table

   b. Contains a PLAN_ID to uniquely identify it

   c. Can be viewed using Enterprise Manager

   d. Can be viewed with SQL by selecting it from the plan table

   e. Is created using the CREATE PLAN statement

15. An execution plan in Microsoft SQL Server

   a. Requires the use of a plan table

   b. Can be displayed using an option in SQL Query Analyzer

   c. Displays the execution plan in a text format

   d. Displays the execution plan in a graphical format

   e. Can be viewed with SQL by selecting it from the plan table

16. When tuning INSERT statements, one should consider

   a. Index maintenance

   b. Row expansion

   c. The CASCADE option

   d. Adequate free space

   e. Query rewrites

17. When tuning UPDATE statements, one should consider

   a. Index maintenance

   b. Row expansion

   c. The CASCADE option

   d. Adequate free space

   e. Query rewrites

18. When tuning DELETE statements, one should consider

   a. Index maintenance

   b. Row expansion

   c. The CASCADE option

d. Adequate free space

    e. Query rewrites

19. Data types should match

    a. For all primary key columns

    b. Between primary key and corresponding secondary key columns

    c. Between primary key and corresponding foreign key columns

    d. Between column values and literal values compared in predicates

    e. For all function-based indexes

20. The most likely cause of query performance problems is

    a. A poorly tuned operating system

    b.   A poorly written SQL statement

    c. Trigger overhead

    d. Index maintenance overhead

    e. Row expansion

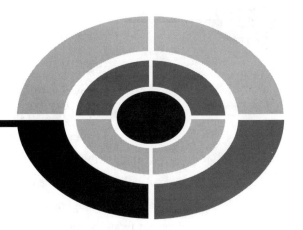

Final Exam

Choose the correct responses to each of the multiple-choice questions. Note that there may be more than one correct response to each question.

1. SQL is a language
   a. Used to define Entity Relationship Diagrams
   b. Used to define web pages
   c. Invented by Dr. E.F. Codd
   d. Used to communicate with relational databases
   e. Used to define and modify database objects

2. A database is
   a. Software provided by the database vendor
   b. A collection of interrelated data items that are managed as a single unit
   c. A named data structure such as a table, view, or index
   d. Defined in the same way by all software vendors
   e. Implemented differently by different vendors

3. A database object is

   a. Software provided by the database vendor

   b. A collection of related records that are stored as a single unit

   c. A named data structure such as a table, view, or index

   d. Defined in the same way by all software vendors

   e. A collection of interrelated data items that are managed as a single unit

4. A database management system is

   a. Software provided by the database vendor

   b. A collection of interrelated data items that are managed as a single unit

   c. Often abbreviated as DBMS

   d. A structure such as a table, view, or index

   e. A named data structure such as a table, view, or index

5. Basic services provided by the DBMS include

   a. Moving data to and from the physical files as needed

   b. Storage of data in tabular form

   c. Security mechanisms to prevent unauthorized data access and modification

   d. Generation of Entity Relationship Diagrams

   e. Support of a query language

6. Components of a relational database include

   a. ERDs

   b. Indexes

   c. Tables

   d. Relationships

   e. Constraints

7. In an ERD, maximum cardinality is shown with

   a. The notation "<pk>" above the relationship line

   b. A "crow's foot" on an end of the relationship line

   c. A circle drawn on the relationship line

   d. A vertical line drawn across the relationship line

   e. No symbol on the end of the relationship line

8. Types of database constraints include

   a. NOT NULL

   b. Unique

   c. Primary key

   d. CHECK

   e. Relationship

9. Normalization is intended to solve the following problems:

   a. Slow performance

   b. Creation anomaly

   c. Insert anomaly

   d. Delete anomaly

   e. Update anomaly

10. To be in third normal form, a relation

    a. Must have a unique identifier

    b. Must have no transitive dependencies

    c. Must have no repeating groups or multivalued attributes

    d. Must be in first normal form

    e. Must be in second normal form

11. SQL

    a. May be pronounced as the word "sequel"

    b. May be pronounced as the letters S-Q-L

    c. May be used to communicate with any database

    d. May be used to communicate with relational databases

    e. May be used to populate web pages with data

12. SQL is

    a. A standard language

    b. A nonprocedural language

    c. A procedural language

    d. An object-oriented language

    e. A declarative language

13. SQL statements

    a. Begin with a delimiter such as a semicolon

    b. End with a delimiter such as a semicolon

    c. Begin with a left parenthesis

    d. Begin with a command keyword

    e. End with a command keyword

14. SQL language elements include

    a. Keywords

    b. Database object names

    c. Constraints

    d. Constants

    e. Operators

15. SQL statements may be divided into the following categories:

    a. Data Definition Language (DDL)

    b. Data Control Language (DCL)

    c. Data Manipulation Language (DML)

    d. Data Selection Language (DSL)

    e. Data Replication Language (DRL)

16. Data Definition Language (DDL) includes the following statements:

    a. CREATE

    b. ALTER

    c. SELECT

    d. UPDATE

    e. DELETE

17. Data Query Language (DQL) includes the following statements:

    a. CREATE

    b. ALTER

    c. SELECT

    d. UPDATE

    e. DELETE

18. Data Manipulation Language (DML) includes the following statements:
    a. CREATE
    b. ALTER
    c. SELECT
    d. UPDATE
    e. DELETE

19. SQL was first developed
    a. By IBM
    b. By ANSI
    c. In the 1980s
    d. In the 1970s
    e. Based on ANSI standards

20. Standard numeric types include
    a. BOOLEAN
    b. INTERVAL
    c. NUMBER
    d. INTEGER
    e. FLOAT

21. Standard temporal data types include
    a. TIMESTAMP
    b. TIMEZONE
    c. TIME
    d. DATETIME
    e. DATE

22. NULL values
    a. Are equal to other NULL values
    b. Are not equal to other NULL values
    c. Are the same as blanks (spaces)
    d. Can be used to represent missing or unknown data values
    e. Are always allowed by default

23. The column definition in the CREATE TABLE statement may include
    a. A DEFAULT clause
    b. A NULL or NOT NULL clause
    c. The table name
    d. A table constraint
    e. The column name

24. A table column name
    a. Must be unique within the database
    b. Must be unique within the table
    c. Must be specified in the CREATE TABLE statement
    d. Must be specified in the ALTER TABLE statement
    e. May only be named in one index

25. A column constraint
    a. Can be used anywhere a table constraint can be used
    b. May reference one or more columns
    c. Uses syntax that is identical or nearly identical to a table constraint of the same type
    d. May be included in either a CREATE TABLE or ALTER TABLE statement
    e. Has syntax that varies little from one constraint type to another

26. The correct syntax for a DEFAULT clause is
    a. DEFAULT [UNIQUE | PRIMARY KEY]
    b. DEFAULT [NULL | NOT NULL]
    c. DEFAULT (*precision, scale*)
    d. DEFAULT (*expression*)
    e. DEFAULT (*column_name*) REFERENCES *table_name* (*column_name*)

27. The correct syntax for a NOT NULL constraint is
    a. *column_name* REFERENCES NOT NULL
    b. *column_name data_type* NOT NULL
    c. *column_name data_type* IS NOT NULL
    d. CREATE NOT NULL INDEX ON *column_name*
    e. DEFAULT [NULL | NOT NULL]

28. The correct syntax for a UNIQUE CONSTRAINT is

    a. DEFAULT UNIQUE (*column_name*)

    b. *column_name* REFERENCES UNIQUE *table_name*

    c. [CONSTRAINT *constraint_name*] UNIQUE (*column_name*)

    d. [CONSTRAINT *constraint_name*] UNIQUE (*table_name*)

    e. DEFAULT [UNIQUE | PRIMARY KEY]

29. The correct syntax for a REFERENTIAL CONSTRAINT is

    a. REFERENCES *table_name* (*column_name*)

    b. *column_name* REFERENCES UNIQUE *table_name*

    c. [CONSTRAINT *constraint_name*] REFERENCES *index_name*

    d. [CONSTRAINT *constraint_name*] REFERENCES *table_name*

    e. FOREIGN KEY *column_name* REFERENCES *table_name* (*column_ name*)

30. The DROP statement can be used to drop a

    a. Table column

    b. Table

    c. Referential constraint

    d. Index

    e. View

31. The UNION operator

    a. Is named JOIN in some SQL implementations

    b. Includes duplicate rows in the result set

    c. Eliminates duplicate rows in the result set

    d. Combines two queries into a single joined query

    e. Combines the result sets of two queries into a single result set

32. The proper syntax for eliminating null values in query results is

    a. = NULL

    b. IS NULL

    c. NOT = NULL

    d. IS NOT NULL

    e. <> NULL

33. An SQL statement containing an aggregate function

   a. Must contain a GROUP BY clause

   b. May not include both GROUP BY and ORDER BY clauses

   c. Must include an ORDER BY clause

   d. May also contain calculated columns

   e. May also contain ordinary columns

34. A subselect

   a. Must be enclosed in parentheses

   b. Is a powerful way of calculating columns

   c. May be corrugated or noncorrugated

   d. Allows for the flexible selection of rows

   e. May be used to select values to be applied to WHERE clause conditions

35. A join without a WHERE clause or JOIN clause

   a. Performs an outer join

   b. Performs an inner join

   c. Results in an error message

   d. Results in a Cartesian product

   e. Returns no rows in the result set

36. A selfjoin

   a. Can be either an inner or outer join

   b. Resolves recursive relationships

   c. Can never result in a Cartesian product

   d. Involves two different tables

   e. May use a subselect to further limit rows

37. A join

   a. Requires the use of a JOIN clause

   b. Requires a comma-separated table name list in the FROM clause

   c. Combines rows from multiple queries into a single query result

   d. Combines columns from two or more tables into a single query result

   e. Occurs whenever the FROM clause references more than one table

38. Column name qualifiers

   a. May be a column alias defined in the FROM clause

   b. May be a table alias defined in the FROM clause

   c. May be a table name

   d. Resolve ambiguous column references

   e. May be a number denoting the relative position of the table in the FROM list

39. A correlated subselect

   a. Has a nested select that references column values from the outer select

   b. Has a nested select that makes no reference to the column values in the outer select

   c. Runs more efficiently than a noncorrelated subselect

   d. Runs less efficiently than a noncorrelated subselect

   e. Has an outer select that references column values from the inner select

40. SQL functions

   a. Can be used in the WHERE clause of an SQL statement

   b. Can be used as a table name alias in an SQL statement

   c. Can be used in the column list of an SQL statement

   d. Return a set of values

   e. Return a single value

41. The RTRIM function

   a. Removes trailing spaces from character strings

   b. Removes leading spaces from character strings

   c. Can be nested with other functions

   d. Replaces null values with other values in character strings

   e. Removes both leading and trailing spaces from character strings

42. CASE expressions

   a. Come in two forms named static and dynamic

   b. Come in two forms named simple and searched

   c. Come in two forms named standard and searched

   d. Come in two forms named searched and nonsearched

   e. Allow for conditional execution of clauses within an SQL statement

43. A DML statement may reference

    a. View columns that come from multiple tables

    b. View columns that come from a single table

    c. Columns from multiple tables

    d. Columns from a single table

    e. A view that contains columns from only one table

44. When forming DML statements, the following types of constraints must be considered:

    a. Referential constraints

    b. Primary key constraints

    c. NOT NULL constraints

    d. Unique constraints

    e. Security constraints

45. An INSERT statement with a VALUES clause

    a. May use the keyword NULL to assign null values to columns

    b. Can insert multiple rows with one statement execution

    c. Must have a column list

    d. Must have a values list

    e. May include a WHERE clause

46. An UPDATE statement without a WHERE clause

    a. Fails with an error condition

    b. Results in a Cartesian product

    c. Updates all rows in the table to null values

    d. Attempts to update every row in the table

    e. Deletes all rows in the table

47. An UPDATE statement

    a. Must include a WHERE clause

    b. May set a column to the value of another column

    c. May set columns of multiple tables to new values

    d. Must include a SET clause

    e. Must provide a new value for at least one column

48. A DELETE statement

    a. May include an optional WHERE clause

    b. May use the FORCE keyword to force deletion of rows

    c. May include an optional column list

    d. Cannot violate any referential constraints on the table

    e. May have a nested SELECT as part of the WHERE clause

49. The SET clause in an UPDATE statement may assign a value to a column that is

    a. A list of values

    b. A constant

    c. Another column name

    d. Any expression that yields a single value

    e. The NULL keyword

50. Security is necessary because

    a. Honest people make mistakes

    b. Databases connected to the Internet are vulnerable

    c. 80 percent of fraud is committed by outside hackers

    d. Application security controls alone are inadequate

    e. Security controls keep people honest

51. Intruders who attempt to penetrate systems connected to the Internet include

    a. Disgruntled employees

    b. Spies from competitors

    c. Bank auditors

    d. Web bloggers

    e. Hackers

52. Components that must be secured include

    a. Networks

    b. Operating systems

    c. Servers

    d. Client workstations

    e. Databases

53. System privileges

    a. Are specific to a database object

    b. Vary across databases from different vendors

    c. Are granted in a similar way in Oracle, Sybase, and Microsoft SQL Server

    d. Are rescinded using the SQL REMOVE statement

    e. Allow the grantee to perform certain administrative functions on the server, such as shutting it down

54. Object privileges

    a. Are specific to a database object

    b. Allow the grantee to perform certain administrative functions on the server, such as shutting it down

    c. Are granted in a similar way in Oracle, Sybase, and Microsoft SQL Server

    d. Are granted using the SQL GRANT statement

    e. Are rescinded using the SQL REMOVE statement

55. Using the WITH GRANT OPTION when granting object privileges

    a. Is a highly recommended practice because it is so convenient to use

    b. Will cascade if the privilege is subsequently revoked

    c. Gives the grantee DBA privileges on the entire database

    d. Allows the grantee to grant the privilege to others

    e. Can lead to security issues

56. Roles

    a. May exist before users do

    b. May contain any number of object privileges

    c. May contain only one object privilege

    d. May be assigned to only one user

    e. May be shared by many users

57. Potential downsides of using roles for security include

    a. They are dropped when the user is dropped

    b. They are dropped when the privilege is dropped

    c. They can be granted without consideration for all the privileges they contain

    d. They are more difficult to administer than individual privileges

    e. Additional training time is required for administrators who must use them

58. Views may assist with security policy implementation by

    a. Storing database audit results

    b. Restricting table rows to which a user has access

    c. Restricting the table columns to which a user has access

    d. Restricting the databases to which a user has access

    e. Monitoring for database intruders

59. A transaction

    a. Changes the database from one consistent state to another

    b. Has properties described by the ACID acronym

    c. May not be partially processed

    d. May be partially processed

    e. Is sometimes called a *unit of work*

60. The process that backs out changes made by a failed transaction is called

    a. Recovery

    b. Savepoint creation

    c. Transaction logging

    d. Commit

    e. Rollback

61. The process that makes transaction changes permanent is called

    a. Recovery

    b. Savepoint creation

    c. Transaction logging

    d. Commit

    e. Rollback

62. Support for transactions in relational databases includes

    a. Distributed database management

    b. Logging each transaction in the transaction log

    c. Identifying the beginning of each transaction

    d. Identifying the end of each transaction

    e. Periodic database backups

63. The amount of data held by a lock (lock granularity) can be a

    a. Column

    b. Row

    c. Table

    d. Block or page

    e. Database

64. The concurrent update problem

    a. Cannot occur when AUTOCOMMIT is set to ON

    b. Occurs when two database users submit conflicting SELECT statements

    c. Occurs when two database users make conflicting updates to the same data

    d. Is a consequence of simultaneous data sharing

    e. Is the reason that transaction locking must be supported

65. A lock

    a. May cause contention when other users attempt to update locked data

    b. May have levels and an escalation protocol in some RDBMS products

    c. Has a timeout set in DB2 and some other RDBMS products

    d. Is a control placed on data to reserve it so that the user may update it

    e. Is usually released when a COMMIT or ROLLBACK takes place

66. A deadlock

    a. Can theoretically put two or more users in an endless lock wait state

    b. Is a lock that has timed out and is therefore no longer needed

    c. May be resolved by deadlock detection on some RDBMSs

    d. May be resolved by lock timeouts on some RDBMSs

    e. Occurs when two database users each request a lock on data that is locked by the other

67. A cursor is

    a. A pointer into a result set

    b. The same as a result set

    c. A method to analyze the performance of SQL statements

    d. The collection of rows returned by a database query

    e. A buffer that holds rows retrieved from the database

68. A result set is

    a. A pointer into a cursor

    b. A method to analyze the performance of SQL statements

    c. The same as a cursor

    d. A buffer that holds rows retrieved from the database

    e. The collection of rows returned by a database query

69. Before rows may be fetched from a cursor, the cursor must first be

    a. Opened

    b. Closed

    c. Deallocated

    d. Declared

    e. Committed

70. Cursors are

    a. Included in the Oracle PL/SQL language

    b. Included in the Sybase Transact-SQL language

    c. Included in the Microsoft Transact-SQL language

    d. Intended to overcome the mismatch between the way object-oriented languages and relational databases handle query results

    e. Intended to overcome the mismatch between the way procedural languages and relational databases handle query results

71. The cursor name is included in

    a. The OPEN statement

    b. The FETCH statement

    c. The CLOSE statement

    d. The DECLARE CURSOR statement

    e. The SELECT statement

72. A cursor OPEN statement

    a. Must include an INTO clause

    b. Must include the cursor name

    c. Must include the table name(s)

    d. May cause the query to be run and some rows placed in the result set

    e. Always causes the query to be run and the result set to be filled with data

73. ODBC is

   a. A Microsoft standard

   b. Independent of any particular language, operating system, or DBMS

   c. A standard API for connecting to DBMSs

   d. Flexible in handling proprietary SQL

   e. Used by Java programs

74. JDBC is

   a. A Microsoft standard

   b. Independent of any particular language, operating system, or DBMS

   c. A standard API for connecting to DBMSs

   d. Flexible in handling proprietary SQL

   e. Used by Java programs

75. A trigger is

   a. Written in a nonprocedural language

   b. Written in a procedural language

   c. Stored in the database

   d. Executed only when called

   e. Executed automatically based on an event in the database

76. A stored procedure is

   a. Written in a nonprocedural language

   b. Written in a procedural language

   c. Stored in the database

   d. Executed only when called

   e. Executed automatically based on an event in the database

77. Performance requirements

   a. Provide a way to know when to stop tweaking a query

   b. Are best when they contain complex criteria

   c. Should be set after the SQL statements are tuned

   d. Provide a way to identify statements that need tuning

   e. Are developed just to make the auditors happy

78. Disk reads and writes can be minimized by

    a. Placing all the database files on one disk drive

    b. Putting the entire database in memory

    c. Spreading files across all available disk drives

    d. Allocating buffers of sufficient size

    e. Adding indexes for all the important table columns

79. Efficient table design includes

    a. Using identical data types for primary keys and their matching foreign keys

    b. Using identical data types for all primary key columns

    c. Using triggers whenever possible

    d. Using VARCHAR for all variable-length character columns

    e. Using the smallest possible numeric data type that holds the data values

80. The query optimizer

    a. May use statistics gathered from the database

    b. May use rules applied to the way the statement was written

    c. Can be cost-based or rule-based

    d. Creates a query execution plan in the plan table

    e. Determines the best way to execute an SQL statement

81. Table scans can be avoided by

    a. Making sure at least one predicate references the leading column of an index

    b. Avoiding unnecessary columns

    c. Using GROUP BY instead of DISTINCT

    d. Including a WHERE clause that references an indexed column

    e. Making sure that statistics are up to date

82. An index cannot be used when

    a. The NOT EQUAL operator is used in a predicate

    b. The NOT operator is used in a predicate

    c. An SQL function is included in a column comparison (except when they match a function-based index)

    d. The WHERE clause references the second column of an index

    e. A LIKE clause references a comparison string that contains a wildcard (except in the first position of the string)

83. Considerations for using indexes include

    a. Avoiding overlapping indexes

    b. Avoiding unique indexes

    c. Placing indexes on all frequently updated columns

    d. Placing indexes on foreign key columns

    e. Creating indexes on columns that have only a few possible values

Write the SQL statement for each of these problems.

84. Find all movies in the MOVIE table where the MPAA_RATING_CODE is either G, PG, or PG-13. Do not use an OR operator.

85. How many movies in the MOVIE table have a title that contains the word "of"? Make sure you handle cases where the word "of" is the first or last word of the title as well as a word in the middle of the title, and cases where it might be capitalized.

86. How many customer accounts are terminated, as indicated by a data value in the DATE_TERMINATED column?

87. Find the minimum and maximum values for the VHS price (RETAIL_PRICE_VHS) in the MOVIE table.

88. Find the average DVD price (RETAIL_PRICE_DVD) for each genre (MOVIE_GENRE_CODE) in the MOVIE table. Round the average price to two decimal places.

89. Use the SUM function to find the total of the CUSTOMER_DEPOSIT_AMOUNT column in the CUSTOMER_ACCOUNT table.

90. Use a subselect to list the Movie ID and Title of every movie that has been rented.

91. Use a join with the join predicate in the WHERE clause to list the Movie ID and Title of every movie that has been rented. Make sure that movies rented multiple times only show up once in the result set.

92. List the Title of each movie along with a count of the number of DVD format copies in the inventory.

93. List each Customer Account ID along with a count of the number of rentals made by the account.

94. Find the average price of a DVD movie (column RETAIL_PRICE_DVD in the MOVIE table), with the calculated average rounded down to the nearest whole dollar.

95. Find the ASCII character set value for a semicolon (;).

96. List the EMPLOYEE_TAX_ID values from the EMPLOYEE table, with hyphens (dashes) translated to spaces.

97. Write an SQL statement that lists each movie title with the DVD price (RETAIL_PRICE_DVD) categorized as follows: None (data value null or 0), Bargain (data value < 20), Moderate (data value >=20 and <30), and Premium (data value>=30).

98. Using an INSERT with a VALUES clause and a column list, insert a new row in the MOVIE table with the following data values:

MOVIE_ID	999
MOVIE_GENRE_CODE	Drama
MPAA_RATING_CODE	NR
MOVIE_TITLE	How the Database Was Won

99. Update the MOVIE table to increase all non-null DVD prices (RETAIL_PRICE_DVD) by 1.00.

100. Delete all rows in the MOVIE_GENRE table that are not referenced by any rows in the MOVIE table.

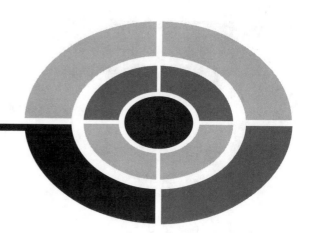

Answers to Quizzes and Final Exam

Chapter 1

1. b, d
2. c, e
3. a, b
4. c, d
5. a, b, c, d, e
6. a, c, d
7. a, b, e
8. c, d
9. a, c, d, e
10. b, c, d
11. a, d, e
12. b, d
13. a, c, e
14. b, d
15. a
16. c
17. a, b, c, d, e
18. b, d, e
19. a, c, d
20. b, e

Chapter 2

1. a, b, c, e
2. c, d, e
3. b, d
4. a, c, d

5. b, e
6. a, d
7. b, c, d
8. c, d, e
9. a, b
10. a, d
11. b, c, d, e
12. b, c, d
13. a, d
14. a, b, c, e
15. c
16. b, c, d
17. a, d, e
18. c, d
19. a
20. b, e

Chapter 3

1. b, d, e
2. a, b, e
3. d, e
4. a, c
5. b, c, e
6. a, d
7. a, b
8. b, d
9. b, d, e
10. a, c

11. b, c

12. c

13. b

14. a

15. d

16. b, e

17. a, c, e

18. a, b, d, e

19. a, c, e

20. b, c, e

Chapter 4

1. c

2. b, d

3. a, c

4. b, e

5. a, b

6. b, e

7. e

8. a, c, d

9. b, e

10. a, d

11.

```
SELECT MOVIE_TITLE
  FROM MOVIE
 WHERE MPAA_RATING_CODE <> 'R';
```

12.

```
SELECT MOVIE_TITLE, RETAIL_PRICE_DVD
  FROM MOVIE
 WHERE RETAIL_PRICE_DVD BETWEEN 19.99 AND 29.99;
```

13.

```
SELECT MOVIE_TITLE, MOVIE_GENRE_CODE, MPAA_RATING_CODE
  FROM MOVIE
 WHERE (MOVIE_GENRE_CODE = 'Comdy' AND
        MPAA_RATING_CODE = 'PG-13')
    OR (MOVIE_GENRE_CODE = 'Drama' AND
        MPAA_RATING_CODE = 'R');
```

14.

```
SELECT COUNT(*)
  FROM MOVIE_RENTAL
 WHERE LATE_OR_LOSS_FEE IS NULL;
```

15.

```
SELECT COUNT(*)
  FROM PERSON
 WHERE UPPER(PERSON_FAMILY_NAME) LIKE '%A%';
```

16.

```
SELECT MOVIE_TITLE
  FROM MOVIE
 WHERE UPPER(MOVIE_TITLE) LIKE '% THE %'
    OR UPPER(MOVIE_TITLE) LIKE 'THE %'
    OR UPPER(MOVIE_TITLE) LIKE '% THE';
```

17.

```
SELECT SUM(RENTAL_FEE) AS TOTAL_RENTAL_FEES
  FROM MOVIE_RENTAL;
```

18. For Oracle and DB2:

```
SELECT DISTINCT SUBSTR(PERSON_FAMILY_NAME,1,5)
  FROM PERSON;
```

For Microsoft SQL Server, Sybase Adaptive Server, and MySQL:

```
SELECT DISTINCT SUBSTRING(PERSON_FAMILY_NAME,1,5)
  FROM PERSON;
```

19.

```
SELECT MOVIE_GENRE_CODE,
       ROUND(AVG(RETAIL_PRICE_DVD),2) AS AVG_PRICE
  FROM MOVIE
 GROUP BY MOVIE_GENRE_CODE
```

20. For Oracle:

```
SELECT MOVIE_ID,
       SUM(RENTAL_FEE + NVL(LATE_OR_LOSS_FEE,0))
          AS TOTAL_FEES
  FROM MOVIE_RENTAL
 GROUP BY MOVIE_ID;
```

For Microsoft SQL Server and Sybase Adaptive Server:

```
SELECT MOVIE_ID,
       SUM(RENTAL_FEE + ISNULL(LATE_OR_LOSS_FEE,0))
          AS TOTAL_FEES
  FROM MOVIE_RENTAL
 GROUP BY MOVIE_ID;
```

For MySQL:

```
SELECT MOVIE_ID,
       SUM(RENTAL_FEE + IFNULL(LATE_OR_LOSS_FEE,0))
          AS TOTAL_FEES
  FROM MOVIE_RENTAL
 GROUP BY MOVIE_ID;
```

Chapter 5

1. a, e

2. e

3. b, d, e

4. b, c, d

5. a, c

6. b, d

7. a, b, e

8. b

9. a, c

10. b, c

11.

```
SELECT PERSON_GIVEN_NAME, PERSON_FAMILY_NAME,
       CUSTOMER_ACCOUNT_ID
```

```
     FROM PERSON JOIN CUSTOMER_ACCOUNT_PERSON
          USING (PERSON_ID)
    WHERE DEATH_DATE IS NOT NULL;
```

   or:

```
SELECT PERSON_GIVEN_NAME, PERSON_FAMILY_NAME,
       CUSTOMER_ACCOUNT_ID
  FROM PERSON A JOIN CUSTOMER_ACCOUNT_PERSON B
       ON A.PERSON_ID = B.PERSON_ID
 WHERE DEATH_DATE IS NOT NULL;
```

   12.

```
SELECT PERSON_GIVEN_NAME, PERSON_FAMILY_NAME
  FROM PERSON
    JOIN EMPLOYEE USING (PERSON_ID)
    JOIN CUSTOMER_ACCOUNT_PERSON USING (PERSON_ID);
```

   or:

```
SELECT PERSON_GIVEN_NAME, PERSON_FAMILY_NAME
  FROM PERSON A
    JOIN EMPLOYEE B ON A.PERSON_ID = B.PERSON_ID
    JOIN CUSTOMER_ACCOUNT_PERSON C
                  ON A.PERSON_ID = C.PERSON_ID;
```

   13.

```
SELECT PERSON_GIVEN_NAME, PERSON_FAMILY_NAME
  FROM PERSON
 WHERE PERSON_ID IN
       (SELECT PERSON_ID FROM EMPLOYEE)
   AND PERSON_ID IN
       (SELECT DISTINCT PERSON_ID
          FROM CUSTOMER_ACCOUNT_PERSON);
```

   14.

```
SELECT C.PERSON_FAMILY_NAME AS EMPLOYEE_NAME,
       D.PERSON_FAMILY_NAME AS SUPERVISOR_NAME
  FROM EMPLOYEE A
       JOIN EMPLOYEE B ON (A.SUPERVISOR_PERSON_ID =
                           B.PERSON_ID)
       JOIN PERSON C ON (A.PERSON_ID = C.PERSON_ID)
       JOIN PERSON D ON (B.PERSON_ID = D.PERSON_ID);
```

   15.

```
SELECT MEDIA_FORMAT, COUNT(*)
  FROM MOVIE_COPY
```

```
         JOIN MOVIE_RENTAL USING (MOVIE_ID, COPY_NUMBER)
     GROUP BY MEDIA_FORMAT;
```

   or:

```
SELECT MEDIA_FORMAT, COUNT(*)
    FROM MOVIE_COPY A JOIN MOVIE_RENTAL B
         ON A.MOVIE_ID = B.MOVIE_ID AND
            A.COPY_NUMBER = B.COPY_NUMBER
    GROUP BY MEDIA_FORMAT;
```

16.

```
SELECT MOVIE_ID, DUE_DATE
    FROM MOVIE_RENTAL
      JOIN MOVIE_COPY USING (MOVIE_ID, COPY_NUMBER)
    WHERE RETURNED_DATE IS NULL
      AND DATE_SOLD IS NULL;
```

   or:

```
SELECT A.MOVIE_ID, DUE_DATE
    FROM MOVIE_RENTAL A JOIN MOVIE_COPY B
         ON A.MOVIE_ID = B.MOVIE_ID AND
            A.COPY_NUMBER = B.COPY_NUMBER
    WHERE RETURNED_DATE IS NULL
      AND DATE_SOLD IS NULL;
```

17.

```
SELECT A.MOVIE_ID, A.MOVIE_TITLE
    FROM MOVIE A
    WHERE MOVIE_ID NOT IN
         (SELECT DISTINCT MOVIE_ID
            FROM MOVIE_RENTAL);
```

18.

```
SELECT MOVIE_TITLE
    FROM MOVIE
    WHERE MOVIE_ID IN
         (SELECT MOVIE_ID
            FROM MOVIE_COPY
            WHERE MEDIA_FORMAT = 'V'
              AND DATE_SOLD IS NULL)
      AND MOVIE_ID NOT IN
         (SELECT MOVIE_ID
```

```
            FROM MOVIE_COPY
          WHERE MEDIA_FORMAT = 'D'
            AND DATE_SOLD IS NULL);
```

19.
```
SELECT MOVIE_TITLE
  FROM MOVIE A
    JOIN MOVIE_COPY B ON
          (A.MOVIE_ID = B.MOVIE_ID AND
           MEDIA_FORMAT = 'V' AND
           DATE_SOLD IS NULL)
  WHERE A.MOVIE_ID NOT IN
      (SELECT MOVIE_ID
         FROM MOVIE_COPY
        WHERE MEDIA_FORMAT = 'D'
          AND DATE_SOLD IS NULL)
```

20.
```
SELECT MOVIE_ID, MEDIA_FORMAT, COUNT(*)
  FROM MOVIE_COPY
 GROUP BY MOVIE_ID, MEDIA_FORMAT
HAVING COUNT(*) >= 2;
```

Chapter 6

1. b, c, e
2. c
3. a, c
4. b, c
5. a, d
6. a, b
7. b, d, e
8. a, d
9. b, c, d, e
10. a, d

11.
```
SELECT REPLACE(MPAA_RATING_CODE,'-',' ')
       AS MPAA_RATING_CODE
  FROM MPAA_RATING;
```

12. Oracle:
```
SELECT MOVIE_ID, MOVIE_TITLE
  FROM MOVIE
 WHERE MOVIE_TITLE LIKE '%' || CHR(39) || '%';
```

Microsoft SQL Server:
```
SELECT MOVIE_ID, MOVIE_TITLE
  FROM MOVIE
 WHERE MOVIE_TITLE LIKE '%' + CHAR(39) + '%';
```

Other SQL implementations:
```
SELECT MOVIE_ID, MOVIE_TITLE
  FROM MOVIE
 WHERE MOVIE_TITLE LIKE '%' || CHAR(39) || '%';
```

NOTE *This statement doesn't seem to work correctly in MySQL 4.*

13.
```
SELECT ASCII('!');
```

NOTE *Oracle requires a FROM clause on all SELECT statements, so the clause "FROM DUAL" must be added to the statement in order to run it in Oracle.*

14. Oracle:
```
SELECT CEIL(AVG(RETAIL_PRICE_DVD)) AS AVERAGE_DVD_PRICE
  FROM MOVIE;
```

Most other SQL implementations:
```
SELECT CEILING(AVG(RETAIL_PRICE_DVD)) AS AVERAGE_DVD_PRICE
  FROM MOVIE;
```

15.
```
SELECT FLOOR(AVG(RETAIL_PRICE_VHS)) AS AVERAGE_VHS_PRICE
  FROM MOVIE;
```

16.
```
SELECT 'ALTER TABLE ' || TABLE_NAME ||
       ' DROP CONSTRAINT ' || CONSTRAINT_NAME || ';'
  FROM USER_CONSTRAINTS
 WHERE CONSTRAINT_TYPE = 'R';
```

17.
```
SELECT NAME FROM SYSOBJECTS
 WHERE XTYPE = 'F';
```

18.
```
SELECT CUSTOMER_ACCOUNT_ID,
   CASE CHILD_RENTAL_ALLOWED_INDIC
      WHEN 'Y' THEN 'Child Rental OK'
      WHEN 'N' THEN 'NO CHILD RENTAL'
      END AS CHILD_RENTAL
   FROM CUSTOMER_ACCOUNT
 ORDER BY CUSTOMER_ACCOUNT_ID;
```

19.
```
SELECT MOVIE_ID, YEAR_PRODUCED,
   CASE
      WHEN YEAR_PRODUCED IS NULL THEN 'Unknown'
      WHEN YEAR_PRODUCED BETWEEN '1980' and '1989'
           THEN '80s'
      WHEN YEAR_PRODUCED BETWEEN '1990' and '1999'
           THEN '80s'
      WHEN YEAR_PRODUCED BETWEEN '2000' and '2009'
           THEN '00s'
   END AS DECADE
   FROM MOVIE
 ORDER BY MOVIE_ID;
```

20.
```
SELECT MOVIE_ID, COPY_NUMBER, TRANSACTION_ID,
   CASE
      WHEN LATE_OR_LOSS_FEE IS NULL THEN 'None'
      WHEN LATE_OR_LOSS_FEE = 0 THEN 'None'
      WHEN LATE_OR_LOSS_FEE < 10 THEN 'Minor'
      WHEN LATE_OR_LOSS_FEE >= 10 THEN 'Major'
   END AS FEE_CATEGORY
   FROM MOVIE_RENTAL
 ORDER BY MOVIE_ID, COPY_NUMBER, TRANSACTION_ID;
```

Chapter 7

1. a, c
2. b, c, e
3. a, c, d, e
4. b, d
5. a, c, e
6. c, d, e
7. b
8. c
9. a, b, d
10. b, d, e
11. a, b, d, e
12. a, b, c, d, e
13.

```
INSERT INTO MOVIE_GENRE
VALUES ('TRAIN','Training');
```

14.

```
INSERT INTO MOVIE
(MOVIE_ID, MOVIE_GENRE_CODE, MPAA_RATING_CODE, MOVIE_TITLE)
VALUES (99, 'TRAIN', 'NR', 'Employee Training Video');
```

15.

```
INSERT INTO MOVIE_LANGUAGE
  SELECT MOVIE_ID, 'ja'
    FROM MOVIE;
```

16.

```
INSERT INTO RENTAL_TOTAL
  SELECT MOVIE_ID, COUNT(*), SUM(RENTAL_FEE)
    FROM MOVIE_RENTAL
  GROUP BY MOVIE_ID;
```

17.

```
DELETE FROM RENTAL_TOTAL;
```

18.

```
DELETE FROM MOVIE_LANGUAGE
  WHERE LANGUAGE_CODE = 'ja';
```

19.

```
UPDATE MOVIE_COPY
   SET DATE_SOLD = '2005-01-15'
 WHERE MOVIE_ID = 1
   AND COPY_NUMBER = 1;
```

20.

```
UPDATE MOVIE
   SET RETAIL_PRICE_VHS = ROUND(RETAIL_PRICE_VHS * 1.1, 2)
 WHERE RETAIL_PRICE_VHS IS NOT NULL;
```

Chapter 8

1. b, e

2. a, b, d, e

3. b, d, e

4. a, b, c, d, e

5. a, c, d

6. b, c, e

7. b, c, d, e

8. b, c, e

9. a, c, e

10. a, b, e

11. a, c, d

12. b, c, d

13. d, e

14. a, c

15. c

16. d

17. c

18. e

19.

```
GRANT SELECT, INSERT, DELETE
   ON EMPLOYEE
   TO manager_1, manager_2;
```

20.

```
REVOKE INSERT, UPDATE, DELETE
   ON MOVIE
   FROM clerk_127;
```

Chapter 9

1. b, c, d, e
2. c
3. b
4. d
5. a
6. c
7. b
8. a, b, e
9. a, d, e
10. a, e
11. d
12. a, b, c
13. a, c, d
14. c, d, e
15. b, d
16. c, d, e
17. a, b, c, d, e
18. a, c, e
19. b, c, d, e
20. b, d, e

Chapter 10

1. b
2. a
3. a, c
4. b, c, d, e
5. a, c, d, e
6. e
7. b, d
8. a, b, e
9. a, d, e
10. b, c
11. a, b, e
12. b, d, e
13. b, c, d, e
14. b, d, e
15. a, d, e
16. c, e
17. a, b, c, d
18. b, d, e
19. a, c, d
20. b, d, e

Chapter 11

1. b, d
2. a, c, e
3. c, e
4. b, d
5. a, c, d
6. b, c, d, e

7. a, b, d

8. a, c, d

9. a, c, d, e

10. b, c

11. b, d

12. a, e

13. c

14. a, c, d

15. b, d

16. a, d

17. a, b

18. a, c

19. c, d

20. b

Final Exam Answers

1. c, d, e

2. b, e

3. c

4. a, c

5. a, c, e

6. b, c, d, e

7. b, e

8. a, b, c, d

9. c, d, e

10. a, b, c, d, e

11. a, b, d, e

12. a, b, e

13. b, d

14. a, b, d, e

15. a, b, c
16. a, b
17. c
18. d, e
19. a, d
20. d, e
21. a, c, e
22. b, d
23. a, b, e
24. b, c
25. c, d
26. d
27. b
28. c
29. a
30. b, d, e
31. c, e
32. d
33. d, e
34. a, d, e
35. b, d
36. a, b, e
37. d, e
38. b, c, d
39. d, e
40. a, c, e
41. a, c
42. b, e
43. b, d, e
44. a, b, c, d
45. a, d

46. d
47. b, d, e
48. a, d, e
49. b, c, d, e
50. a, b, c, d, e
51. a, b, e
52. a, b, c, d, e
53. b, c, e
54. a, c, d
55. b, d, e
56. a, b, e
57. c, e
58. b, c
59. a, b, c, e
60. e
61. d
62. b, c, d
63. a, b, c, d, e
64. c, d, e
65. a, b, c, d, e
66. a, c, d, e
67. a
68. e
69. a, d
70. a, b, c, e
71. a, b, c, d
72. b, d
73. b, c, d
74. c, d, e
75. b, c, e
76. b, c, d

77. a, d

78. b, c, d

79. a, e

80. a, b, c, e

81. a, d, e

82. a, b, c, d

83. a, d

84.

```
SELECT MOVIE_ID, MOVIE_TITLE
  FROM MOVIE
 WHERE MPAA_RATING_CODE IN ('G','PG','PG-13');
```

85.

```
SELECT COUNT(*)
  FROM MOVIE
 WHERE LOWER(MOVIE_TITLE) LIKE 'of %'
    OR LOWER(MOVIE_TITLE) LIKE '% of'
    OR LOWER(MOVIE_TITLE) LIKE '% of %';
```

86.

```
SELECT COUNT(*)
  FROM CUSTOMER_ACCOUNT
 WHERE DATE_TERMINATED IS NOT NULL;
```

87.

```
SELECT MIN(RETAIL_PRICE_VHS) AS MIN_PRICE,
       MAX(RETAIL_PRICE_VHS) AS MAX_PRICE
  FROM MOVIE;
```

88.

```
SELECT MOVIE_GENRE_CODE,
       ROUND(AVG(RETAIL_PRICE_DVD),2) AS AVG_PRICE
  FROM MOVIE
 GROUP BY MOVIE_GENRE_CODE;
```

89.

```
SELECT SUM(CUSTOMER_DEPOSIT_AMOUNT) AS TOTAL
  FROM CUSTOMER_ACCOUNT;
```

90.

```
SELECT MOVIE_ID, MOVIE_TITLE
  FROM MOVIE A
```

```
WHERE EXISTS
  (SELECT MOVIE_ID
    FROM MOVIE_RENTAL B
    WHERE A.MOVIE_ID = B.MOVIE_ID);
```

91.

```
SELECT A.MOVIE_ID, A.MOVIE_TITLE
  FROM MOVIE A, MOVIE_RENTAL B
 WHERE A.MOVIE_ID = B.MOVIE_ID
 GROUP BY A.MOVIE_ID, A.MOVIE_TITLE;
```

The DISTINCT keyword may be used in place of the GROUP BY clause but is usually less efficient.

92.

```
SELECT MOVIE_TITLE, COUNT(*) AS DVD_COPIES
  FROM MOVIE JOIN MOVIE_COPY
       ON MOVIE.MOVIE_ID = MOVIE_COPY.MOVIE_ID
 WHERE MEDIA_FORMAT = 'D'
 GROUP BY MOVIE_TITLE;
```

93.

```
SELECT CUSTOMER_ACCOUNT_ID, COUNT(*) AS NUM_RENTALS
  FROM CUSTOMER_TRANSACTION A JOIN MOVIE_RENTAL B
       ON A.TRANSACTION_ID = B.TRANSACTION_ID
 GROUP BY CUSTOMER_ACCOUNT_ID;
```

94.

```
SELECT FLOOR(AVG(RETAIL_PRICE_DVD)) AS AVERAGE_DVD_PRICE
  FROM MOVIE;
```

95.

```
SELECT ASCII(';');
```

For Oracle, the clause FROM DUAL must be added.

96.

```
SELECT REPLACE(EMPLOYEE_TAX_ID,'-',' ')
       AS EMPLOYEE_TAX_ID
  FROM EMPLOYEE;
```

97.

```
SELECT MOVIE_TITLE,
  CASE
    WHEN RETAIL_PRICE_DVD IS NULL THEN 'None'
    WHEN RETAIL_PRICE_DVD = 0 THEN 'None'
    WHEN RETAIL_PRICE_DVD < 20 THEN 'Bargain'
```

```
      WHEN RETAIL_PRICE_DVD < 30 THEN 'Moderate'
      WHEN RETAIL_PRICE_DVD >= 30 THEN 'Premium'
   END AS PRICE_CATEGORY
 FROM MOVIE
 ORDER BY MOVIE_TITLE;
```

98.

```
INSERT INTO MOVIE
  (MOVIE_ID, MOVIE_GENRE_CODE, MPAA_RATING_CODE,
   MOVIE_TITLE)
 VALUES (999, 'Drama', 'NR',
   'How the Database Was Won');
```

99.

```
UPDATE MOVIE
   SET RETAIL_PRICE_DVD = RETAIL_PRICE_DVD + 1
 WHERE RETAIL_PRICE_DVD IS NOT NULL;
```

100.

```
DELETE FROM MOVIE_GENRE
 WHERE MOVIE_GENRE_CODE NOT IN
   (SELECT DISTINCT MOVIE_GENRE_CODE
      FROM MOVIE);
```

The DISTINCT is not absolutely necessary, but it makes the list of values in the subselect much shorter, which makes the statement far more efficient.

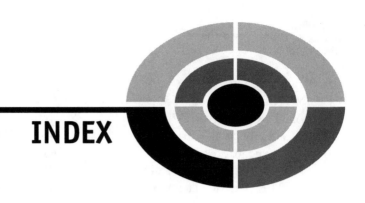

INDEX

References to figures and illustrations are in italics.

% (percent), 103
_ (underscore), 103
<> (not equal operator), 140
, (commas), 46
- (hyphens), 46
; (semicolons), 45
' (single quotes), 46

A

aggregate functions, 117–118
ALTER TABLE statement, 78–80
American National Standards Institute.
   See ANSI
AND operator, 97
ANSI, 43, 44
answers to quizzes and final exam, 281–301
APIs, 226
application programming interfaces. *See* APIs
applications, 221
approximate numeric data types, 57
arithmetic operators, 108–109
arrays, 69
ASC keyword, 77
ASCII function, 153
asynchronous I/O, 241
attributes, multivalued, 13–16

autocommit mode, 207, 208, 209, 210
AutoNumber data type, 61

B

BETWEEN operator, 101–103
BFILE data type, 64
big integer data types, 58
BIGINT data type, 61, 66, 68
BIGSERIAL data type, 68
BINARY data type, 62
binary large object types, 60
BIT data type, 62, 67, 69
BIT VARYING data type, 69
bit-map indexes, 248–249
BLOB data type, 63, 64, 67
BOOLEAN data type, 60, 66, 68
Boyce-Codd normal form, 21
buffers, 223–224, 240–241
BYTEA data type, 68

C

Call Level Interface (CLI), 226
Cartesian product, 128–129
CASE expression, 166
    searched, 168–169
    simple form, 166–168
case sensitivity, 45, 104

The fast and easy way to understanding computing fundamentals

- *No formal training needed*
- *Self-paced, easy-to-follow, and user-friendly*
- *Amazing low price*

0-07-225454-8

0-07-225363-0

0-07-225514-5

0-07-225359-2

0-07-225370-3

0-07-225364-9

0-07-225878-0

0-07-226134-X

0-07-226171-4

0-07-226170-6

0-07-226141-2

0-07-226182-X

0-07-226224-9

0-07-226210-9

For more information on these and other McGraw-Hill/Osborne titles, visit www.osborne.com.

OSBORNE DELIVERS RESULTS!

McGraw Hill Osborne

3/06

mL